D0056471

Peace through Entrepreneurship

Peace through Entrepreneurship

Investing in a Startup Culture for Security and Development

STEVEN R. KOLTAI

with

MATTHEW MUSPRATT

BROOKINGS INSTITUTION PRESS

Washington, D.C.

The Brookings Institution is a private nonprofit organization devoted to research, education, and publication on important issues of domestic and foreign policy. Its principal purpose is to bring the highest quality independent research and analysis to bear on current and emerging policy problems. Interpretations or conclusions in Brookings publications should be understood to be solely those of the authors.

Library of Congress Cataloging-in-Publication data are available
ISBN 9-780-8157-2923-5 (cloth : alk. paper)
ISBN 9-780-8157-2924-2 (ebook)

9 8 7 6 5 4 3 2 1

Typeset in Electra

Composition by Westchester Publishing Services

To Lorraine Hariton
for enabling me to do this work

To Darrell West
for enabling me to tell the world about it

To Ivan
for enabling me

Contents

Preface ix

Acknowledgments xix

1 Introduction 1

PART I **THE PROBLEM**

2 It's All about Jobs 19

3 A Million Reasons Entrepreneurship Is Good for You 37

4 American Made 51

5 Through the Looking Glass 65

6 Turning a Screw with a Rubber Screwdriver 85

PART II **THE SOLUTION**

7 It Takes an Ecosystem 101

8 How It Works and Who Does It 119

9 A Business Plan 145

Notes 173

Index 201

Preface

TWENTY-FOUR HOURS. THAT'S HOW much time the young parents had to plan their departure. They packed two suitcases, stuffing them with identity papers, diplomas, and the few clothes they could carry. They picked up their two-year-old son and, on their way out the door, grabbed his teddy bear. They left food in the fridge and dishes in the sink. They seemed to be heading on a quick errand. In fact, they were going out for the rest of their lives.

Of course they were scared. Who wouldn't be? It was freezing cold, soldiers were firing real bullets, and they had never been abroad, except for the one time the father journeyed in a cattle car to the Theresienstadt children's work camp courtesy of the Nazis. But the family believed that whatever future lay ahead would be better than the present of communism or the horror they had lived during the Second World War.

This was Hungary in November 1956. As Soviet tanks rumbled through Budapest, suppressing the largest armed insurrection in the half-century history of the Soviet-occupied countries of Eastern Europe, some 200,000 Hungarians fled the violence, degradation, surveillance, and economic straightjacket of the so-called Hungarian People's Republic. Too young to have escaped during World War II, the parents now had a chance to slip through a brief parting in the iron curtain. Just weeks before, students from Budapest's Technical University had led tens of thousands of protesters to the city center, where they had sliced the communist coat of arms from

Hungarian flags and yanked down a statue of Joseph Stalin. The young couple had been part of those demonstrations. Euphoria had flowed through the city. The communist government quickly fell. However, after a tantalizing and deceptive five days of freedom, the Soviet occupiers returned. This time it was clear they were staying.

The young family made their way through the dark, slick streets to the Western Station (ironically, in Hungarian, the "tranquil" station) and boarded one of the last westbound trains to Vienna. It stopped about eight miles short of the Austrian border. There the parents bundled their son into a knapsack and handed him his teddy. They gave him some brandy to ensure a nice long sleep and joined two dozen other families for the final miles of their trip, a nighttime walk across the Austro-Hungarian border.

A few weeks and several stops later, the family arrived in the United States. They eventually settled in Los Angeles and began to live the American dream. The father worked in a wallpaper factory by day and went to community college to learn English by night. He earned a B.A., M.A., and Ed.D. at UCLA and became a highly successful educator, eventually running the community colleges of Kansas City and then Los Angeles. The mother, never losing her blond, blue-eyed Hungarian beauty, became the perfect American wife, managing an immaculate home and epitomizing the adage, "Behind every successful man, there is an even more successful woman." They gave the child with the teddy bear two siblings, a girl and another boy.

The child with the teddy bear, of course, is me. My family's story, from children of the Holocaust to the flight from Soviet-occupied Eastern Europe, is not unique. In fact, across America you will find many similar stories of refugees and immigrants from almost every corner of the world.

But my family's background shaped the course of my life and, particularly, inspired a vital belief that I hold today: war is to be avoided at all costs, and the key driver of war is not actually religious or political difference; it is economics. Karl Marx was right about one thing. Economics is the foundation of all politics and, as just about every politician knows, the most important economic condition is jobs. Joblessness is the root cause of most of the worst political disasters to have befallen mankind, thus, job creation is the foundation of political stability and a civil society. And I believe there is no better way to create jobs than through entrepreneurship. In fact, for many immigrants, first-generation and beyond, entrepreneur-

CBS publicity still of the Koltai family for 1957 television
program on Hungarian refugees

ship has been the path to fulfilling the promise of America, the land of opportunity. Entrepreneurship and the American dream are inextricably intertwined.

Back to my family. My father was a voracious reader. Almost everything he read was about World War II. As a child, I could never understand how there could possibly be anything new for him to learn about the war. But he kept reading. When I asked what more he wanted to find out, he would answer, "I was in the war, but never understood it. We never understood what was happening outside the blackened windows, what was happening outside the ghetto walls or the concentration camp barracks. Now, I want to know it all." The war, its causes, and its consequences defined what were supposed to be my father's high school and college years. He never wanted to see such catastrophe happen again.

Like my father, I sought to understand, as well. I gravitated quickly toward the idea of economics as the cornerstone of security and politics, the antidote to the two world wars that had upended my family's life in Hungary. I became a European history major at Tufts University and studied international economics in graduate school at Tufts' Fletcher School of Law and Diplomacy. I believed then, and believe now, that Europe could only avoid repeating its terrible, violent history through economic union and linked prosperity. I won a Fulbright to study and work in Brussels, and wrote my master's thesis on the creation of the European Economic Community, the precursor to today's European Union (EU), which banked on economic integration to "lay the foundations of an ever-closer union among the peoples of Europe" and "to preserve and strengthen peace and liberty."[1]

Indeed, economic failure was, in my opinion, the root cause of the two world wars. Inter-war Germany was economic chaos. While the Weimar era was a great time for culture (see Kurt Weil, Thomas Mann, and the world of cabaret), it was a terrible time to find a job. The Treaty of Versailles that ended World War I saddled the Germans with reparations of some 130 billion gold marks, 400 billion in today's U.S. dollars, with the final installment of $94 million paid only in 2010.[2] The defeated country suffered from mass unemployment and hyperinflation. The German people were buried under a crippled economy, backed into the belief that they had no political choice other than a very strong state that could provide jobs, security, and dignity. This was the poisonous brew from which the Nazi Party could rise to power.

That disastrous rise is what my father and I were trying to understand. What fascinated me most, and what carried real, personal significance, was the key role of institutions in securing economic order and enabling prosperous and civilized societies, in preventing apocalyptic economic collapse and destruction.

And yet, though I was familiar with the workings of European and world institutions, and despite a long-held dream of joining the U.S. State Department, I embarked after graduate school on an international business career. I began my professional life as a banker, worked in consulting, and logged many years on the strategy and business side of the entertainment industry with Warner Bros.

Sprinkled throughout these "normal" jobs were several entrepreneurial ventures; some successful, some not. In starting and running businesses,

I raised money, delivered products, met payrolls, and hired and fired employees. I learned that being an entrepreneur was exhilarating, lonely, terrifying, rewarding, and completely exhausting. It was much harder than being a corporate executive (or, later, I would learn, a government official) but also much more satisfying, at least to me. One of the main reasons entrepreneurship was more satisfying was that it created jobs.

Coronet, a satellite firm I cofounded in Luxembourg with Clay T. Whitehead (who, in addition to being a brilliant entrepreneur, engineered numerous policies deregulating the telecommunications and cable TV industries as a Nixon administration official), has evolved to become one of the world's largest telecommunications satellite operators. Its current incarnation, SES S.A., today claims total assets in excess of €9 billion and operates fifty-four satellites carrying communications and television channels, reaching 99 percent of the world's population. The firm employs over 1,200 people.[3] It has spawned further thousands of jobs indirectly. Another of my startups, an online event management service, employed over 200 people at its peak, and over the life of the company created some 600 jobs before turning south and ending in failure. I learned as much from the failure as from the success; probably more.

These entrepreneurial experiences changed my views on government and international institutions. After all, foreign missions, currency unions, and trade agreements cannot create jobs in and of themselves. That was something my startups did, and which the corporations I worked for did. Certainly, international organizations try to establish regulatory environments (the EU), help foster security and stability (the United Nations), and provide budgetary support and project-specific loans (the World Bank and the International Monetary Fund), all important and necessary activities. But the underlying desperation of inter-war Germany was, at its root, caused by a lack of jobs. It is new businesses that create jobs at a meaningful scale. And it is entrepreneurs who create new businesses. In fact, it was from the very milieu of pre–World War II hyperinflation and hyper-unemployment that Viennese American economist Joseph Schumpeter emerged to espouse the basic economic theory of "creative destruction" and the critical role entrepreneurs play in generating jobs and growth.[4]

By the time I had semi-retired to Maine—quiet, coastal Maine—I had become convinced that entrepreneurship is more than a means of building wealth. It is a powerful force for good around the world. I saw a straight-line connection between entrepreneurship, job creation, economic growth, political stability, and a civil society. This sequence inspired my mantra today: peace through entrepreneurship.

There is no better evidence of this powerful equation than the success of the United States itself, economically, politically, and culturally. And there is no better personification of its inverse than the desperate vegetable seller Mohamed Bouazizi, who set himself on fire in the streets of Sidi Bouzid, Tunisia, out of severe economic frustration from a lifetime of shakedowns and confiscation of goods by authorities that stifled any hope of meaningful work or entrepreneurialism. Bouazizi's act of despair resonated in a region wracked by youth unemployment rates exceeding 30 percent, and touched off the Arab Spring of 2010–11.[5]

Exacerbating that ongoing employment crisis is an increasingly youthful population. Two of every three Arabs are age twenty-nine or younger.[6] Thus the largest, fastest growing, and, arguably, most politically active segment of the population in the Middle East and North Africa (MENA) struggles to find gainful employment, leaving it angry, frustrated, and with lots of time to spare. This pattern holds true outside of MENA, as well, of course, from Afghanistan to Sahel Africa, to the *banlieues* of Paris and the favelas of Latin America. The ramifications for peace are obvious and ongoing, from 9/11 to Tahrir Square, to Nairobi's Westgate mall attack, to the rise of the Islamic State of Iraq and Syria, to Paris on November 13, 2015. Just as the economic turmoil of inter-war Germany fostered Nazism, the joblessness of today's troubled economies breeds radical ideology and unrest.

A confluence of events encouraged me to pursue this idea of entrepreneurship as a tool for peace and to write this book. In fact, I finally got to work at the State Department. My entrée was the Franklin Fellowship, a federal program designed to get old people into government. (They actually use words like "experienced" and "mid-career" and "more senior," but they really mean "old.") When first presented with the Franklin Fellowship offer I was at home in Maine. Mulling over the opportunity, I happened to flip on the TV and witness a U.S. president talking about entrepreneurship and foreign policy in the same breath, perhaps for the first time.

This was June 4, 2009, before the Arab Spring, and Barack Obama was at Cairo University in Egypt to deliver the key foreign policy speech of his first term. It was titled "A New Beginning" and was addressed to the Muslim world. From Maine I heard Obama propose a "broader engagement" between Muslim communities and the United States, one that looked beyond oil, terrorism, and unrest. This engagement, Obama said, would begin with "a Summit on Entrepreneurship . . . to identify how we can deepen ties between business leaders, foundations, and social entrepreneurs in the United States and Muslim communities around the world."[7]

Fortuitously, I had recently met a new political appointee in Hillary Clinton's State Department, a woman from Silicon Valley who understood entrepreneurship. Lorraine Hariton and I had immediately connected. We shared a worldview and a common perspective on the ultimate cause of chronic political and social instability in the MENA region—youth unemployment—and a view that entrepreneurship was part of the solution.

Hariton's commitment to entrepreneurship as a policy tool was clear. At the same time, Secretary Clinton was directing a major strategy review that saw economic development as important as diplomacy to the State Department's work. This review had a decidedly un-sexy name: the Quadrennial Diplomacy and Development Review (QDDR). Led by foreign policy expert Anne-Marie Slaughter, the QDDR was a policy document that should stand as one of the crowning (if not headline-grabbing) achievements of Secretary Clinton's tenure, one of the key contributions by Secretary Clinton to twenty-first-century American foreign policy. It recognized the connection between economics and peace and security in the world's trouble spots, and the consequences of poverty and instability abroad for peace and security at home. QDDR announced that economic development should be elevated as a foreign policy tool.

So I joined Hariton at State. As a first step, I helped organize the very Presidential Summit on Entrepreneurship that Obama had described in Cairo. We brought 200 Muslim entrepreneurs from more than fifty countries to Washington for the conference. But I also believed we needed to actually do something. Hariton's openness and absence of ego, coupled with some great mentoring from a truly exemplary foreign service officer, Sue Saarnio, allowed me to bring my prior experience and a degree of creativity to State's approach to entrepreneurship, and I soon launched the Global Entrepreneurship Program (GEP), a program I felt could showcase the power of entrepreneurship as a tool for foreign policy.

The idea driving GEP was job creation. By promoting entrepreneurship in Muslim-majority countries, GEP could spur new businesses and new jobs. We implemented packages of programs that supported startups in a variety of ways, providing real entrepreneurs with real business assistance, from mentoring relationships to access to capital. GEP had a special focus on Egypt, Indonesia, and Turkey, with additional, secondary programs in Lebanon, Jordan, Tunisia, Algeria, and Morocco. During my tenure heading GEP we helped attract seed investment to over three dozen companies in seven countries, established hundreds of mentoring relationships, and helped launch new venture funds and angel investor networks.

Unfortunately, for this international businessman and entrepreneur from L.A.—by way of Kansas City, Luxembourg, and Maine—Washington and the State Department turned out to be a very different world. Despite a few successes and backing from Secretary Clinton, Slaughter, and Under Secretary for Economics Bob Hormats, GEP suffered from a lack of budgetary and bureaucratic support right from the beginning, most prominently from the very bureau in which we were housed, what was then called the Bureau of Economic, Energy, and Business Affairs.

I was stunned that after the presidential summit so few people were interested in taking action or doing anything at all beyond convening a conference and merely talking about job creation, entrepreneurship, and Muslim countries. In the business world I knew, when the CEO of a company announced the launch of a new initiative, managers tripped over each other to carry out the directive (in no small measure because their bonuses often depended on it). In Washington, no such thing happened. In fact, it became apparent that putting on the conference amounted to "mission accomplished" when it came to implementing what the country's CEO, President Obama, meant when he talked about entrepreneurship in the context of a "broader engagement" with the Muslim world. The institutional response was all about "convening" and "developing the brand." It was not about actual content.

GEP never became the program it could have been (and, hopefully, one day will be). My time in Washington exposed me to the myriad ways that the U.S. government can stymie entrepreneurship promotion as a foreign policy tool—from a bureaucratic ethos that stifles creativity to procurement processes that prevent America's most talented from performing America's most important work. That big government has significant problems is hardly a revelation. Yet my stint at State did not dissuade me from the idea of entrepreneurship in the service of foreign policy, that entrepreneurship promotion is a vital tool for addressing unemployment and economic stagnation in at-risk parts of the world. Entrepreneurship is not just a vital tool but, perhaps, the best tool for repairing the economic malaise that creates risks to American security.

Today's employment, demographic, and economic crises put more and more people into a corner, deprived of dignity and hope, like Mohamed Bouazizi, like an inter-war German, like an Islamic State foot soldier. Leveraging entrepreneurship as a foreign policy tool can effect enormous positive change, not just within foreign economies, but internationally. Entrepreneurship can bring us closer to world peace. This book explains why and how.

Acknowledgments

THERE ARE FEW ENTREPRENEURIAL ventures whose successes can be attributed to a single person—be it the first product prototype, the first dollar of revenue, reaching breakeven, or acquisition. This book is no exception. I am fortunate to have encountered scores of people during my career in entrepreneurship and government whose encouragement, support, and friendship have resulted in this book. I wish to thank:

— Greg Behrman, for helping me develop the Six+Six Entrepreneurship Ecosystem Model and being my partner in building the Global Entrepreneurship Program, GEP, when few others believed

— Anne-Marie Slaughter, for taking the time to understand what GEP was about and helping both to shape it and move it forward

— Melanne Verveer and Wenchi Yu, for teaching me about the unique power of, and problems faced by, women entrepreneurs

— Jonathan Alan at the State Department, who was a model of "intrapreneurship" in a very large, very bureaucratic organization

— Ambassadors Cameron Hume, Scot Marciel, Margaret Scobey, and Anne Patterson, who understood the outsized importance of entrepreneurship development in the countries to which they were posted

—Tara Sonenshine, who encouraged me throughout and contributed directly to the creation of this book

—Friends and supporters at the State Department, USAID, and throughout the U.S. government who were among the few to step forward and really want to do something about joblessness in fragile states: Secretary Hillary Clinton, Bob Hormats, Cheryl Mills, Tom Nides, Bambi Arellano, Peggy Keshishian, Quintan Wiktorowicz, John Wasielewski, Jackie Strasser Higgins, Peter Ballinger, Eric Postel, Maura O'Neill, Alex Dehgan, Jeff Margolis, Steve Radelet, Anthony Cotton, Kapil Gupta, Travis Hunnicutt, Brenda Rios, Anne Park, Vanessa Holcomb Mann, Cleveland Charles

—Sue Saarnio, Richard Boly, and Karen Volker, who were staunch supporters of what I tried to do at State and role models of what a foreign service officer could be

—Everyone in each of the major GEP countries who made the program possible. In Egypt: Mike Ducker, Tarek el-Sadany, Marianne Siemietkowski-Needham, Sherif Kamel, Wael Fakharany, Tarek Kamel. In Indonesia: Shinta Kamdani, Martin Hartono, Eka Ginting, Sati Rasuanto, Cindy Koh. In Turkey: Ussal Sahbaz, Guven Sak, Esen Caglar, Didem Altop, Mete and Canan Cakmakci, Ali Karabey, Selcuk Kiper, Emir Ozen, Nihan Siriklioglu, Elmira Bayrasli, Ali Sabanci

—GEP Entrepreneurship Delegation members who made such a difference on the ground in the places we visited: Chris Schroeder, Mike Cassidy, Loretta McCarthy, Faysal Sohail, Laura Brightsen, Martin Gedalin, Bob Stringer, Magid Abraham, Shervin Pishevar, Jonathan Smith

—Ashraf and Haytham ElFadeel, who became the "poster children" of what is possible in terms of world-class entrepreneurs coming from developing countries

—From the global entrepreneurship world: Ahmed El Alfi, Leslie Jump, and Hany Al Sonbaty of Sawari Ventures in Egypt; Linda Rottenberg of Endeavor, who modeled what it was to be the "Rolls Royce" of global entrepreneurship in action; Jan Piercy of ShoreBank/Enclude; Natalia Pipia and Ovi Bujorean of CRDF; Randall Kempner of the Aspen Network of Development Entrepreneurs; Jonathan Ortmans of the Kauffman Foundation and Global Entrepreneurship Week; Shahid Ansari,

Donna Kelley, and Cheryl Kiser of Babson College; Jim Maxmin and Vimala Palaniswamy of Demeter; Audrey Selian and Ken Hynes of Artha Networks; Sean Griffin of Startup Cup; Maria Pinelli and Giuseppe Nicolosi of EY; Alix Landais, James Reeves, Nigel Penfold, and Daniel Idowu of IMC International; Harold Rosen and Agnes Dasewicz of Grassroots Business Fund; Mildred Callear, Jim Sosnicky, and Peter Righi at SEAF/CEED

—My teachers, especially at Tufts and Fletcher, who taught me how to think and write: Tony Smith, Robert Legvold, George Marcopoulos, Sol Gittleman, Janice Green, Daniel Mulholland, Lynda Shaffer, Pierre Laurent, Leo Gross

—Randy Glass, my childhood friend and the most amazing artist I've ever known, for the terrific sketches capturing my ideas and that appear in electronic and marketing materials associated with this book.

—A long list of friends who provided both intellectual and emotional guidance and support, including: Diane Hessan, Rik Kranenburg, Jim Berliner, Bill Simon, Buffy Bondy, Des FitzGerald, Lucinda Ziesing, Liv Rockefeller, Ken Shure, Alissa Stern, Louis Boorstin, Lisa Hook, Peter Gillon, Brett Trueman, Mark Miller, Dave Ferguson, Mark Humphreys, Anthony Garrett, Jane Mayer, Julie Salamon

—Friends, advisors, and guides from the worlds of journalism and books, including Bennett Ashley and Paul Lucas at Janklow & Nesbit, Wayne Kabak, Gail Ross, David Rohde, Kate Zentall, and Shoshana Zuboff

—Michael Crowley, Jason Noah, Wouter Takkenberg, Rebecca Kullman, and Noam Rifkind for important research and fact-checking assistance

—Pete Beatty for incredibly sharp, thorough, and insightful editing

—The Smith Richardson Foundation and, especially, Nadia Schadlow, for believing in me and this concept of entrepreneurship as a foreign policy tool and for providing the only outside financial support, without which this book would never have been written

—My family, including my mother, Katherine Koltai, my sister, Marian Koltai-Levine, and my sons, Nicholas and Benjamin

—And finally, but probably most importantly, my collaborator, Matt Muspratt, without whom this book certainly would not have been possible

ONE

Introduction

IN THE UNITED STATES, a 10 percent unemployment rate is a catastrophe, the kind of number that gets presidents and parties booted from office. In much of the world, especially in the Middle East and North Africa, a rate three times that—unemployment greater than America's at the height of the Great Depression—is a fact of life.

From Yemen to Turkey, Algeria to Iraq, young men face staggering odds against finding work. The job market is even worse for job-seeking women, who are not even counted in unemployment figures in some countries. Twenty-eight percent of young people[1] in Saudi Arabia are unemployed. Over 30 percent in Tunisia. Thirty-five percent in Egypt. Nearly 40 percent in the Palestinian Territories. As a whole, the MENA region is home to the highest youth unemployment rates in the world. And those rates are rising.[2]

This is not merely a crisis of percentage. MENA is absolutely teeming with young people. Today, of the roughly 420 million Arabs in the world, two-thirds are age twenty-nine or younger. Half of those hundreds of millions are under fifteen years old.[3] By 2025, the populations of Iraq, Syria, Yemen, Jordan, Oman, Kuwait, the West Bank, and the Gaza Strip will be double the 1995 levels.[4] In the words of regional expert Vali Nasr, "Looking at the population numbers in the Middle East today, it is hard to see anything but youth."[5] Hard to see anything but youth without jobs, he might have said.

1

Millions of unemployed young people makes for millions of lives stunted by economic despair. It makes for legions of frustrated, idle, angry, and impressionable teenagers and twenty- and thirty-somethings. It makes for instability and chaos that spills over borders—into Jordan, into Israel, and into Turkey. And, as we know from Paris, more and more, it makes for threats that spill into Europe and into America.

Today, the lands of breathtakingly huge numbers of jobless youth are the lands of extremism and the lands where threats to peace and prosperity spawn. These lands are often "failed states" or, at the very least, "failing states," especially from the standpoint of their increasingly hopeless and disaffected youth. From al-Qaeda to the Islamic State, terror and instability breed where young men cannot find jobs. Joblessness, not religious, cultural, or tribal strife, is, I believe, the root (though not the only) cause of the chaos that today challenges international security and American foreign policy. The Peruvian economist Hernando de Soto, whose groundbreaking work ties peace and prosperity to economic opportunity, wrote in 2014 that the "West must learn a simple lesson: economic hope is the only way to win the battle for the constituencies on which terrorist groups feed."[6]

De Soto is right. This book advances his point and argues that the United States government has utterly failed to deal with the foremost underlying cause of extremism: economic dysfunction. But this book also argues that the hope de Soto speaks of can come in great part—in most part, in fact—from a quintessential American value and underutilized foreign policy tool that offers a tremendously potent solution: entrepreneurship.

Entrepreneurship is a job-creating machine. Jobs are the foundation of peaceful, civil societies. In the United States the youngest firms, not our established corporations, account for nearly all net job growth.[7] The same is true in poor states and emerging markets, where small- and medium-size businesses predominate.[8] By bolstering entrepreneurship in fragile and developing states, by supporting the innovators, startup companies, and job creators of the Arab world, the United States can generate truly viable economic opportunities for jobless youth and alternatives to the chaos and extremism that threatens America today.

Until now, our response to the problems wrought by massive youth unemployment has been warfare, military advisors, drones, Guantanamo Bay detentions, and vast amounts of military spending. These have not made America more secure. Every year (or every month) it seems we face a new question about invading a Middle Eastern country, bombing a terrorist cell, arming a repulsive rebel group, or ratcheting down on our own civil liberties. We spend trillions and lose thousands of American lives. And, as British diplomat and author Rory Stewart writes of coalition efforts to combat the Islamic State: "We already tried counterinsurgency and state-building in the same area of Iraq in response to a very similar group—al-Qaeda in Iraq—in 2008. We invested $100 billion a year, deployed 130,000 international troops, and funded hundreds of thousands of Sunni Arab militiamen. And the problem has returned, six years later, larger and nastier."[9]

In other words, the return on our anti-terror investment is negative. It is time for a new strategy for dealing with the threats that dominate our fears and headlines: terror groups running amok across the Middle East; shootings in Paris and Ottawa; beheadings in Syria (and Oklahoma); hatchet attacks in London; Denver schoolgirls flying abroad to jihad.

As we say in the business world, "Don't tell the market what it wants; listen to what the market is telling you." The United States must move away from military-heavy solutions (and military-leaning humanitarian solutions) and away from low-yield traditional economic development projects. We must rebalance our portfolio of investments in fragile and developing regions toward job creation—that is, toward entrepreneurship—and redeploy our agencies and staffing to do so effectively. Simply, the United States must elevate entrepreneurship as a foreign policy tool.

What Is Entrepreneurship?

In chapter 2 of this book we will look closely at how entrepreneurship can solve the unrest that plagues and threatens so many people today. The short answer: Entrepreneurship creates jobs in great numbers and generates economic growth; jobs and growth are the underpinnings of a stable, civil society. But, first, we need to understand what kind of entrepreneurship we are talking about. Who is an entrepreneur? Let's get this straight. We are not talking about rural microfinance. We are not talking about lemonade stands. We are talking the stuff of Silicon Valley and Sam Walton, the stuff of Walt Disney and Thomas Edison.

This is my definition of *entrepreneur*: An entrepreneur is a person with the vision to see a new product or process and the ability to make it happen.

Not every small business owner on Main Street or in a Marrakesh market is an entrepreneur according to this definition. Walk down stretches of

Sepulveda Boulevard in my home town of Los Angeles (one of the longest streets in America, by the way) and you will spot quite a few restaurants serving Central American fare—pupusas, fajitas, rice and beans. Street vendors stroll the sidewalks, too (along those few blocks where there are actually pedestrians), perhaps dicing mangoes for passersby on a sweltering day. Catering to, and often owned or operated by, first- and second-generation immigrants living nearby, few of these establishments are "entrepreneurial" by my definition. Why? There is nothing new about them, as enjoyable, tasty, or income generating as they may be. Such establishments, and their menus, exist all across the country.

There are also plenty of nail salons and cheap furniture stores along Sepulveda Boulevard, as well as countless other businesses with signage in Korean, Farsi, Vietnamese, Hmong, Russian, Hebrew, Armenian, Arabic, Hindi, and Tagalog. Even English! The owners (or franchisees) of these, too, are not entrepreneurs by my definition, even if it is the first shop they have run and even if they have sunk their life's savings into its launch. They are certainly inspiring, determined businessmen and women, but they have not brought to life a new product or service. Opening a barbershop; opening a café; starting a retail store . . . this is not entrepreneurship in and of itself. For similar reasons, the Lebanese and Indian enterprises across West and East Africa do not necessarily fall under my definition of entrepreneurship. Their owners are typically traders, not entrepreneurs. Traders, shop owners, and small businessmen and women are very important to economic growth, so I am not detracting from their work or their contribution to jobs and growth. But I am making a distinction. In this book, when I talk about entrepreneurship, I am talking about new products and processes. It's about innovation. And innovation isn't the same thing as technology, although they often go hand in hand. Show me a growing chain of dry cleaning operations that offers drive-thru service or ensures 100 percent environmentally sensitive chemical processes and carbon-neutral energy consumption, and I will show you an entrepreneur.

What about the hawkers along Jalan Sudirman in Jakarta, Indonesia? There, as in other bustling mega-cities across the globe, when a traffic light turns red, dozens of men, women, and children sweep up to captive drivers offering bottled water, handkerchiefs, maps, encyclopedias, live animals, lottery tickets . . . you name it. Some yank back windshield wipers and immediately begin washing and buffing windows in hope that an acquiescing customer will pay a few coins. These street vendors often provide a convenient service, responding to a demand in a hot, traffic-choked city. They are enterprising. But they are not entrepreneurs for the purposes of this book.

Many of Jakarta's street vendors are what entrepreneurship watchers like the Global Entrepreneurship Monitor (GEM) or the Omidyar Network refer to as "necessity entrepreneurs."[10] These vendors have no other options for making money. My definition in no way precludes the necessity entrepreneur who makes it big off an innovation, but GEM's other category, the "opportunity-driven" entrepreneur, speaks more to the innovator who will generate commercial success under my criteria. My definition of entrepreneurship is about disruption, high growth, scalability, and serious job creation.

Thought leaders in the field of entrepreneurship who are far more accomplished than I have offered various definitions of "entrepreneur," several of which resemble my thinking. Joseph Schumpeter, widely credited with coining the term "entrepreneur" and fathering the study of the phenomenon, also thought the creation of new products or processes, or new markets for products and processes, was the hallmark of entrepreneurship.[11] Peter Drucker speaks of someone who "upsets and disorganizes" and William Baumol of "the bold and imaginative deviator from established business patterns and practices."[12] Carl Schramm and Bob Litan would describe L.A.'s restaurants and Jakarta's street vendors as "replicative entrepreneurs" and anoint businessmen and women who create new products, services, and processes as "innovative entrepreneurs."[13] For some, myself included, true entrepreneurship requires employing more than oneself.[14] Entrepreneurship is about growth and creating jobs.

My definition of entrepreneur is driven not by necessity but by opportunity. Entrepreneurs innovate a product or a process rather than replicate an existing offering. Entrepreneurs envision scalable, high-growth businesses. But they also possess the ability to make those visions a reality. They are not merely inventors. As mentors tell startup founders all the time, "It's 5 percent inspiration and 95 percent perspiration." Entrepreneurs get things done. They go over, under, and around obstacles, do not take no for an answer, and have a fire in their belly, a fire to make their endeavor succeed.

There is another way of thinking about this criterion. Entrepreneurship is the bridge between innovation and commercialization. Innovation without entrepreneurship stays in the university lab or on the garage workbench.[15] In fact, I have always felt that only about one in five entrepreneurs are innovators, while the remaining 80 percent (including me) are commercializers of other people's innovations. Entrepreneurship brings the new thing to market. It does not always mean being the genius with the idea. My version of entrepreneurship actually delivers a product or process to the marketplace. Someone takes a risk and launches a firm; someone pitches for capital; someone sweats to meet payroll; someone hires and fires; someone makes late-night runs to FedEx to ensure a customer is happy. Someone makes it happen.

Despite the limitations I have drawn around "entrepreneur," my definition—a person with the vision to see a new product or process and the ability to make it happen—is, in fact, hugely broad. Here's why. First, I strongly believe that entrepreneurs are everywhere. Entrepreneurs are men and women, rich and poor, Christian and Muslim and otherwise; they are found in every country, be it democratic or authoritarian, industrialized or developing. Second, my version of entrepreneurship doesn't require an engineering degree. Innovation can be high-, low-, or no-tech. Entrepreneurship is by no means synonymous with apps and software, Facebook and Google.

Entrepreneurs are everywhere. In fact, they are among today's top celebrities, at least in the United States. Most people most of the time think of today's entrepreneurs as high-profile supermen and superwomen, people like Steve Jobs, Mark Zuckerberg, Bill Gates, Oprah Winfrey, and Richard Branson. My view is slightly different. Sure, these are all exceptional people and extraordinarily successful entrepreneurs. But, to me, they are a rare breed, like a prize-winning rose that has grown in ideal conditions. In my experience, entrepreneurs are not so much well-groomed flowers as they are crabgrass. Crabgrass is everywhere. It does not require good soil, fertilizer, or careful tending. Crabgrass pushes through the cracks in broken pavement in abandoned lots littered with broken glass and detritus. I see entrepreneurs finding a way all over the world, in rich and poor countries, from Jakarta to Jordan, Maine to Morocco, Accra to Ankara. The *New York Times* has even reported on entrepreneurship penetrating Jordan's "squalid, barren" Zaatari refugee camp for Syrians, in the form of camp-tailored pet stores and pizza delivery.[16]

But, as I will discuss later, strengthening the ecosystems in which entrepreneurs work greatly boosts the odds that more crabgrass (more startups) can fully flourish and, perhaps, become prize-winning roses. Just because an entrepreneur does not enjoy an ideal enabling environment with liberal access to startup capital, great intellectual property laws, and plentiful, inexpensive, trained staff does not mean that the entrepreneur does not exist.

I strongly second the sentiments of Erik Hersman, cofounder of the messaging app Ushahidi and a key player in putting Kenya on the global innovation map: "The truth is that innovation in Africa is everywhere. My theory is that there is an even distribution of innovation globally, in the same proportion in Africa as any other continent in the world."[17]

So we should not be surprised when *The Economist* tells us that "in Beirut, Cairo, Dubai, Riyadh or even Gaza City, small technology firms are multiplying."[18] We should not be surprised that in many Middle East cities women comprise 35 percent of Internet entrepreneurs, three times the global rate for such startups.[19] We should not be surprised that in high-growth industries twice as many entrepreneurs are over fifty as are under twenty-five.[20] Entrepreneurs are everywhere. Opportunities to nourish them are everywhere, too.

The second point—about no-, low-, and high-tech entrepreneurship—is one of my favorite subjects. In the West, all too often "innovation" is used as synonymous to "technology." Our rock star entrepreneurs include Jobs, Zuckerberg, Gates, and other Silicon Valley stalwarts. But my definition of entrepreneurship is also open to the likes of talk-show pioneers (Oprah) and travel innovators (Branson). And look at Starbucks. It serves a centuries-old drink, but it innovated the coffee shop experience and is now on every street corner in every city. That is a process innovation and very much an example of no-tech entrepreneurship. Travis Kalanick and Garrett Camp, founders of Uber, are low-tech entrepreneurs. They did not invent taxis or even using a mobile phone to call one. But their innovative end-to-end mobile process, including the way in which drivers are recruited and graded, has changed the way an ancient business (carriage for hire) works.

That entrepreneurship is tech-agnostic becomes absolutely critical when we consider what this whole book is about: jobs. No- and low-tech companies often create far more jobs than the techie darlings of Silicon Valley. Instagram, for all its buzz and popularity, boasted only thirteen employees when it was famously acquired by Facebook for $1 billion. As Jaron Lanier points out in *Who Owns the Future?*, Kodak, a company that serviced that same snapshot market, employed a whopping 140,000 people during its day in the sun.[21] Today, Starbucks employs 182,000 people.[22] That is nearly 50,000 more than Facebook,[23] Google,[24] and Apple[25] combined. And when you consider social ramifications, no- and low-tech innovations are often more consequential than tech breakthroughs. For example, economist Ha-Joon Chang has argued that the washing machine has changed the world more than the Internet, since it helped liberate women into the labor force.[26]

So it's quite likely that no-tech and low-tech innovators, not the high-tech rock stars, will create the bulk of the jobs in the future. This is doubly true in the emerging and developing markets we are most concerned with. These countries, though saddled with youth unemployment, often possess burgeoning urban middle classes who want what entrepreneurs are typically good at figuring out how to deliver in the local context: housewares, furniture, textiles, convenience food, and the like. In Ghana, my consulting firm met Albert Osei of Koko King, who sells packaged breakfast foods roadside and by delivery to Accra's traffic-bound commuters and professionals; he has grown from two employees to over 100 locations in the greater Accra area.[27]

As another example, agriculture, decidedly no- and low-tech, is crucial to developing economies. Perhaps you have noticed quinoa claiming increasing space on the shelves at Trader Joe's and Whole Foods. The protein-packed grain has been grown in Bolivia for centuries, but it has only become commonplace in foreign (for example, American) markets over the past few decades due to clever marketing, partnership initiatives, and the all-around entrepreneurial resolve of smallholder Bolivian farmers, like those of Nor Lipez province. There, starting in the 1970s and 1980s, a local cooperative won several grants and loans to improve the efficiency with which quinoa is debittered, trained its members to improve production, and partnered with American agricultural scientists to expand to U.S. markets. Today, the Nor Lipez co-op has doubled the size of its farmer membership and been part of a quinoa boom that has seen exports climb from next to nothing in the 1990s to $80 million in 2012.[28]

So, entrepreneurs are everywhere and they excel at bringing innovative, no-, low-, and high-tech products and services to market. Again, we're not concerned with just any small business or microfinanced enterprise. We're interested in the innovators who are developing scalable enterprises and who will create significant numbers of jobs. I take the time to explain my definition of entrepreneurship for a reason. This is the kind of entrepreneurship at which the United States excels and for which it is famous, and it is the kind of entrepreneurship our government can use as a foreign policy tool. That is because scalable, high-growth entrepreneurship is amenable to turbo-charging. It is "influenceable." It does not happen by accident; it can be proactively, consciously, and deliberately spurred.

Doing Entrepreneurship

Turbo-charging entrepreneurship and turning crabgrass into a vibrant garden is about more than making money. It can also change the world. The United States, respected throughout our history as a world leader in innovation, from Ford to Facebook, is uniquely positioned to leverage its expertise in entrepreneurship for the force of good. At home, our entrepreneurs in many (though not all) parts of the country enjoy the advantages of a supportive ecosystem, from early-stage financing that allows entrepreneurs to borrow against their homes and max out credit cards to a generally favorable regulatory environment, rule of law with minimal corruption, cutting-edge research universities, low-cost shared workspaces, incubator and mentorship programs, and, perhaps most important, a culture that extols starting your own business. We "do entrepreneurship" so well because our entrepreneurship ecosystems are so strong. This is experience we can bring to the dozens of developing countries suffering from 30 percent youth unemployment (and unrest). Doing entrepreneurship is not about picking winners, but about bolstering the ecosystems—influencing them—so that more young firms have more chances for more success over more time, and so they can generate more jobs and more economic hope in the places that need it most (and the places where America needs it most).

Building these ecosystems is precisely what I tried to do when I created the Global Entrepreneurship Program at the State Department. GEP's first pilot country was Egypt and, in 2011, just days before the Arab Spring swept through Tahrir Square, I was in Cairo. One moment on that fateful trip in January sticks out in my mind. Two young, awkward guys, looking like they might be presenting to the principal at a high school science fair, came onto the stage to make their pitch at GEP's business plan competition finale.

Ashraf and Haytham ElFadeel certainly deserved their spot in the finals, but the brothers were not cut out to stand in front of a crowd and deliver "wow." At the time, Ashraf did not seem to speak English very well and Haytham did so with an accent that occasionally turned "problems" into "broblems" and "product" into "broduct." The unassuming twenty-something siblings from Port Said were a bit shy, and the room was a bit weary from the competition's slate of thirty-two finalists.

But then the ElFadeels pitched Kngine. Their idea, Haytham explained, was a new, smart search engine, a voice-activated mobile search tool for iOS and Android that relied on natural language, context, and word relationships—as the human brain does—to derive its results. Kngine would provide users with true answers to search questions, not a catalog of links. The ElFadeels had a plan to deliver cutting-edge semantic search.

I sat riveted, eyes on the Kngine pitchmen. Haytham, on stage, essentially laid out his plans to build a back-end engine to compete with Wolfram Alpha, the engine behind Apple's Siri. Google's Mike Cassidy was there, along with Austin Ligon, the CarMax cofounder turned angel investor, and a dozen other savvy American investors and top entrepreneurs, all delegates on GEP's tour of the Egyptian startup scene. Kngine had their attention and they had questions. Watching from the wings was diaspora Egyptian Ahmed El Alfi along with his partner, Hany Al Sonbaty, and their American colleague, Leslie Jump, the founders and principals of Sawari Ventures, the venture capital and startup equity stalwarts of Egypt. They, along with the American Chamber of Commerce and American University in Cairo, were partnering with GEP to sponsor the business plan competition.

Haytham and Ashraf had taken Kngine as far as they could on a shoestring budget. It had been three years of coding and platform development. The brothers had reached the classic make-or-break moment for technology startups, and all entrepreneurial ventures, really, when the backing of friends and family is exhausted and more capital is required to further a product, to hire additional employees, and to expand.

The appearance at GEP's competition turned into precisely the catalyst the ElFadeels needed. The brothers were the stars of the event and claimed one of the top cash prizes of $20,000. Buoyed by the independent validation Kngine garnered from the GEP delegation, the ElFadeels were soon in negotiations with Sawari Ventures. Sawari, indeed, decided to invest in Kngine—to the tune of $275,000 and, later, $150,000 more—thereby attracting further investors, including Samsung and Vodaphone in 2014.[29] TechCrunch profiled Kngine, noting that an independent consultant had run tests pitting Kngine against Siri and another natural-language competitor, United Kingdom-based Evi. Kngine outperformed them both.[30] The ElFadeels opened a Palo Alto office.

Yet Kngine's creators were hardly the only winners in Cairo. The business plan competition and "entrepreneurship delegation" (EDel, for short) to Egypt, both arranged by GEP, brought together accomplished American business veterans and investors, people like Cassidy and Ligon, as well as their regional counterparts, to get Egypt's entrepreneurial and investment juices flowing and mixing. The EDel participants met with hosts of start-ups, ran workshops for budding Egyptian angel investors, dropped by the Egypt office of Google and Cisco, interacted with the Ministry of Communications and Information Technology, and learned much about the Egyptian entrepreneurial ecosystem.

These investors and mentors won, too. Especially so Sawari Ventures. "Having eight outside people look at the company, and the fact that they won, helped with my decision," El Alfi later said, referring to how the EDel drove his investment in Kngine.[31] Sawari, in fact, used the momentum of the EDel to announce at the closing ceremonies additional investments in mobile app and services companies as well as the creation of a new venture capital fund focused on Egyptian startups.[32] El Alfi and Al Sonbaty were also in the midst of launching Cairo's first serious startup accelerator program, Flat6Labs, in conjunction with American University in Cairo.[33] Since its launch on the heels of the EDel, Flat6Labs has incubated more than seventy-five businesses and spurred the creation of over 400 jobs, nurturing companies in search of investment as well as those that have already secured funding and are growing. In 2013 Flat6Labs opened a second office, in Jeddah, Saudi Arabia, and in 2014 a third, in Abu Dhabi. A Flat6Labs Beirut is slated for 2016.[34]

GEP was shooting for just this sort of catalytic effect. Companies like Kngine secured deals with investors like Sawari Ventures. Professors of development and entrepreneurship mingled with government officials. International investors discovered the Egyptian market. The business competition helped *identify* aspiring entrepreneurs; workshops *trained* entrepreneurs on pitch dos-and-don'ts; mentoring relationships were established between seasoned businessmen and young entrepreneurs, ensuring innovators *connected* with one another and could *sustain* their efforts; investors made *funding* commitments to startups; discussions with government officials tackled regulatory issues that *enable* business growth; and the closing ceremony *celebrated* Egypt's entrepreneurial culture, broadcasting the success of the ElFadeel brothers and, we all hoped, inspiring the next Kngine. One American delegate, Chris Schroeder, was making his first trip to the Arab world startup scene. What he saw inspired him to write a widely acclaimed book, *Startup Rising*, about the bubbling entrepreneurial activity of the Middle East.[35] Thanks in part to GEP, companies were sprouting, jobs were being born, and Egypt's economy made a quarter turn forward.

This is entrepreneurship ecosystem building, and EDels have proven to be one of the most successful programs in that effort. The key words above—*identify, train, connect and sustain, fund, enable, celebrate*—are the crucial elements of a healthy ecosystem. Later in this book I will discuss these elements, and who pays for and implements them, and what I call the Six + Six Entrepreneurship Ecosystem Model. For now, suffice it to say that Egypt's entrepreneurship ecosystem, and Egypt itself, was clearly a GEP and EDel winner, too.

After the GEP EDel to Egypt, the events of Tahrir Square and ensuing months of Arab Spring turmoil highlighted the importance of entrepreneurship to the Middle East and North Africa. As Hernando de Soto has argued, those revolutions were less about democracy and ideals than they were about "a massive economic protest."[36] It became abundantly clear, at least to me, that a generation of young Egyptians had had enough; they wanted economic hope, not the same old same old. Programs like GEP are one way, perhaps the best way, to deliver economic hope.

Elevating Entrepreneurship

Unfortunately, today, the U.S. government does very little GEP-style ecosystem building. In fact, it barely does GEP anymore at all. GEP-Egypt itself was shut down in 2014. We're not shy about spending in Egypt. We just don't spend it on effective entrepreneurship programming. The United States has funneled $1.3 billion in arms and weapons annually to successions of Egypt's military governments since the mid-1980s,[37] while all but ignoring the budding entrepreneurial class. GEP closed shop after stretching its paltry (and hard-won) budget of $2.3 million across three-plus years, a veritable rounding error relative to Egypt's military aid package.

Guns and drones aside, it is clear that our aid and international economic development budgets do not "think entrepreneurship," either. Remarkably, less than 1 percent of our government's foreign aid budget is devoted to programs that have something to do with entrepreneurship, and we can assume that only a fraction of that supports the scalable, job-creating entrepreneurship we really want to see.[38] The impact of GEP, the State Department, the U.S. Agency for International Development (better known as USAID), and many other agencies pales in comparison to the potential.

And so this book is about flipping this around, or at least balancing the tables. This book does not ask you to imagine billions in entrepreneurship assistance to Egypt, but it does ask you to consider what might happen if just a bit more U.S. foreign assistance were diverted to the sort of entrepreneurship ecosystem building that helped launch Kngine. The result, I believe, would be peace, or at least a big step toward that dream.

The first part of this book will explain the power of entrepreneurship, and why the U.S. government routinely fails at entrepreneurship. Chapter 2 discusses how promoting entrepreneurship in foreign countries answers America's national security threats through sheer job-creating power, sopping up unemployment abroad and generating the kind of opportunity that underpins political stability and a civil society. "Doing entrepreneurship" abroad also generates investment opportunities for Americans, opening up markets and investments in today's fastest-growing economies. Entrepreneurship empowers, enabling the undereducated and underserved in weak economies to better themselves. As I say in chapter 3, there are "a million reasons entrepreneurship is good for you." Don't worry; I don't list them all. But some of the benefits will surprise you.

Chapter 4 focuses on entrepreneurship as a key, universally respected American value. Even in the countries that dislike America the most (a growing list), almost all admire the spirit of American innovation and entrepreneurship.[39] They want some of our secret sauce for business success. This is our in.

Chapters 5 and 6 will turn to the bad news. No administration, Democratic or Republican, has ever effectively leveraged entrepreneurship as a foreign policy tool. President Obama's 2010 Summit on Entrepreneurship birthed programs, including GEP, but did not sustain them. Funding and staffing for real pro-entrepreneurship work has remained pitifully small. Even with funding, the convoluted chain of contractors, procurement guidelines, and bureaucracies virtually guarantees entrepreneurship programming will fail.

Beyond stingy funding, critical elements of government functionality are broken; we are turning the economic development screw with a rubber screwdriver. Programs for foreign economic development assistance are scattered across dozens of federal agencies with little coordination, almost always devised by people who have zero "subject matter expertise" (government-ese for "actually knowing what the hell you're talking about"). Government contracting and procurement processes lack the hallmarks of entrepreneurialism: flexibility, innovation, boundary pushing, the ability to "work around" an obstacle. The vast majority of procured government work goes to a small set of large "beltway bandit" firms that are really good at winning government contracts, not to firms that are really good at substantive work.

During my stint with the State Department, I witnessed all the oxymoronic inefficiencies of a bureaucracy doing entrepreneurship. This book will tell these stories, and they are not all about disappointing budgets. Much like Alice's observations of Wonderland through the looking glass, I found that how things are done in Washington is quite different from how things are done in the rest of America. The State Department is different from the real world of business; bureaucracies know little about startup culture.

After that downer, we'll begin the second part of the book by lifting your spirits. It doesn't have to be this way. I'll explain how to do entrepreneurship, highlight examples of entrepreneurship done well, and outline how the U.S. government, warts and all, can do the job.

Chapter 7 outlines my ardent belief that bolstering entrepreneurship requires an ecosystem approach rather than narrow or one-off efforts (for example, seed capital or hit-and-run training), and that startups and small and medium enterprises thrive when multiple actors play multiple roles. As described by my Six + Six Model, business mentoring, regulatory climate, and making entrepreneurship "cool" are also essential to entrepreneurial success. There are proven programs that help build healthy entrepreneurship ecosystems. Chapter 8 examines a host of these. EDels are one example, but as we know from ecosystems in America, there are many ways to bolster entrepreneurship and spark startups, from incubators to television shows like *Shark Tank*.

Chapter 9 brings things together with a roadmap for the U.S. government. Tilting economic development spending toward entrepreneurship, consolidating our entrepreneurship programming into a specialized agency, and reinvigorating "Washington" with "America's" entrepreneurial spirit are vital steps. There is no need to spend more money, just to spend better. But we do need to upgrade two Ps, *procurement* and *people*, to do entrepreneurship right. Redeploying America's entrepreneurship and job-creating talents in the service of foreign policy is part of what might be considered a new approach to "economic statecraft." The United States has been woefully slow to recognize that economic development (and democratic development) and American security and prosperity are inextricably linked. And so the concept and tools of economic statecraft, of which entrepreneurship is a vital part, are at a critical juncture.

I write from the vantage point of an entrepreneur with a keen interest in foreign policy. This is not an academic book. It is not designed to "boil the ocean" with sweeping ideas on bureaucratic reform in the American foreign affairs cluster, detailed blueprints for reforming the government procurement apparatus, or exhaustive surveys of case studies on the role of entrepreneurship in economic development. It is a business guy's view on what entrepreneurship can do, as well as a statement for why and how, based on my tour of duty in Washington, the U.S. government must elevate entrepreneurship as a foreign policy tool and core strategy to preserve American security and prosperity.

PART I

The Problem

TWO

It's All about Jobs

The West thought it recognised what was happening in the Arab world: People wanted democracy, and were having revolutions to make that point. . . . Could it be that the Arab Spring was about something else entirely? I believe so. The Arab Spring was a massive economic protest: A demand that the poor should have the basic rights to buy, sell, and make their way in the world. . . . If the West places Egypt and the Arab Spring into the category of "Islamist uprising," it will not only misunderstand the hopes of millions but miss a remarkable opportunity.

HERNANDO DE SOTO, *The Spectator*, 2013

It is logical that the United States should do whatever it is able to do to assist in the return of normal economic health in the world, without which there can be no political stability and no assured peace.

SECRETARY OF STATE GEORGE C. MARSHALL
on the Marshall Plan, 1947

To succeed in the twenty-first century, we need to integrate the traditional tools of foreign policy—diplomacy, development assistance, and military force—while also tapping the energy and ideas of the private sector and empowering citizens, especially the activists, organizers, and problem solvers we call civil society, to meet their own challenges and shape their own futures.

SECRETARY OF STATE HILLARY R. CLINTON,
Hard Choices, 2014

COUNTRIES WITH SKY-HIGH UNEMPLOYMENT dominate the roster of the world's most unstable and un-peaceful places. This is not a coincidence. In fact, the primary driver of instability in many countries is chronic jobless-ness, the 30 and 40 percent unemployment rates for young people that hamstring many Middle Eastern and North African economies. When you consider that unemployment rates for young people are rising in the re-gions where the number of young people is rising, the future is already in trouble.[1]

Destabilizing unemployment plus a very young population is a brutal combination. This combination produced Mohamed Bouazizi, the des-perate Tunisian vegetable seller who set himself afire out of sheer economic frustration, launching the Arab Spring. The same combination rallied hun-dreds of thousands to Tahrir Square in Egypt. It also spawns foot soldiers for the Islamic State in Iraq and Syria[2] and for Boko Haram in northern Nigeria.[3] The combination creates pools of young men open to radical ide-ology and susceptible to recruitment to uprisings and rebel groups and ter-rorist cells.[4]

The social unrest wrought by unemployment is clearly not just a local matter confined to the world's chaotic neighborhoods. Fragile states are fer-tile ground for terrorism, with immensely real consequences for the United States. Most observers agree that today's threats to American security come not from strong nation-states with standing armies (like Nazi Germany and the Soviet Union) but from unstable, politically shaky regions of the world and from "non-state actors," men in caves outside of Kandahar plot-ting world-changing terrorist attacks, for instance. Building a nuclear sub-marine fleet or army of invasion takes a massive economic foundation. But the weapons of hide-and-seek terrorist groups like ISIS and al-Qaeda re-quire far more modest startup costs. The West—America, mostly—fights these elusive enemies with boots on the ground and (after trillions of dol-lars and hundreds of thousands of lives consumed) drones. With mixed results. (It is, of course, very possible for Western milieus of unemployment to foster terror. The Paris attacks of November 2015 were perpetrated by men from or connected to Molenbeek, Belgium, a Brussels neighborhood beset by a 25 percent unemployment rate, greater than the city's average, and a MENA-like youth unemployment rate of 37 percent.[5]).

"American security and prosperity is increasingly and inextricably linked to economic growth in developing countries," warns a 2013 Center for Strategic and International Studies report.[6] In those parts of Africa with bleak economic prospects—Niger, Mali, northern Nigeria, and elsewhere—

terrorist havens are hardly a concern for the future. They are a clear and present danger. As the *Christian Science Monitor* reports of Africa: "Widespread unemployment, corruption, poor governance, and lawlessness have offered Islamist militants a foothold. Frustrated young men make good recruits, while criminal networks can be tapped as sources of funding."[7] Trouble brews in troubled lands.

But frequently the root cause of instability is misdiagnosed. In the Middle East and North Africa, centuries-old conflicts between religious sects, and the fact that ethnic identities often trump national ones, are blamed for the region's problems. While these factors clearly matter, they alone are not at the heart of MENA's challenges. The core problem—one that doesn't discriminate about religion, ethnic identity, or age—is unemployment and lack of opportunity. As economists Adeel Malik and Bassem Awadallah noted of MENA's uprisings:

> Arab revolutions had a clear economic underpinning; they were fuelled by poverty, unemployment, and lack of economic opportunity. Without a concrete economic response, therefore, the hopes generated by these revolutions can easily give way to despair, raising the spectre of future political volatility. . . . A singular failure of the Arab world is that it has been unsuccessful in developing a strong private sector that is connected with global markets, survives without state crutches, and generates productive employment for its young.[8]

This analysis echoes Hernando de Soto, the Peruvian economist whose groundbreaking work on formal and informal economies ties peace and prosperity to economic opportunity, not to religious and cultural harmony.[9] *New York Times* columnist Thomas L. Friedman, an astute commentator on Arab–Israeli and Middle East strife, says modern nations exist in either of two worlds, one of "order" or one of "disorder." But, he says, disordered-world states blow up today not because of deep ethnic conflict, but "thanks to rapid advances in the market (globalization), Mother Nature (climate change plus ecological destruction) and Moore's Law (computing power)":

> You can't understand the uprising in Syria unless you understand how a horrendous four-year drought there, coupled with a

demographic explosion, undermined its economy. . . . You can't understand Egypt's uprising without linking it to the 2010 global wheat crisis and soaring bread prices. . . . You also can't understand Egypt's stress without understanding the challenge that China's huge labor pool poses in a globalized world to every other low-wage country. . . . You can't understand the spread of ISIS or the Arab Spring without the relentless advance in computing and telecom.[10]

As the saying goes, "It's the economy, stupid." And within the economy, it is specifically jobs—or the lack thereof. In essence, foreign policymakers and the Johnny-come-lately governments emerging from MENA's upheavals often scratch the wrong itch. What most protesters and agitators on the Arab street really care about is not whether Shias or Sunnis rule, but economic change—and the political normalization and rule of law required as ground conditions for such change. (In 2015, French economist Thomas Piketty, whose widely read and acclaimed *Capital in the Twenty-First Century* analyzed tendencies toward extreme inequality and wealth concentration in capitalistic economies, floated a slight variation of my argument, that inequality is also a driver behind terror and the rise of ISIS in the Middle East. As reported by Jim Tankersley of the *Washington Post*, Piketty argues "economic deprivation and the horrors of wars that benefited only a select few of the region's residents have, mixed together, become . . . a 'powder keg' for terrorism. . . . Terrorism that is rooted in inequality, Piketty continues, is best combated economically."[11])

The Cliff's Notes version of joblessness and instability revolves around MENA: Tahrir Square and the Arab Spring, the costly wars in Iraq and Syria (and their regional and global tentacles, including the rise of ISIS). But the plague and symptoms of unemployment are widespread. The gang-ridden and chaotic states of Central America endure high youth unemployment rates, as well, and drive tens of thousands of children to the Arizona border.[12] At the height of the Tamil Tigers' suicide attacks and assassinations in the early 1990s, Sri Lanka's youth unemployment exceeded 40 percent.[13] A lack of employment options is a primary driver for young people to join militias and terror groups, especially in sub-Saharan Africa.[14] In Kenya, in early 2014, a month before authorities intercepted an explosives-laden car operated by suspected Somali Islamist militants,[15] the port city of Mombasa was unsettled by clashes and disputes between police and the Muslim community. Over one hundred Muslims were arrested in a police raid of a mosque reputed to be a home for radical Islamists. While such unrest could easily be framed as religious or ethnic friction—or a response to Kenya's military presence in Somalia—many had a different analysis: jobs. The chairman of Kenya's Muslim Human Rights Forum, Al-Amin Kimathi, attributed the success of Islamist recruiting to a simple fact: "They lack a basis for living. Many young people have no work."[16] He is right. Mombasa's youth unemployment rate is estimated at 44 percent.[17]

From East Africa to the Sahel to the Middle East, or Central America, or Southeast Asia, the instability that afflicts the world stems from unemployment, first and foremost. Even in regions that are calm—for now—the need for job creation is monumental. The government of India has estimated that 10 million to 15 million jobs must be created each year for a decade to accommodate the vast numbers of Indian youth seeking employment.[18] The promising economies of Africa, from Ghana to Zambia to Tanzania, have earned positive media attention,[19] but analysts temper the enthusiasm with evidence that the growth is largely jobless. Observers point out that a decade of rising GDPs has done nothing for poverty at the grassroots level and that the African manufacturing sector has failed to create jobs in the manner seen elsewhere in the world.[20] As economists for the Organization for Economic Cooperation and Development (OECD) Jan Rieländer and Henri-Bernard Solignac-Lecomte explain:

> This is a tough time to be young in Africa. Growth is up but good jobs are scarce. . . . Forty million young people are estimated to be out of work and many more in poor employment. . . . In some countries, like South Africa, the unemployment rate of young people is as high as 50 percent. In other countries most young people work, but do not make enough to put food on the table . . . . Within the next ten years, 130 million young people will be leaving the education system and looking for jobs.[21]

Tens of millions of youth—tens and tens of millions—lack jobs, opportunity, and hope across the developing world. And millions more are due to join those ranks. In the Muslim Arab world, some analysts see a coming "demographic time bomb" that can only be defused by the creation of

80 million new jobs by 2020. That rate of job growth roughly doubles the pace experienced in the United States during the long boom of the 1990s.[22]

Are economic miracles possible?

A New Beginning . . . and a New Answer

In 2009 President Obama delivered his "New Beginning" speech in Cairo. There, he spoke of a "broader engagement" between America and Muslim communities around the world. He talked about what the U.S. government would actually do ("deliverables," in government-ese), like "a new corps of business volunteers to partner with counterparts in Muslim-majority countries;" "a new fund to support technological development in Muslim-majority countries, and to help transfer ideas to the marketplace so they can create more jobs;" and a "Summit on Entrepreneurship."[23]

This was hardly the Marshall Plan, but the fact that an American president was even talking about the value of supporting innovation and entrepreneurship abroad was historic. And Obama's Cairo address was very much in line with my passion for entrepreneurship in the service of foreign policy, and my experience as a startup founder and business guy. The Arab world needs jobs, and the best job creator of all is entrepreneurship.

Inspired by Obama's speech, I abandoned semi-retirement in Maine, cashed in on a standing Franklin Fellowship offer to volunteer at the State Department, and moved to Washington to work on this issue of spurring entrepreneurship. Importantly, at the time, President Obama was not the only one talking about economic engagement with troubled regions like MENA. I discovered that similar ideas were brewing right in Hillary Clinton's State Department.

When I arrived at State in 2009, Secretary Clinton was working with her policy planning director, Anne-Marie Slaughter, to produce the first Quadrennial Diplomacy and Development Review. Called the QDDR for short, this report may ultimately stand as one of Secretary Clinton's most important accomplishments while in office.[24] It did not have the bright-and-shiny-object characteristics of, say, ending a war or transitioning a chunk of the world from totalitarianism to democracy, but it was an important strategy statement that homed in on "trends reshaping the global context of U.S. foreign policy."[25] Translation: Here was a belated acknowledgement that the post-9/11 world is different from the postwar and Cold War world.

Noting a sea change from the threats of old, Secretary Clinton's QDDR identified what truly endangers American security and prosperity today: "Power in the international system was once exercised more or less exclusively by states, but it is now shared with a wide array of non-state actors. These actors . . . have an ever greater ability to impact international affairs. [Some of them] pose deadly threats."[26]

Secretary Clinton saw new circumstances—especially economic chaos and the shift from state to non-state actors—as key U.S. concerns and advocated a shift from a foreign policy based solely on military muscle to one that highlighted "soft power" assets like economic, social, and political development.[27] This amalgamation she would call "smart power."[28] Like President Obama's Cairo speech, the intent that QDDR signaled was news in itself. Ideas about what foreign policy could do were changing. Discussing QDDR publicly a month after President Obama's visit to Cairo, Secretary Clinton explained her goal of elevating economic development as a foreign policy tool: "A central purpose of the Quadrennial Diplomacy and Development Review that I announced last week is to explore how to effectively design, fund, and implement development and foreign assistance as parts of a broader foreign policy."[29]

Music to my ears. For if shaky regions and non-state actors are America's top threats and we all agree that smarter development assistance could be a solution, then, boy, do we have a useful gizmo in the toolbox: entrepreneurship. Secretary Clinton's QDDR and Obama's Cairo Initiative opened the door for my kind of programs. My first gig upon settling in at Foggy Bottom (aka the State Department, known as "Foggy Bottom" for reasons that made a lot of sense to me after I had been there a while) was helping organize the Presidential Summit on Entrepreneurship that Obama mentioned in Cairo. But I realized there would be "no there there" if we did not have a real program of real activity to pursue afterward (another "deliverable"). And since my ultimate boss, Secretary Clinton, would be the final speaker at the entrepreneurship summit, it seemed she would be the perfect person to talk about what we, the U.S. government, were actually going to do about entrepreneurship in the Middle East and North Africa beyond a confab over snacks and coffee in Washington, D.C. So I set about trying to figure that out. Not long after, I founded the State Department's Global Entrepreneurship Program (GEP), an initiative designed to support entrepreneurs in several key Muslim countries.

The idea behind GEP was to stimulate job creation in countries whose instability and youth unemployment could threaten America. We would do this by promoting entrepreneurship. We would engage the real factors that affect real entrepreneurs by providing real business assistance directly to startups, as well as addressing some of the behind-the-scenes issues important to entrepreneurs, like regulatory environments and media coverage. (In many emerging markets, business journalists know how to cover happenings at Coca-Cola, but are clueless about approaching a two-man software startup.)

Also, I had noticed that programs were completely uncoordinated and, very often, poorly executed. This was true across State, USAID (our government's primary foreign aid vehicle, responsible for projects in over 100 countries), and the dozens of other government agencies that throw their hat into the international economic development ring. USAID might brag (and does) about hundreds of millions of dollars spent on entrepreneurship programming, but those millions were spread over a hundred programs worldwide that had little to do with one another and little evidence of success. These scattered initiatives were more often than not actually initiated and funded by individual USAID offices ("country missions"), and almost never shared lessons learned (unless coincidentally carried out by the same USAID contractor). It was the first example of something I was to see often in Washington, what I call "groundhog day": Every idea in every location is new for the first time. Government efforts at business development lacked institutional memory, cross-fertilization, consistency, and coordination.

Typically, these programs were operated by a rotating cast of "usual suspect" contractors who knew little, if anything, about startups but a lot about winning and managing USAID contracts (including through court action). I will say more in chapters 5 and 6 about how USAID and other government agencies underperform on entrepreneurship promotion, but my focus now is the new approach of the GEP initiative I founded. America could provide sustained, comprehensive, customized packages of entrepreneurship programs to countries.

GEP would take a holistic approach, one that bolstered "ecosystems" that foster entrepreneurship and worked in partnership with both for-profit and not-for-profit groups. Successful entrepreneurship ecosystems consist of multiple activities undertaken by many kinds of actors. They include entrepreneurs, of course, but also universities, investors, governments, and other entities. Everyone's favorite ecosystem is Silicon Valley; think of all the startups, shared workspaces, elite educational institutions, and venture capital firms up and down Route 101 and across the Bay Area.

Strong entrepreneurship ecosystems also feature multiple pillars of activity: mechanisms to identify promising entrepreneurs, to train them, to mentor them, and to fund them. This was the basis of what became my Six+Six Entrepreneurship Ecosystem Model, described fully in chapter 7, and I wanted to design programming that targeted all of the actors and all of the pillars in particular ecosystems.[30]

For instance, entrepreneurship delegations, like the one described in chapter 1 that connected Kngine with investors, exemplify a program that strengthens an ecosystem. Business veterans and seed-stage investors visit a particular ecosystem, meet local entrepreneurs, hold workshops, judge a business plan competition, and generally churn the fledgling ecosystem. Not only do entrepreneurs need training, but so do investors, especially those new to very early-stage investments. At the time of GEP's founding, the angel investment movement in the United States was at least fifteen years old. Angels, who make earlier and smaller investments in startups than venture capitalists, are critical to startup activity. I have both received and made angel investments myself, and I wanted GEP to develop angel groups in some of the places the program worked to activate local wealth in the ecosystems.

With programming like this in mind, we designed GEP to focus on Muslim-majority (though, importantly, not just Arab) countries, which were the focus of Obama's Cairo Initiative. The countries were, in order of rollout: Egypt (the world's largest Arab population), Indonesia (the world's largest Muslim population), and Turkey (widely considered to be the "poster child" of a democratic, free-market Muslim country). We planned secondary programs for Lebanon, Jordan, Tunisia, Algeria, and Morocco. Secretary Clinton announced GEP in the closing speech at the Presidential Summit on Entrepreneurship, saying it would "provide concrete support to new entrepreneurs, starting in Muslim-majority communities" and that "we plan to expand to a dozen countries within the next two years."[31]

Despite her resounding words, GEP struggled to make a significant stamp in its three primary countries, let alone "a dozen countries." This is a story for chapters 5 and 6, a big story, and one very much about "good idea, bad execution." It's also a story for which this book aims to write a better ending.

Nevertheless, GEP was not without its successes. We implemented programs like entrepreneurship delegations (in Lebanon, Jordan, Egypt, and Turkey), investor trainings, and journalism workshops. Our activities served some 2,500 entrepreneurs and helped secure seed investment for dozens of companies in seven countries. GEP enabled hundreds of mentoring relationships between successful American entrepreneurs and those in target countries across the Middle East. We helped launch new venture funds and angel investor networks. Our entrepreneurship delegation rosters boasted veteran investors in A-list firms as well as highly successful entrepreneurs and representatives of boundary-pushing companies like Google.[32] As GEP partner and Sawari Ventures principal Ahmed El Alfi says of Egypt, "The GEP program was a kick-starter to accelerate the entrepreneurial activities that were present in the country."[33]

Entrepreneurship = Jobs = Growth = Stability

Can an initiative like GEP be part of the solution to 30 percent youth unemployment rates and bring hope to millions of frustrated, jobless young people? Yes. But, of course, not on its own. GEP is not a silver bullet, but it is precisely the kind of concrete program that the United States government needs to implement on a large scale to address the roots of twenty-first-century threats. The U.S. government has learned to "talk the talk" on entrepreneurship promotion. Executing on GEP and similar programs represents "walking the walk."

The main reason I believe so strongly in this is because entrepreneurship can be a job-creating machine. Promoting entrepreneurship means not just that companies in Egypt, Turkey, and Indonesia exist, but that they flourish and create jobs. When startups flourish and create jobs, economies grow, men and women productively contribute to society, political stability reigns, and life is good. Of course, it takes many of these companies (and not all startups will be successful), but we have to start somewhere. It may not be the last word in world peace, but creating jobs for young people is certainly a big first step to creating the hope and optimism that are essential to that peace.

Entrepreneurship = jobs = growth = stability. This sequence stands at the very core of this book and my conviction that entrepreneurship must be leveraged as a foreign policy tool. Entrepreneurship creates jobs and generates economic growth; jobs and growth are the underpinnings of a stable, civil society. More than anything else, the central tenet of this book is the power of this direct-line connection between entrepreneurship and a peaceful society.

So this chapter and the next will discuss entrepreneurship's powerful effects. For example, in recent decades, firms less than five years old accounted for nearly all net job creation in the United States.[34] Such entrepreneurial energy is very much a core American value. It is no coincidence that for two-and-a-half centuries the United States has prospered, maintained a stable democracy, and stood tall as "the land of opportunity," the one nation that the world's aspiring emigrants most often want to reach.[35] It is similarly no coincidence that a region plagued by rampant youth unemployment and economic frustration—the Middle East and North Africa—is home to never-ending strife and exports terrorism.

Remember our definition of entrepreneurship: An entrepreneur is a person with the vision to see a new product or process and the ability to make it happen. Entrepreneurship of this kind—innovative and scalable—leads off the jobs–growth–stability sequence at the heart of this book.

So how strong are the relationships in this sequence? The first, that entrepreneurship creates jobs, may seem obvious. A new company hires new employees. But just how important are startups and young firms on the macroeconomic scale? I just mentioned the impressive calculation from economists at the Kauffman Foundation, perhaps the world's foremost entrepreneurship think tank, that American firms less than five years old were responsible for nearly all net job creation in the United States from 1980 to 2005. Kauffman also reports that in 2007 alone firms between one and five years old (that is, excluding the youngest startups) created 8 million of the 12 million new jobs added to the American economy that year.[36] That is two out of every three.

The consulting firm McKinsey & Company (one of my former employers) also keeps a close eye on entrepreneurship and has a stack of factoids demonstrating the critical role entrepreneurship plays in employment. For instance, if new businesses had kept forming at 2007 rates, the United States would have had 1.8 million more jobs by the close of 2010 than it did after the financial crisis; a drop in startups means a drop in jobs, and research in the last few years suggests new business formation continues to be anemic in the United States.[37] In France, firms less than five years old account for 16 percent of employment in all industry, trade, and services.[38] In the United

Kingdom it is a tiny fraction of high-growth, innovative firms that generate the majority of new jobs.[39] Economists from the OECD recently surveyed data from the United States and seventeen other rich countries and concluded: "Young firms (five years of age or younger) are the primary source of job creation in all eighteen countries over most of the 2000s. This is driven to a large extent by the entry of new start-ups as well as higher growth rates of young firms that survive."[40]

Bottom line: entrepreneurship creates jobs.

But does the same effect of entrepreneurship on job creation hold true for poorer and emerging countries as well? Yes. In fact, reports McKinsey & Company, when it comes to startups and new businesses, "What holds true for a mature economy such as the U.S. is likely to be even more applicable in emerging economies where the economic and business fabric is less robust."[41] For starters, small- and medium-size enterprises (SMEs) account for the vast majority of jobs in emerging economies. This means governments and economists often target young firms and entrepreneurs as a means to boost employment.[42] In India, which needs 10 million to 15 million new jobs every year to absorb its ever-growing working-age population, the government commissioned a study of the role that angel and early-stage venture capital investing might play in sopping up job seekers. The report was blunt: "Accelerating entrepreneurship and business creation is crucial for such large-scale employment generation. . . . Large Indian businesses— both in the public and private sector—have not generated significant employment in the past few decades and are unlikely to do so in the coming decade or two."[43]

The same is true across the world. Calls for entrepreneurship to do battle with unemployment, especially youth unemployment, resonate from Nigeria[44] to the Middle East.[45]

The key to entrepreneurship's job-creating power is that startups and SMEs are like seedlings. You have to start with the seed before you get a tree, and you need lots of seedlings to get a handful of survivor trees. Scatter an entrepreneurship ecosystem with a number of startups and the future will yield at least a few big, full-blown trees that employ big numbers. Of course, individual startups will create jobs themselves. Such firms tend to be more innovative and nimble than their established counterparts. Bringing new and improved products and processes to market, and hiring new employees to do so, they are the embodiment of what the economist who arguably "discovered" the power of entrepreneurship, Joseph Schumpeter, calls "creative destruction."[46] But entrepreneurship mainly creates jobs by seeding the economy with startups that are churning and developing, waiting in the wings, with a tiny but hugely important few ultimately exploding and creating significant numbers of jobs.[47] As an example, according to a study in the United Kingdom: "A small minority of high-growth businesses hold the key to job creation and wider prosperity. New research . . . shows that the 6 percent of U.K. businesses with the highest growth rates generated half of the new jobs created by existing businesses between 2002 and 2008."

It is important to note that not all entrepreneurs and the businesses they start create jobs. Indeed—putting on my mentor hat—the last thing you want your company to do is hire more people than absolutely necessary. The goals of public policy and the private sector do not always overlap on this point. (Further, clearly, not all startups succeed; trial-and-error at the firm level and within an ecosystem of startups always yields winners and losers, lucky and unlucky both. Still, more seedlings, more trees.)

Entrepreneurship is a primary driver of jobs, but it is also a serious driver of economic growth. Again, this might seem obvious. More businesses and more jobs should correlate with, perhaps even cause, economic activity. We know that countries with higher rates of startups typically have superior economic growth,[48] and that there is a strong positive correlation between the size of a country's SME sector and its economic growth.[49] The Legatum Institute has published a Prosperity Index for the past several years that aggregates and weighs country data from sources like the World Bank, Gallup, and the United Nations. Scandinavian countries (as you would expect) top the prosperity list, with sub-Saharan African countries at the bottom. Across the board, Legatum finds that, of its eight indicators, it is "entrepreneurship & opportunity" that correlate most strongly with a country's overall prosperity.[50] Separately, economists Norbert Berthold and Klaus Gründler wrote in a 2012 paper: "Using data of 188 countries between 1980 and 2010, we show that entrepreneurship has a significantly positive effect on growth. . . . Entrepreneurship matters."[51]

Why it matters isn't hidden away in a black box. Entrepreneurship means business creation, and these businesses, more efficient than their predecessors,[52] are creating good jobs that are part of the formal economy. In developing and emerging market contexts, formal jobs typically yield higher incomes than careers in the informal economy.[53] Workers are consumers, too, and newly employed people add to an economy's consumer base, paving the way for further growth. Similarly, startups are consumers, as well, since they become customers of and suppliers to other businesses. One of my favorite pro-entrepreneurship programs, and many will be discussed in Part II, connects startups as customers and suppliers for each other. Investors are great, but customers are better!

The history of international entrepreneurship is filled with amazing examples of entrepreneurship driving economies forward. One of my favorite history lessons, the contrasting fates of Jamaica and Singapore, was outlined by Josh Lerner in *Boulevard of Broken Dreams.*[54] In 1965, Jamaica and Singapore, both resource-poor, former British colony island nations, had similar populations[55] and per capita GDPs, about $2,700 (in 2006 U.S. dollars). Forty years later, Jamaica had bumped up its per capita GDP to $4,800 and had gained about a million people. Singapore? After independence, the island city-state implemented reforms and incentives to create one of the most innovative and pro-business economies not just in Asia, but the world. By 2006, in great contrast to Jamaica, the Asian Tiger had 4.4 million people enjoying a per capita GDP of $31,400. As Lerner puts it: "In explaining Singapore's economic growth, it is hard not to give considerable credit to its policies toward entrepreneurship."[56] (Of course, effective governance underlies the ability to implement any policy, including entrepreneurship. Clearly, its presence in Singapore helped allow many policies to actually succeed.)

Governmental emphasis on business creation has similarly keyed jobs and growth in diverse economies around the world. Israel and Rwanda stand as particularly interesting examples of entrepreneurship's vital influence on growth.[57] This is in part because of the disparity in their current wealth, and in part because they demonstrate that entrepreneurship is influenceable. Both countries—one rich, one poor—have entrepreneurship to thank for gains in their populations' welfare; both countries' governments took conscious pro-entrepreneurship steps to bolster their entrepreneurship ecosystems.

The role of government and the role of ecosystems will be further explored in chapters 4 and 7. For now, let us continue to the latter portion of the entrepreneurship = jobs = growth = stability equation: Entrepreneurship is a powerful tool not just because it creates jobs and grows economies, but because jobs and growth bring political stability and underpin a civil society.

When there aren't enough jobs, the consequences are serious, from civil strife to international conflict and terror. We know how bitter economic conditions and resulting spite fueled Nazism's rise in inter-war Germany. Economic ruin and decimated dignity are recipes for extremism. Recall Tunisian street vendor Mohamed Bouazizi, whose intense economic frustration drove him to set himself on fire in 2010, an act that set off the Arab Spring. Bouazizi was protesting a system that offered him little chance of earning a meaningful living. By 2013 it was clear the Arab Spring was, in fact, the wrong term; it was really more like the Arab *rolling thunder*, as the Muslim Brotherhood that emerged from post–Arab Spring elections was no more able (many would say even less able) to spur the Egyptian economy than the sclerotic Mubarak regime. The Brotherhood government soon fell under pressure from mass demonstrations and Egypt's military. In Egypt (and Tunisia, Turkey, and several other Muslim countries), political tension amplifies the underlying malaise that comes from high unemployment, gross income distribution inequality, and dim prospects for change. I would argue, however, that more often than not economic despair is the cause, not the result, of political, religious, and cultural friction.

In fragile states, lack of jobs and slow economic growth pose real threats to social cohesion and peace.[58] Among young people who join rebel movements, one in every two do so because they cannot find a job.[59] Unemployment stands at the very heart of hopelessness, and when political remedies don't exist, violence is often the recourse for young men.[60] Studies of recent African conflicts show a worrying negative correlation between GDP growth and civil violence, with the likelihood of civil war increasing by more than one-half with a 5 percentage-point drop in annual economic growth.[61] There is little doubt that depressed income levels and sluggish growth lead to civil strife in poor and fragile countries.[62]

On the flip side, jobs and growth tend to stabilize societies, diffuse unrest, provide people with hope for mobility, and encourage a civil society free from disruption. Some studies suggest that rising incomes correlate with democratic governance, and that countries sporting per capita GDPs over $6,000 are likely to lean toward democracy, with democracies over $10,000 unlikely to ever give it up.[63] Entrepreneurship grows a middle class, and a middle class always represents a society's anchor of political stability and civil society, a society's core. That is the message behind Middle East expert Vali Nasr's *Forces of Fortune: The Rise of the New Muslim Middle Class and What it Will Mean for Our World*,[64] and behind the optimistic "Africa rising" message from that continent's high-growth economies.[65] A middle class is an economy's core set of consumers, core set of workers, and core set of voters. A strong middle class links the economic elite of a country with its young entrepreneurs, its next generation of businesses leaders. It encompasses the citizens who have real stakes in their country's political environment.

Diffusing unrest and stabilizing societies is all about jobs and growth. Jobs and growth start with entrepreneurship.

A Different Role for Government

In entrepreneurship, the U.S. government has at its disposal an extraordinary tool, one that creates jobs and directly addresses the youth unemployment crisis that underlies threats to American security and prosperity. This tool, as examined in chapter 4, is quintessentially American. Our government must spend more of its development funds on supporting entrepreneurs in fragile and developing economies.

But the answer is clearly not just spending more on entrepreneurship. We have to spend it more wisely. My observations from my time creating and running the Global Entrepreneurship Program—coupled with over thirty years of experience in investment banking, telecommunications, and entertainment—showed me that there is often a huge gap (chasm, really) between policy and execution. I do believe that government is often inept and frequently inefficient and wasteful. I believe government often fails to back up talk with action, and that many parts of government are broken, from human resources practices to procurement policy—all issues discussed at length in chapters 5 and 6.

Nevertheless, there are some things that only government can do and must do, things that the private sector cannot or will not do on its own. And just because government does some things badly does not mean government is totally ineffective in all realms. It does not follow that we should slash taxes and slash bureaucracy, starve the beast and let the private sector "do it all." That would be throwing the baby out with the bathwater. Instead, government must elevate entrepreneurship as a foreign policy tool, which will require government getting its act together.

Why is this government's responsibility? Because what we have here is a national security situation. Youth unemployment in fragile states, as noted throughout this chapter and chapter 1, poses the real core threat to America and the "ordered" world today. And everyone from the most fanatic Tea Party member leftward would agree that failing states and terrorism are threats to America and that dealing with threats to America is the responsibility of the federal government. The framers of the Constitution distinctly put the task to "provide for the common defense" in federal hands.[66]

Dealing with economic disaster in troubled nations, work best done by entrepreneurship programming, is a matter of national security. When youth unemployment, instability, and terror came home to roost on 9/11, we decided to invade Afghanistan and Iraq. Now we have discovered that those invasions, Guantanamo Bay detentions, drones, and vast military expense have not and will not make America more secure in the long run. The Middle East is as unstable as ever, probably more than it was fifteen years ago, before the United States spent more than $1.5 trillion—some calculate a figure three to four times that—on wars that killed 45,000 American soldiers, allies, and contractors and, at a bare minimum, 175,000 civilians across Iraq, Afghanistan, and Pakistan.[67]

We can chase ISIS, al-Qaeda, al-Shabaab, Hamas, Hezbollah, Boko Haram, AQIM, and whoever else all over the globe for a very, very long time. But there will be a virtually limitless supply of desperate, unemployed young (mostly) men living in shaky states, until truly viable economic opportunities present themselves. Those opportunities will come, at least in part, through entrepreneurship. Right now, foreign diplomats laugh at America's naïve Afghanistan policies,[68] and post-conflict reconstruction efforts have been sloppy affairs, with the Special Inspector for Iraq Reconstruction estimating that U.S. government programs "wasted at least $8 billion" of the $60 billion of rebuilding and development funds in that country.[69] Public, insider, and foreign disillusionment with Washington's approach to fragile states and economic development is heavy and widespread. It is time for another strategy.

If we really want to respond to twenty-first-century threats to America, and if we really want to prevent another 9/11, we must try entrepreneurship. Job creation for the sake of national security is not a private sector specialty, I am afraid. The private sector is beholden to shareholders and core business purposes; it has no direct interest in getting Pakistani teenagers off the streets. Our very own federal government is the only entity with the interest, the duty, and the means to solve the joblessness and hopelessness in faraway lands that breed extremism.

Both President George W. Bush ("war on terror") and President Obama (Cairo Initiative) could see how instability and non-state actors in difficult parts of the world affected America. But Bush only saw nails and swung a hammer. And while Obama and Secretary Clinton looked for more nuanced tools, it turned out they were using a rubber screwdriver. Sure, the U.S. government has not mastered economic statecraft or done entrepreneurship, aid, or even Healthcare.gov very well. But in entrepreneurship promotion we have a discrete area where I strongly believe our track record can improve, and that it must. This will cost a fraction of a fraction of a fraction of a war on terror. And no one gets killed. They get jobs, instead.

Job creation is entrepreneurship's most powerful weapon. But there are actually a million more reasons why entrepreneurship is good foreign policy. These reasons are examined more closely in the next chapter because there are a bunch of benefits that derive from supporting entrepreneurs besides job creation. After that we will turn to why there is no one better than us, Americans and the American government, to promote entrepreneurship abroad.

THREE

A Million Reasons Entrepreneurship Is Good for You

LORNA RUTTO COLLECTS PLASTIC. She started doing this as a kid, crafting bits and pieces into earrings. Today she gathers a bit more. Like about 1,500 pounds of it. Per day. And instead of making earrings, she sorts and shreds the pieces, melts them down, pours the molten liquid into an injection molder, and manufactures plastic lumber. She makes poles, beams, and planks. These she sells for fencing; for flooring; for picnic tables; for livestock enclosures; for signage; for shipping pallets; for decks; for garden planters; for roofing. Rutto's lumber does not rot. It does not need any chemical treatment, does not splinter, and is of no interest to termites and mold. It can outlive and outperform conventional wood timber.

Rutto's lumber can be found all over the place. Municipalities affix road signs to it. Fancy hotels, international banks, and national parks use it for fencing. Rutto has done well for herself. Newspapers, conference panels, and awards ceremonies have celebrated her story and innovative business model. And 100 percent recycled plastic lumber offers huge environmental benefits. Trash is recycled and trees saved. Rutto estimates that for every twenty-five posts made from recycled materials, she saves a mature cedar tree.[1]

Like many manufacturing operations, Rutto's factory is in an industrial part of town. But the town is not Seattle, San Francisco, Copenhagen, Amsterdam, or any eco-friendly, innovative metropolis. The town is Nairobi, Kenya.

When Rutto founded EcoPost in 2010, the news out of Kenya was focused on the International Criminal Court's (ICC) decision to investigate election-related violence that had killed 1,500 people and displaced hundreds of thousands in 2008. Those events had startled a world that viewed Kenya as East Africa's economic rock. Tourism dropped off precipitously, decimating the country's primary source of foreign currency.[2] The ICC went on to charge Kenya's leadership with crimes against humanity. In the next few years, tourism began to recover and a general election went off smoothly (despite an expectant, almost eager-for-failure Western press). But then came the September 2013 Westgate terror attack, in which more than sixty civilians were killed in an assault and subsequent siege at an upscale Nairobi shopping mall. The militant Islamist group al-Shabaab claimed responsibility, saying the attacks were retaliation for Kenya's military incursion into Somalia, where Kenyan and Somali forces were pursuing an al-Qaeda cell.

Today, on top of environmental challenges (Nairobi generates over a million pounds of plastic trash a day), Kenya sits uneasy, facing worrying demographic and economic trends: "500,000 youth enter the job market every year with limited employment prospects," laments EcoPost's website. Unemployed youth are thought to be prime recruiting material for Kenya's radical Muslim groups. Those who feared that Westgate was just a prelude were proven right in April 2015, when al-Shabaab struck Garissa University College in Kenya's North Eastern Province toward the Somali border, killing at least 150.[3]

Lorna Rutto is doing something about the jobs crisis. Her factory pumps out plastic building materials a few miles from the Westgate site, adjacent to a horrific slum and near Eastleigh, a neighborhood dominated by Somali migrants, who, these days, fear harassment from Kenyan forces ostensibly on anti-terror patrol.[4] Part of EcoPost's mission is to "create sustainable jobs for people in marginalized communities," and these entrepreneurial efforts are making an impact. Rutto employs a core staff of fifteen, but over 500 people pick plastic trash off of Nairobi's streets and bring it to EcoPost. Rutto buys the scrap plastic at a per kilogram rate, thus providing wages to vast numbers who otherwise might be idle.

EcoPost is good for Kenya. As we will soon see, EcoPost—and the kind of entrepreneurship it represents—is also good for you, me, and the United States of America.

This book is about why the U.S. government should spend more money supporting entrepreneurs like Rutto. If the United States could shift its international economic development resources—even slightly—so that more American aid dollars were directed to bolstering the entrepreneurship ecosystems that are essential to nurturing startups like EcoPost, then we would see a lot more EcoPosts. And that would be a very good thing.

I jokingly say there are a million reasons entrepreneurship is good for you. The most important reason was discussed in the last chapter: jobs. According to our entrepreneurship equation, entrepreneurship creates jobs and economic growth, and jobs and growth are the underpinnings of stable, civil, peaceful societies. It hardly seems necessary to explore any of the other million reasons entrepreneurship is good for you—world peace ought to be good enough—but many of these reasons are ancillary to and reinforcing of this core entrepreneurship − jobs = growth = stability equation, and many demonstrate the far-reaching influence entrepreneurship has on a society.

Here are a few examples. Entrepreneurship links innovation with commercialization, transforming a neat concept in a lab into a can't-live-without-it product for the retail consumer. Plastic lumber is an innovation. But without entrepreneurs like Lorna Rutto who bring ideas to market, Kenyans would not have an alternative to wood fencing (often stolen for firewood) or wood water-tank platforms (which rot and weaken in heavy rains). Without the entrepreneurial efforts of Spencer Silver and Art Fry, the semi-adhesive glue that Silver developed in his 3M lab in 1968 would never have led to the Post-it note we find in every office today.[5]

Entrepreneurship also empowers, enabling a poor woman in a poor country to generate income, secure a good home, and send her children to school. This is also the promise of microfinance, but full-blown entrepreneurship takes it to a meaningful, lasting level. Entrepreneurship is the first step up the economic ladder, providing access to both well-being and social respect for those who are normally denied such access, including women (see, for example, Lorna Rutto), ethnic minorities, and those lacking friends in high places.

Different kinds of entrepreneurship yield different benefits. For example, the "traditional" high-tech entrepreneurship we hear so much about does create jobs, but usually not at the scale that no- and low-tech entrepreneurship can achieve. But high-tech entrepreneurship does drive attention to improving the quality of tertiary educational institutions. It sparks regulatory reform to improve business-enabling environments.

As a huge believer in the power of entrepreneurship, I am tempted to list all one million reasons that entrepreneurship is good for you. But I'll spare you and cite just a baker's dozen:

1. Entrepreneurship is one of the most important job creators in any economy.
2. Entrepreneurship links innovation to commercialization.
3. Promoting entrepreneurship helps post-conflict and fragile states create hope, heal their wounds, and turn toward reconstruction and stabilization.
4. Entrepreneurs respond to actual market needs, not the whims of development "experts" who often are based far from the action on the ground.
5. Entrepreneurship organically promotes a regulatory environment that is hospitable to business and a justice system that respects things like contracts, intellectual property rights, and labor mobility by enlisting a society's very own citizen-entrepreneurs as advocates for change and proponents of successful state institutions.
6. In the long run, entrepreneurs turn "informal" economies "formal." You can borrow against, finance, sell, or take public a legal asset, but not an illegal (informal) one. Governments also want to move businesses from the informal to the formal sector so they can be taxed, which (at least theoretically) enables government to become more professional and provide more services.
7. Entrepreneurship mobilizes existing resources, encouraging local investors to vet and consider startups in their own region, thereby keeping money local and creating local pro-entrepreneurship constituencies.
8. Entrepreneurship is often the only "way up" for women and girls in societies where they are traditionally excluded from economic opportunity. Similarly, entrepreneurship can allow those not born to privilege to better their lives.
9. Growing companies in emerging economies create financial return opportunities for investors, domestic and foreign alike. In fact, for both

entrepreneurs and investors, startups are often the single greatest wealth creator in any economy.

10. Entrepreneurs are the "same person" all over they world. As a result, they tend to get along with each other. More than any other group in society, entrepreneurs from vastly disparate cultures—even warring cultures—usually care more about their startups than their differences. If they see a benefit to collaboration, which all but the least creative and least likely to succeed will, they will reach out to even their worst "enemies."

11. Entrepreneurs get things done and bring an energy and focus that can move an economy out of neutral and toward growth, be it a poor country or stagnant developed one.

12. Education drives innovation, and innovation drives entrepreneurship. Nations that value entrepreneurship quickly find that this direct connection encourages greater emphasis on supporting educational institutions. The result is often increased government-funded research and development spending, which accelerates innovation.

13. Entrepreneurship is a shining example of all the very best America has to offer the world. Even those who most dislike our politics or other aspects of America's projected image view our entrepreneurial culture favorably. Playing to this strength can win over hearts and minds in developing markets.

I aim to convince you by the end of this chapter that elevating entrepreneurship as a key element of U.S. foreign policy is a no-brainer. To do this, I would like to elaborate on a few of the above points and extract themes that I think are especially interesting to both the U.S. government and the taxpayers it is supposed to serve. Consider this:

—Entrepreneurship is good for you because it is a highly effective and efficient tool for foreign economic assistance. Private foundations, NGOs, and corporations, from the Omidyar Network to Endeavor to Google, realized this first. However, some official development institutions—like the United Kingdom's Department for International Development (DFID), the Dutch development bank FMO, the World Bank's infoDev, and (in smaller ways) even USAID—are beginning to realize this.

—Entrepreneurship is good for you because it creates investment and trade opportunities for Americans. Money spent on entrepreneurship promotion is not, to paraphrase former Senator Jesse Helms, foreign aid thrown down a "rat hole." It is a true win–win.

—Entrepreneurship is good for you because it is a cross-cultural common ground that wins new friends for entrepreneurs and governments alike. Entrepreneurship opens doors; it even *creates* doors and then opens them.

Inside the Tent

Let us start with "effective foreign assistance," something of an oxymoron for some people. Investing in entrepreneurship ecosystems makes for smart foreign aid spending, not just because it generates economic activity. It also activates demand-driven change. Entrepreneurs are not implementing aid projects designed in D.C., London, or Geneva, nor are they responding to an RFP (request for proposal) drafted by USAID bureaucrats (who, in my experience, have rarely had real experience in creating a single job, and who are frequently forbidden from pre-bid consultation with relevant subject-matter experts). Entrepreneurs are innovating and commercializing because they have identified a market opening for a new product or service. Whether a new innovation is good or useful is determined by a country's investors and consumers, not D.C.'s aid dollars. This is reason number 4; entrepreneurship listens to the market.

But entrepreneurship as demand-driven change plays out in more subtle ways, as well, which is what reason number 5 is about. For example, entrepreneurs are a ready-made pro-education constituency since they draw their workforce from local schools. Good companies need good workers. Consider, too, rule-of-law and regulatory issues (which, like education, are often targets of aid projects). Though usually apolitical, entrepreneurs— and the investors who support them—care deeply about effective government. They know that a successful ecosystem cannot exist without political stability and sensible regulatory frameworks. They, therefore, tend to press for modernization of legal systems, sane intellectual property rules, and stable currencies. Coincidentally, these issues are what rich donor countries generally are trying to impose via carrot (that is, aid) and stick (that is, sanctions). Entrepreneurs are also a strong constituency for reducing corruption, one of the biggest problems in developing countries. If corruption is too great and the cost it imposes on startups too high, entrepreneurs will simply leave or close up shop.

The salutary effects of entrepreneurship on the regulatory environment are important for both homegrown and foreign companies, especially those based in knowledge or innovation economies. Here is a specific example: intellectual property rights. Be they in pharmaceuticals, computer software, or movies, entrepreneurs want to protect their own innovations and will be strong campaigners for the relevant causes. This happens to align well with U.S. interests, as enforcing U.S. intellectual property (IP) rights—on software, movies, music, and other material—is one of the great challenges for American business and government abroad. Endlessly exhorting foreign governments to respect U.S. patent, copyright, and other IP protections is not terribly effective. But highlighting to those same governments the benefits of IP protection for their own citizens' innovations is effective. A colleague at an American embassy in a large developing country notorious for piracy of American patented and copyrighted material once remarked to me that by working with entrepreneurs he had a new opportunity to find in-country allies on IP protection. It was clear to local entrepreneurs that "what was good for the goose was good for the gander." The locals would benefit if their own government started observing international standards of intellectual property protection, so they supported reform.

Another major boon of entrepreneurship promotion as foreign policy is its encouragement of formal economies (reason number 6). The disadvantages of informal economies are many. Hernando de Soto has articulated how wealth creation relies on clear, regularized ownership of property and strong protection of property rights. One particular de Soto insight, that "the single most important source of funds for new businesses in the United States is a mortgage on the entrepreneur's house,"[6] describes my experience exactly. I used a second mortgage on my home to fund one of my own startups, Event411.com, an online event management service used at the 2000 Democratic National Convention in L.A. I was able to do so because my company operated in the formal economy and my home was duly registered, titled, and taxed, so I could offer legitimate, documented collateral for seed capital. I will discuss this further later, but for now, the key point is that an entrepreneur's own resources are almost always the source of an entrepreneur's first dollars, not VCs or banks or angel investors. That's true in Peru, and in America, and everywhere else.

But if you cannot get a second—or first—mortgage, you do not get seed capital. Indeed, de Soto estimates that "the total value of the real estate held but not legally owned by the poor of the Third World and former communist nations is at least $9.3 trillion." That is trillions of dollars of property locked up that cannot be leveraged to create businesses and jobs; trillions of dollars of "dead capital." But when economies are formalized, citizens (that is, entrepreneurs) can obtain collateralized credit, trade stock, and perform exits, mergers, and acquisitions. For governments, clear property rights and formalization lead to increased tax revenues, which help governments provide basics such as infrastructure (power, roads, water, sanitation), education, and, all too often, security.[7] The stakes for governments can be mighty. In Indonesia, only 14 percent of the country's 250 million citizens are registered to pay taxes,[8] which caps government coffers and hobbles financing mechanisms.

Enter entrepreneurship. Entrepreneurs want to be part of the formal economy. Startups require capital to grow—both debt and equity—and to be eligible, they need to be formal (investors tend to like documentation for their investment). They want to leverage their assets, and they want their investors to be able to leverage theirs. Further, there are limits to growth if you are informal. It is hard to export as an unregistered business, for example. So entrepreneurs tend to want, and agitate for, formalization. Entrepreneurship, therefore, builds the formal economy and pushes for sound property rights regimes so that capital may readily flow. In turn, a government's tax revenue grows. A de Soto–designed scheme in Peru saw 276,000 informal entrepreneurs voluntarily legalize their businesses. Four years later, the government had tallied an additional $1.2 billion in revenue from previously informal businesses.[9]

When foreign assistance takes the form of entrepreneurship promotion, startups begin to emerge in meaningful numbers. This administers "stress tests" on the institutions required for economic growth. New entrepreneurs push the government to make it easier to register a business; they push financial regulators to enable investors to get their money in and out; they push for streamlined permitting processes. While traditional development fumbles around with vague workshops and junkets for government officials, entrepreneurs demand specific action on specific issues that are important to them and to the real businesses that will create real jobs.

A final example of how entrepreneurship makes for effective foreign assistance lies in the local resources that it activates. When entrepreneurship promotion is done well—this is discussed in Part II—it prompts local investors to think about startup companies within their own countries (reason number 7). That does not occur as often as you would think. A vibrant startup scene keeps money "on shore." But there is another, perhaps more important, local resource that entrepreneurship deploys in the cause of economic development: people. Entrepreneurship empowers and creates opportunity, providing entrée to paths of success and improved livelihoods. It does this not just for the privileged, but for everyone, including the young, women, and those born without traditional middle-class advantages or political connections (reason number 8). Women have embodied the promise and comprised the majority of success stories of microfinance over the past decade. The same phenomenon is now playing out at a much larger, more effective scale with entrepreneurship. Even in the Middle East, entrepreneurship, especially in tech, is drawing women to the workforce and business in greater proportions.[10]

I became especially aware of the importance of supporting women entrepreneurs during my time at Secretary Hillary Clinton's State Department. Surely no leader on the world stage has focused more on the importance of empowering women and providing them with unique and appropriate tools than Secretary Clinton. In fact, she, her policy strategist Anne-Marie Slaughter, Global Women's Issues Ambassador Melanne Verveer, and the woman who actually hired me and allowed me to build a entrepreneurship program, Lorraine Hariton, all taught me a great deal about the power of women in shaping societies. Entrepreneurship is about moving an entire economy forward, and that means providing opportunities for whole categories of individuals previously left out.

Enlightened Self-Interest

For all the benefits that entrepreneurship brings to a nation's startup scene, there are countless upsides for the foreign investor as well (reason number 9). When America promotes entrepreneurship abroad it also seeds investment and trade opportunities for Americans. This is the Marshall Plan phenomenon. After World War II, with the disaster of post–World War I reparations as a cautionary example, the U.S.-led Allies decided to invest in Germany rather than belittle it. To the tune of $13 billion (about $125 billion in today's dollars), the United States invested in European, including West German, economies, helping resurrect agricultural and industrial sectors. Today, of course, Europe is one of the world's primary economic engines and a leading U.S. trading partner and investment target. Indeed, American goods exports to Germany exceed $4 billion per month.[11]

We can run the Marshall Plan playbook again. Later in this book, I argue that we don't have to spend more on aid; we just have to spend what we already spend smarter. Just by rebalancing foreign economic assistance toward entrepreneurship promotion we could unlock massive potential for foreign economies and enormous opportunities for American trade and American investors. In fact, while the traditional conversation revolves around seeding markets for U.S. exports, international entrepreneurship promotion boasts prospective financial returns to U.S. investors who put equity into new companies in the world's emerging economies. We all know that these emerging economies are expected to grow at many times the rate of the United States and other OECD countries for some time. That means tomorrow's startup billionaire founders, tomorrow's Dellionaires, and tomorrow's Instagrams may well be Mexican or Turkish or Kenyan or Egyptian; they will be the ones creating way-above-market returns for their investors. We should want some of those investors to be Americans.

The roadmap for this Marshall Plan approach already exists in many parts of the world. For example, Rwanda, a country torn apart by genocide, explicitly describes its renewal and development strategy as based heavily on entrepreneurship and foreign investment. (Rwanda also embodies yet another of the million reasons why entrepreneurship is so important: It is an essential tool for rebuilding shattered societies.[12]) As Rwandan President Paul Kagame has said, "Things won't happen without investment, without capital coming in. And that capital must benefit those who invest and also those who are on the ground where the investment is being made."[13] In 2010 Rwanda jumped from 143rd to 67th in the World Bank's *Ease of Doing Business* rankings—in 2013 it was up to 52nd—and the East African country has enjoyed business relationships with the likes of Starbucks, Costco, BNSF Railway, JPMorgan Chase, Visa, and Google. Smaller firms from the United States, especially those interested in Rwanda's coffee beans, have also sought to establish a presence.[14] All of these American firms are trying to make money. These are not charity or corporate social responsibility plays; these are efforts to take advantage of a new market. American investments— and its returns—occur when developing and emerging markets offer thriving entrepreneurship ecosystems.

Therefore, the more the U.S. government can do to enable such investment environments, the better for those countries and the better for America. As we have discussed, middle classes—consuming classes—are burgeoning in developing and emerging markets at velocities far greater than the original benchmark industrialized nations. Review economic data from the year 1700 onward and you will find that Britain and the United States took about 150 and 50 years, respectively, to double their per capita GDPs. Japan took thirty years. China and India will do so in a mere twelve and sixteen years, with millions upon millions more people. By 2025, annual consumption in emerging markets will hit $30 trillion, with non-BRIC (Brazil, Russia, India, and China) nations contributing half of the growth.[15]

The United States must pay attention. And it should pay attention to the entrepreneurs in these growing economies. For American investors, the word from McKinsey is straightforward: "It's easier to grow where the markets are growing."[16] Participation in developing and emerging market entrepreneurship may well be the next "big thing" in terms of earning financial returns for U.S. investors. Such markets can no longer be viewed merely as export destinations or sources of raw materials. Entrepreneurship represents one of the major pathways for the American economy to interact with and benefit from international connections and engagement.

This is increasingly important as more and more "south-south" and "south-north" innovation supplements traditional "north-south" models of trade and investment. Remember, entrepreneurs are everywhere; innovation comes from all corners. Gone are the days when the United States could simply export clones of what worked domestically—the "Facebook of country x," "the eBay of y, "the Walmart of z." Increasingly, "south" innovation is where it's at. As just one example, consider that about half of the world's users of mobile payments systems live in sub-Saharan Africa.[17] The global leader in mobile payments is the now-famous M-PESA of Kenya's Safaricom, which processes payments for 70 percent of the country's adult population and handles more transactions just within Kenya than Western Union does worldwide.[18] This is not an industry that has taken off in richer countries (for a host of reasons, including the deep penetration of banking and credit cards), but it represents a great opportunity, one that is recognized by the countless East African entrepreneurs who are leveraging M-PESA to create businesses and platforms that exploit the mobile money movement.[19] (And, by the way, M-PESA was birthed thanks in part to support from a foreign government's development agency: the United Kingdom's DFID.) Combine M-PESA's smashing success—and that of the startups it has spawned—with the prospect of a $30 trillion emerging market, and you quickly realize that the "north's" lack of interest in domestic mobile payments is irrelevant to earning returns abroad in the "south."

The truth is, whole new categories of investment activity have opened in the global south, and U.S. investors and entrepreneurs should—must—take part. Entrepreneurship is good for you, especially if you go to where entrepreneurship is happening.

The Same People the World Over

Finally, but not last or least, entrepreneurship makes friends. This is good for entrepreneurs and their broader societies, and good for governments.

Entrepreneurs are the same the world over. They tend to be like-minded folks who get along with one another because they value innovation, product development, and business over social and political differences. The result? Entrepreneurs are natural peacemakers, and entrepreneurship is a network of bridges, linking nations and cultures. (Huge reason number 10.) Entrepreneurship knows no borders, connecting young Arabs and Israelis, Sunnis and Shias, Russians and Ukrainians, Irish Catholics and Protestants, and warring clans and factions around the world. The SESAME physics lab in Jordan attracts Israeli, Iranian, and Palestinian scientists, and Arabs are increasingly joining Israel's famed tech-based startup culture.[20] The world of entrepreneurship promotes peaceful collaboration, international investment, and shared expertise and learning.

Entrepreneurship also acts as a conversation starter. This proves useful in international diplomacy. As I described in the intellectual property story, a U.S. foreign mission engaging in entrepreneurship promotion will interact with segments of a foreign country's population that it does not usually encounter, namely the innovative, young, cool, job-creating, tech segment—an increasingly important element of society.

I saw this firsthand in Egypt, where our 2011 GEP entrepreneurship delegation engaged with both young, aspiring entrepreneurs and successful local figures. When the first riots in Tahrir Square began in January 2011, local Google executive Wael Ghonim was detained by the frightened Mubarak government, apparently on the rather naïve theory that since the young demonstrators were using social media, locking up executives of social media companies would break their network. When the American embassy in Cairo tried to help Google free Ghonim, it was not the traditional sources of embassy information that stepped up, but rather our tiny GEP team (including our extraordinary partners from Sawari Ventures), who already had Ghonim's mobile phone number and Twitter handle at the ready. Ghonim was released unharmed and continues to inspire countless young Egyptian entrepreneurs today.

Thus entrepreneurship enables the U.S. government to connect more meaningfully with foreign populations. The upheavals of Egypt in 2011 and Ukraine in 2014 were fuelled by social media, with young, entrepreneurial classes in leading roles.[21] If the U.S. government has no connection to these people it could find itself hamstrung in its ability to execute foreign policy.

Entrepreneurship = jobs = growth = stability. The direct-line connection between entrepreneurship and peaceful, civil societies is the number one reason we should all advocate for programs that support startups. But entrepreneurship also yields a vast array of other benefits—to startups, to investors, to governments, to the young woman from a poor family with a great idea.

The million arguments for entrepreneurship demonstrate why the United States should elevate entrepreneurship in its foreign economic assistance. Exactly how this can be done is the subject of Part II of this book. Before that, however, we must consider one more reason that entrepreneurship is an especially useful tool for the U.S. government: Entrepreneurship is quintessentially American.

FOUR

American Made

BUCKFIELD, MAINE, IS ABOUT as far as you can get from Silicon Valley, both geographically and culturally, without leaving the lower forty-eight. It is a secluded, small town that is spectacularly beautiful and quaint, with a hard-to-pin-down mystery about it. One of those mysteries is that Buckfield, Maine—not Menlo Park or Cupertino—is home to one of the greatest Internet sensations of the past decade. Buckfield is where you will find "the Coke and Mentos guys."

EepyBird Studios, founded by Fritz Grobe and Stephen Voltz, is the firm that turned a popular middle-school cafeteria game—mixing Mentos candies with Diet Coke to explosive effect—into a viral YouTube video featuring 200 liters of Diet Coke and 500 Mentos gushing in monstrous, choreographed geyser displays. People could not look away. Grobe and Voltz's Coke-and-Mentos videos have been viewed no fewer than 120 million times. Grobe and Voltz have put on spectacular displays across the world and for *Late Night with David Letterman*. Thanks to EepyBird's handiwork, Coca-Cola, easily the world's most recognizable brand and already sold all over the world, enjoyed a 5 percent bump in sales of two-liter Diet Coke bottles.[1] Mentos sales spiked 15 percent. Grobe and Voltz graced the cover of *Advertising Age* magazine.

Now, after their breakout, EepyBird is a successful video and advertisement studio, responsible for the production of several viral campaigns for major American brands. Grobe and Voltz's book, *The Viral Video Manifesto*, offers a recipe for producing hit web videos and was ranked a top-ten business book of 2013 by *The Globe & Mail* of Toronto. Coca-Cola's Director of Interactive Marketing says EepyBird's work has "the impact of a Super Bowl ad."[2]

Grobe and Voltz are truly innovative; they are true entrepreneurs. But note that they do not live in Silicon Valley. Note, also, that neither Diet Coke nor Mentos are high-tech materials. Grobe and Voltz have built a company far from Silicon Valley, and done so in low- and no-tech industries. Grobe, Voltz, and EepyBird illustrate, in some ways even better than Steve Jobs and Mark Zuckerberg, a key, continuing thread in American entrepreneurship. As creative and wacky as Grobe and Voltz may be, they are actually quite typical of most American entrepreneurs now and throughout our history.

Americans have a penchant for turning highways and byways into symbols. Wall Street is the home of our stock exchanges. Main Street is the spiritual address of mom-and-pop enterprises. Washington D.C.'s K Street denotes lobbyists, and Park Avenue in New York means white-glove privilege. Route 66 came to symbolize the West. And Interstate 101 rolls through the heart of Silicon Valley, with Sand Hill Road the literal and figurative home of venture capital.

But we could also take a trip on a road with less symbolic importance. U.S. Route 1, which wriggles along the Maine coast and up to Canada, originates in Key West, Florida, just a block from a Starbucks and Jimmy Buffett's Margaritaville Café. Key West is compact, barely spanning five square miles of land, and Route 1 cuts through quickly, never far from ocean waters, before arcing up the Florida Keys toward Miami. The funky Key West streets that Route 1 bisects are home to over 5,000 businesses.[3] Starbucks, yes, and Walgreens, too. But also family-owned B&Bs, boat rental shacks, tackle shops, and the Original Ghost Tours—and its knock-offs.

In Miami, Route 1 encounters another 85,000 firms.[4] Miami-Dade County boasts over 400,000.[5] One of these is Ryder System, Inc., whose yellow rental trucks have moved Americans and their belongings across the nation's highways for decades. Jim Ryder's first truck was a Model A Ford, acquired in 1933 with a $35 down payment to haul concrete. Diversifications, innovations, and acquisitions later, Ryder System today focuses on commercial clients and posts annual revenues in excess of $6 billion while employing over 25,000 people. Around the corner from Ryder headquarters is Elete Salon & Spa, whose website advertises men's haircuts for $15.

A day's drive north of Miami, Route 1 enters North Carolina and the Research Triangle of Raleigh-Durham-Chapel Hill, a dynamic ecosystem of universities and technology and life sciences companies that has proven staunchly recession-resilient. The anchor of the area is Research Triangle Park, conceived in the late 1950s to jolt a region flatlining in stagnant industries like tobacco and textiles. The fruit of government, academic, and business concerns, the Research Triangle Park complex today hosts some 40,000 workers who work at world leaders like IBM and Cisco. The Triangle region as a whole—population 2 million—routinely tops "best places" lists for entrepreneurs and small and growing businesses.[6]

In fact, the length of Route 1, from Key West to Maine, repeats these American stories of entrepreneurship writ small, medium, and large millions of times over. It tells those stories through the country's most established corporations and through recent garage startups and public–private partnerships, from the Campbell Soup Company (Camden, New Jersey, founded 1869, today employing 17,000+), to the TechStars startup accelerator in New York City (sixty-plus alumni companies since 2011 employing hundreds), to Boston-Cambridge's biotech cluster (50,000+ employed, over $1 billion in annual venture investments).

Route 1's entrepreneurship is important precisely because it is not Route 101's. We often think of Apple or Google or the dozens of other household Silicon Valley success stories when we think of American innovation. But our entrepreneurship, like entrepreneurship all over the world, is also low-tech and no-tech. American entrepreneurship is also the leather-and-rubber Maine Hunting Boot, which Leon Leonwood Bean first innovated and sold in 1917 in Freeport, 3,200 miles from Silicon Valley and just thirty-five miles from Buckfield, Maine.

Entrepreneurship is in America's DNA. America is certainly not perfect, but our heritage of innovation and our entrepreneurial spirit are integral to the American story of prosperity, democracy, and stability. This chapter serves as a reminder of this fact. Because of our unique relationship with entrepreneurship, because entrepreneurship is such an American thing, we can credibly claim serious expertise in the matter at hand: promoting entrepreneurship and startups in emerging, developing, and fragile economies abroad.

The American entrepreneur is a familiar figure here at home, but what positions us so well to export this idea is the fact that almost everyone else admires the American entrepreneur, too—even people in the countries that like us least. Wars, drones, torture, and spying have surely undermined the United States' reputation abroad, but when it comes to economic opportunity, our reputation is intact. In light of the security and foreign policy challenges the United States faces today, it is critical that the world remember all the amazing things about America. Innovation, entrepreneurship, and the general "can do" spirit are high on that list. U.S. foreign policy must leverage this genuinely American trait—entrepreneurship—that is so widely admired.

The case for the U.S. government's active support for entrepreneurship is strengthened by another truth, albeit one that can be difficult to swallow. The U.S. government is no stranger to entrepreneurship. Government has no business "picking winners," but it most certainly has a role to play in entrepreneurship promotion. In fact, it always has. The U.S. government fills a critical role in American entrepreneurship as an enabler—ensuring that rule of law and transparent regulations reign—and as an "investor" in high-risk industries or fields that require heavy R&D (research and development) or that feature distant time horizons (for example, pharmaceuticals, defense, or nanotechnology).

The reasons and methods by which the U.S. government should be involved in promoting entrepreneurship at home are different from the reasons and tools for supporting entrepreneurs in the Middle East and elsewhere, but they converge on the same point. The private sector can't do entrepreneurship entirely on its own. Government must play a role if startups are to innovate and proliferate.

All of these points stand for the same proposition: Entrepreneurship is as American as apple pie. We're experts at business innovation. We should be exporting this expertise.

Give Me Your Poor, Your Tired, Your Huddled Masses . . . and Your Entrepreneurs

The first chapters of this book extolled the job-creating power of entrepreneurship. Our youngest firms account for the majority of job creation in America, not established blue-chip companies like Boeing or GM,[7] and the stories of Route 1 and Route 101 are replicated up and down highways and Main Streets all across the United States. We glorify the high-tech exploits of Steve Jobs and Bill Gates—and the EepyBirds far from Silicon Valley—but we all know the entrepreneurial heroes of days past: Henry Ford and the Model T; the Wright brothers and flight; Alexander Graham Bell and the telephone. Our country was built on entrepreneurship. Entrepreneurship is so American, in fact, that it is increasingly one of the few issues that is truly bipartisan. Politicians will denounce entrepreneurship just as soon as they will denounce baseball.

That entrepreneurship is quintessentially American, or that entrepreneurship is the quintessential American trait, is not some fuzzy American myth. It is how the rest of the world views us, as well. And it is why people want to come to America. For all the America-bashing out there, for all the American flags burned in MENA cities, for all the work that Republican and Democratic administrations do to get people really mad at America, for all the enjoyment Europeans get in pounding American golfers at the Ryder Cup, our entrepreneurial heritage stands tall, respected, and admired.

This is true even in the most unlikely of places. A poll from the Pew Center's Global Attitudes Project finds that the United States' highest marks in terms of appreciation for our "technological and scientific advances" and "American ways of doing business" come not from allies in Europe, but from Arab world countries like Lebanon, Egypt, Jordan, and Tunisia, as shown in table 4-1.

People around the world also vote with their feet, or would like to. Gallup has found that the United States is "the number one desired destination for potential migrants," and attributes that sentiment to "economic opportunities."[8] Moreover, as my own family history can attest, immigration is very much a part of America's and American entrepreneurship's story. Entrepreneurship itself is a magnet for attracting people to America. They come to study in the United States and they migrate to the United States to start businesses because they respect America's ability to nurture entrepreneurs.

Evidence of this has emerged in recent campaigns to ease visa processes and expand the number of U.S. visas available to foreign-born entrepreneurs (especially the H-1B visa). The Kauffman Foundation has published interesting data demonstrating just how much the world's emigrants revere and strive to join the American entrepreneurship ecosystem. For example, in 2010, immigrants or children of immigrants were listed as founders of

TABLE 4-1. *Worldwide admiration for American entrepreneurship*

	Percent admiring U.S. "technological and scientific advances"	Percent admiring "American ways of doing business"
Tunisia	82	59
Lebanon	77	63
Egypt	72	52
Jordan	65	59
Britain	77	41

Sources: Pew Research Center Global Attitudes Project, "American Business (All)— Indicators Database | Pew Research Center's Global Attitudes Project," www.pewglobal .org/database/indicator/44/survey/all; Pew Research Center Global Attitudes Project, *Global Opinion of Obama Slips, International Policies Faulted, Drone Strikes Widely Opposed* (Pew Research Center, June 13, 2012), www.pewglobal.org/2012/06/13/ global-opinion-of-obama-slips-international-policies-faulted.

over 40 percent of the Fortune 500 companies. In 2011, nearly half of America's top fifty venture-funded companies boasted a foreign-born founder, and these immigrants created about 150 jobs per company.[9]

Of course the United States does not have a monopoly on entrepreneurship. Innovation occurs everywhere, and clearly the United States, as a relatively young country, has piggybacked on some of mankind's greatest entrepreneurial efforts, be it the developments of England's industrial revolution or the mathematical breakthroughs from the medieval Muslim world. But the fact remains that we do have a special sauce. America today is revered as the land of entrepreneurship, not just the land of opportunity. Other nations respect us for it, and this respect is one of the primary reasons the U.S. government can and should elevate entrepreneurship in its foreign policy.

Setting the Table

Entrepreneurship is, indeed, as American as apple pie. But it was not baked by the private sector alone. The government was very much in the kitchen. Lest I be accused of an Obama-esque "you didn't build that" statement, let us consider what the president was trying to say on the campaign trail in 2012:

> Somebody helped to create this unbelievable American system that we have that allowed you to thrive. Somebody invested in roads and bridges. If you've got a business, you didn't build that. Somebody else made that happen. The Internet didn't get invented on its own. Government research created the Internet so that all the companies could make money off the Internet.[10]

Though I am not a political speechwriter, I believe the gist of Obama's words is that entrepreneurship is not something the private sector does alone. Government enables, and government invests. Very few of America's successful entrepreneurs have innovated and commercialized without some assistance in some form from the U.S. government, even if they didn't realize it; often, foundational innovation behind a new business's existence derives from research that was, once upon a time, funded by the government.

Even die-hard free market types will concede that government plays a role in nurturing business creation and growth. State institutions lay the ground rules by which businesses play. Governments create a regulatory environment and enforce laws (and contracts, and both real and intellectual property rights) that entrepreneurs rely on. This is Obama's "unbelievable American system that we have that allowed you to thrive." When I launched my second startup, I rented a facility to incubate a few ideas and pilot a few projects. Easy. I signed a rental agreement and, boom, I moved in and rolled up my sleeves. I know an entrepreneur in Kenya who rented land from a government agency and, boom, was blindsided by third parties claiming conflicting leases, a mess that cost thousands of dollars in delayed construction, renegotiated agreements, and legal investigation into title. The U.S. government did not build my startup, but it sure as heck was easier to build it in Southern California than East Africa.

Mary Shirley, president of the Ronald Coase Institute, which studies how laws and customs affect the efficiency (or inefficiency) of economies and markets, puts it this way:

> What determines which economy lags or prospers? The answer, according to Schumpeter, is entrepreneurship: The constant creation of new goods, new markets, new methods of production, and new

ways of organizing. And what determines whether entrepreneurship flourishes? The answer, I submit, is institutions, institutions that nourish rather than stifle innovation and change, as we can see in the history of the modern market economy.[11]

Shirley, as befits her position, leans on Coase's "transaction costs" concepts, but there are many ways to consider government's role in entrepreneurship. We have already talked about the importance of clear, transparent property rights; banks are far more likely to give you a business loan if proving ownership of your collateral is straightforward.[12] Government also develops a tax and regulatory regime around benefits and incentives for certain investments, long-term capital gain, inheritance for multi-generational family businesses (like L. L. Bean), and more. Government passes and tweaks legislation. The Patent Act of 1836 created a patent office, enabling the registration of innovation and institutionalizing patent protections; the Bayh-Dole Act of 1980 spurred university-led commercialization of innovation, allowing retention of royalties for breakthroughs developed with federal research funds.

Now we can certainly argue whether or not a government has hit the sweet spot with certain regulations—some taxes and licensing requirements could be struck; banks could use closer supervision and more incentives to lend to young and small businesses—but what we are talking about here is government's role in the enabling environment, government's role in creating an ecosystem that nurtures entrepreneurship. We all agree government has a role here, and we all agree some governments do a better job than others. In fact, the World Bank ranks precisely that in its *Doing Business* report, evaluating which governments do better than others when it comes to the environment for forming and growing a business. As of this writing, Singapore was number one, Eritrea dead last, and the United States number seven.[13]

DARPA and Its Cousins

More difficult to accept is the fact that, when it comes to entrepreneurship, the American government has done more than write a rule book and referee the game. It has made direct and indirect investments into entrepreneurship and it has done so with great success. This is Obama's comment that "somebody invested in roads and bridges" and "the Internet didn't get invented on its own. Government research created the Internet so that all the companies could make money off the Internet." The private sector simply will not, cannot, or should not invest in certain areas. Sometimes government is the only source for large amounts of patient capital capable of withstanding substantial failures on the way to unknowable future benefits.

Defense technologies with civilian applications, advanced research, and high-risk industries are all areas where the American government has given entrepreneurs a strong helping hand. Look at our public universities, especially the schools descended from the 1862 Morrill Land-Grant Act. This was more than "investing in education;" this was investing in agricultural and technical schools that evolved into the cutting-edge research universities of today.

In fact, R&D is a real government strong suit. The National Institutes of Health have invested some $750 billion into the pharmaceutical industry since NIH's founding in 1938, and over $625 billion into biotech since 1976. Mariana Mazzucato, author of *The Entrepreneurial State: Debunking Public vs. Private Sector Myths*, says that the venture capital and private equity funding that has since chased after pharma and biotech firms really "'surfed the wave,' rather than created it." Pointing out that NIH-backed research, not private companies, is responsible for three-quarters of new molecular entities, Mazzucato explains that "while the state-funded labs have invested in the riskiest phase, the big pharmaceutical companies have preferred to invest in the less risky variations of existing drugs."[14]

Mazzucato's best example of government's role in innovation is Apple's iPhone. All the principal technologies that comprise the iPhone—GPS, the touchscreen, SIRI voice recognition, the Internet itself—had their roots not in Apple's private investment but in government-funded research projects, especially at federally backed research universities. Steve Jobs' innovation was adapting the technologies and combining them in a new and useful way. Jobs' personal innovative role was certainly decisive, but prior government research provided the foundation for it. He did not pull the iPhone out of thin air.[15] Note, too, that Larry Page and Sergey Brin were able to do the early research on Google's search algorithm thanks to grants and fellowships from the National Science Foundation.[16]

Of course, much government investment in entrepreneurship has roots in the defense industry, around which our government has created entire organizations devoted to innovation. The poster child here is the Defense Advanced Research Projects Agency (DARPA), which was founded in 1958 in response to the Soviet launch of the Sputnik satellites. DARPA has contributed to a broad range of military technologies, many of which made their way to the civilian retail consumer; most famously, the Internet. DARPA is seen as such an institutional success that a bipartisan movement during George W. Bush's presidency led to the creation of ARPA-E, an agency modeled on DARPA, housed under the Department of Energy, and geared toward advanced and clean energy technologies.

Other examples of defense-seeded innovation include GPS (Global Positioning System), which the Department of Defense developed for military navigation purposes, but now ensures we walk in the right direction when we're running late for a meeting and emerge disoriented from a subway stop. As far back as the 1990s, the RAND Corporation, in an assessment of GPS policy, remarked that "GPS has evolved far beyond its military origins" and has "spawned a substantial commercial industry in the United States and abroad with rapidly growing markets for related products and services."[17]

The U.S. government has also entered into successful public–private partnerships aimed at spurring innovation. Semiconductors are a good example. In the 1980s, when Japan was eating America's semiconductor lunch, fourteen manufacturers, including Intel and Texas Instruments, formed SEMATECH and negotiated a five-year, $500 million research grant from DARPA (matched by SEMATECH companies' research budgets) to bolster chip research and manufacturing. SEMATECH (short for "semiconductor manufacturing technology") was headed by an industry CEO, Robert Noyce, a cofounder of Intel. The *MIT Technology Review* has described this public–private partnership as "a model for how industry and government can work together to restore manufacturing industries, or jump-start new ones."[18]

One of the most important, and under-heralded, U.S. government entrepreneurship investments is the ongoing Small Business Administration's SBIR program (Small Business Innovation Research). Launched by President Ronald Reagan and designed to support the commercialization of scientific and technical innovation, SBIR dishes out grants of up to $1 million (depending on the stage of R&D) to American-owned businesses with fewer than 500 employees. More than 100,000 Americans firms have taken advantage of close to $30 billion in SBIR grants. Funded by our government's largest agencies (especially the Defense Department), SBIR has benefited such companies as telecommunications giant Qualcomm.[19] Thanks to programs like SBIR, Mazzucato tells us, our government's funding for early-stage tech firms equals the funding from angel investors and exceeds that from private venture capitalists.[20]

Table 4-2 provides just a sampling of the innovative products Americans engage with daily in the private sector whose developments were government-stimulated.

There are several themes running through this list. Among them: government gets involved in entrepreneurship where risk and/or investment requirements are intolerably high for the private sector; where national defense is implicated; and where results (that is, commercial benefits) come far down the road. John Maynard Keynes said this better than President Obama: "The important thing for government is not to do things which individuals are doing already, and to do them a little better or a little worse; but to do those things which at present are not done at all."[21]

A Matter of Policy

Entrepreneurship is our thing. It is not a big deal if France or Japan or Germany does not promote entrepreneurship in their economic development policy; one thinks of wine, good cars, and even better cars, respectively, when thinking of those countries. But it is absolutely ridiculous for the United States not to leverage our heritage and expertise in entrepreneurship to the hilt. As discussed in the next chapter, at least one of the aforenamed countries appears to actually do more to support entrepreneurship abroad than does the United States right now.

Entrepreneurship represents an area where America boasts serious credentials. Our country was built on innovation and commercialization. People around the world, friends and enemies alike, revere America for its ability to nurture entrepreneurs. They come to America to be entrepreneurs. Entrepreneurship stands right up there with democracy and human rights as leading American values, and bears none of the recent scars and dents suffered by those other attributes.

Importantly, our history also demonstrates that government can aid innovation and entrepreneurship. As Mazzucato says: "Despite the perception of the U.S. as the epitome of private sector-led wealth creation, in

TABLE 4-2. *American innovation stimulated by government*

Year	Technology	Government investment
1798	Firearms	Congress funds private contractors (including inventor Eli Whitney) to manufacture military weapons
1860	Telegraph	Pacific Telegraph Act funds a $40,000 transcontinental telegraph line
1862	Railroads	Pacific Railway Act funds a thirty-year bond issue to Union Pacific and Central Pacific rail lines to fund transcontinental railroad
1890	Counting machines	After developing counting machines for the Census Bureau, employee Herman Hollerith founds a company to build the machines for the 1890 census (and co-founds IBM)
1915	Aircraft	Naval Appropriations Act of 1915 establishes the National Advisory Committee, the first U.S. government agency to support aeronautical research
1950s	Jet engines	Government-funded research drives Boeing's development of jet engine technology
1964	GPS	Transit, a Navy satellite program to track ship and submarine positions, is a forerunner to GPS

reality it is the State that has been engaged on a massive scale in entrepreneurial risk taking to spur innovation." Citing government investments in areas like defense, the SBIR program, and pharmaceuticals, she argues that "the U.S. has spent the last few decades using active interventionist policies to drive private sector innovation in pursuit of broad public policy goals."[22]

Today's major "broad public policy goal" is dealing with the disorder of troubled regions around the world. This disorder has its roots in joblessness, and entrepreneurship is the number one job creator known to man. Fighting wars and chasing splintered terror groups can do nothing to treat the underlying causes of instability and violence. But entrepreneurship can.

Year	Technology	Government investment
1972	Internet	The Internet, a project that began as ARPANET, linking computers within DARPA, is demonstrated at the International Conference on Computer Communication
1980s	Semiconductors	The government helps form SEMATECH, providing $100 million annually to drive innovation at companies such as Intel
1980s	Lithium batteries	The military underwrites R&D and procures initial lithium battery technology
1990s	Nanotechnology	The National Science Foundation creates the National Nanotechnology Initiative to coordinate government support for the sector

Sources: IEEE Global History Network, "A Brief History of the U.S. Federal Government and Innovation (Part I): From Independence to World War I (1787–1917)," www.ieeeghn. org/wiki/index.php/A_Brief_History_of_the_U.S._Federal_Government_and_Innova-tion_(Part_I):_From_Independence_to_World_War_I_(1787_%E2%80%93_1917); Simon Winchester, *The Men Who United the States: America's Explorers, Inventors, Eccentrics and Mavericks, and the Creation of One Nation, Indivisible* (Harper, 2013); Jesse Jenkins, Devon Swezey, and Yael Borofsky, *Where Good Technologies Come From: Case Studies in American Innovation* (The Breakthrough Institute, December 10, 2010), http://thebreakthrough.org/archive/american_innovation.

When it comes to peace through entrepreneurship, the policy reasons for U.S. government involvement in foreign entrepreneurship differ from those that motivate domestic involvement. The methods our government employs to promote international entrepreneurship will differ, as well. Yet, fortunately, not only does the United States have a policy and national security interest in promoting entrepreneurship abroad, our domestic track record demonstrates our government has regularly promoted entrepreneurship for policy reasons. This can serve it well internationally.

In Part II, we will discuss the methods—the specific programs—in which the U.S. government can invest and participate abroad. We are not talking about building DARPA-esque facilities in Guatemala and Qatar. What we are talking about is business incubators and mentorship networks that cost far less than a single F-14 Tomcat and an entire order of magnitude less than a year's worth of SBIR grants. These are the kinds of programs that enable entrepreneurs to create jobs and grow an economy, to create opportunity for thousands of jobless youth and give them at least a shot at lives preferable to joining a rebel militia. In Part II we will return to government's role again, but this time to the responsibilities of local governments in entrepreneurship. Just as the U.S. government plays a role in the larger ecosystem, so, too, must local governments enable local entrepreneurs.

One might well ask why the United States has not already spread our entrepreneurship goodness around the world. If our special sauce is so special, wouldn't we have already successfully exported it far and wide? Our entrepreneurship is such a powerful economic development tool and so American, surely USAID and the State Department have given this a go? Alas, they—we—have not yet solved the question of scaling our business innovation to other countries. In the next chapter, we will look at exactly why, drawing in part on my experience at State and my trials and tribulations in the world of entrepreneurship ecosystem development. Our government does talk about entrepreneurship, but it does very little in the way of comprehensive entrepreneurship programming or spending. There are institutional obstacles, too, that make it next to impossible for our government to use our special sauce to create effective pro-entrepreneurship activities.

These problems, as we will see, are surmountable. American-made entrepreneurship is loved around the world. And while "results may vary" and "past performance is no guarantee of future success," there absolutely are things we know how to do—and can help others to do—toward increasing the quantity and quality of entrepreneurship. We really can do this.

FIVE

Through the Looking Glass

IF YOU ARE AN entrepreneur in America, even one lucky enough to live in a part of the country that provides a great ecosystem, you know that nothing works out as planned. An investor backs out. Your prototype falls short of expectations. The container from China will be two weeks late. You need to skip paychecks to slow your burn rate. Or, most horrifying of all, a key employee (and in a startup they are all key) asks if they can come in to your office and shut the door for a minute. Nothing good ever happens after that!

The successful entrepreneur's *modus operandi* is to deal with changes, setbacks, and the unforeseen. He or she finds workarounds when things don't go as planned, when obstacles sprout up. When told "You can't do that," or "The system doesn't allow for that," the intrepid entrepreneur's instinct is to find a workaround—to figure out what the system does allow for, or as they say these days, "to pivot." But when I left the world of business and startups to join the State Department in 2009, I soon found myself through the looking glass. As Alice once said to the Queen of Hearts, "What a strange world we live in."[1] The concept of "workarounds" serves as a great example of the difference between the private sector and government.

At State, my main project was launching the Global Entrepreneurship Program (GEP) under the auspices of the Office of Commercial and

65

Business Affairs (CBA) in the State Department's Bureau of Economic, Energy, and Business Affairs (EEB). (Everything at State has an acronym, and acronyms change! EEB, where I worked, is today EBA, the Bureau of Economic and Business Affairs.) At its inception GEP was facing that age-old startup problem: money. We needed it. We had good ideas for entrepreneurship programming that we wanted to roll out in several countries, programs that would identify leading entrepreneurs in Muslim-majority regions and support them with mentorship, training, and access to capital. But nobody in the State Department, let alone EEB, had any money for us. We were desperate to locate a government funding source just to establish a budget.

I approached EEB's senior administrative officer in hope of finding an experienced ally to solve this problem. I explained the big picture of why GEP was important to creating jobs for unemployed Arab youth; how President Obama and Secretary Clinton were speaking about just such programs and, in fact, were asking for deliverables; and how it would be really important work for our bureau to support our leadership in this way. In the entrepreneurial spirit, I suggested figuring out a "workaround" for our funding problem. Taking this tack turned out to be a big mistake. The officer, a twenty-plus-year State Department employee, immediately straightened up and said, "This is the State Department. We don't do workarounds."

At that moment, I understood something. I realized that, in the mind of a career government worker, when you hit an obstacle, you stop. You do not figure out how to go over it, under it, or around it. You just stop. This turned out to be a big lesson in the difference between the way America works and the way the U.S. government works.

In this particular case, I learned that government workers not only stop, but stop and block. At one point, we discovered that GEP was eligible for some funding and that EEB, in fact, had unspent money in its own budget. But our administrative office, called the EX, was completely uninterested in securing the funds for GEP, and, instead, erected roadblock after roadblock to justify inaction. GEP could not, in fact, access the funds because the sub-office in which we were housed, CBA, did not have a certified grants officer authorized to manage the money. Fair enough. Time for a workaround. I figured out that the Foreign Service Institute, the in-house training center for the government's foreign affairs crowd, held regularly scheduled workshops precisely to train such grants officers. Contractors and consultants (like myself at that early point) were not eligible, but no matter; we sent to the training a "borrowed" foreign service officer on loan to us while awaiting new assignment (called a "Y tour," standing, I think, for "Don't ask me why"), which he successfully completed. Now we had a certified grants officer!

But we still could not apply for or even use the unspent money in EEB's budget because EX itself would be unable to properly account for and report on program funding. EX did not want to manage the process of running bid competitions for vendors who would implement GEP programs. EX did not want to oversee funds awarded to vendors. EX did not want to use another State Department arm to run its programs. (Such a capacity does exist.) The bureau, EX said, simply did not "do programs." It "did policy." Even though everyone knows that the State Department does, in fact, manage millions and millions of dollars and countless contracts, no one in the EEB EX—with probably hundreds of years of combined experience— could help us figure out how to do just that.

Imagine if EX's attitude were the norm in America. We would still be hunting wild turkeys and picking cranberries.

My experience at State and working with USAID—and since then as a sometime-contractor to other development institutions like the World Bank and the United Kingdom's DFID—taught me two things. First: The U.S. government does not "do" entrepreneurship. That is the whole point of this book. All the wonderful things about entrepreneurship discussed in the last few chapters, all the wonderfully American things, go effectively unutilized by the U.S. government abroad, either as pure development programs or as foreign policy tools. The second thing life at Foggy Bottom taught me was this: With its current processes, staffing, and attitude, the U.S. government cannot do entrepreneurship effectively.

Why is it impossible for the American government to do entrepreneurship? Three reasons:

—Often, the U.S. government doesn't put its money where its mouth is. This is a funding problem.

—Washington is a through-the-looking-glass land complete with its own lexicon. Government bureaucrats are sometimes punished for innovation that might fail, so the only safe thing to do is do nothing. This is a people problem.

—The government's contracting process is grossly broken and prevents America's best from doing America's most important work. This is a procurement problem.

We are going to look at each of these reasons closely, the funding issue in this chapter and "the two Ps," people and procurement, in chapter 6. The United States spends on the order of $35 billion each year on foreign aid, yet only a miniscule amount goes toward entrepreneurship promotion. By my estimate, we spend less than 1 percent of our foreign aid budget on entrepreneurship. And since our foreign aid budget is less than 1 percent of the total federal budget, entrepreneurship promotion abroad makes up less that one ten-thousandth (0.01 percent) of the federal budget. This is not an impressive outlay for an area many would argue is the cornerstone of the "American way," and, as I argue here, goes to the root cause of the primary foreign threats to the United States. Even if entrepreneurship programming were lavishly funded, Washington lacks the private-sector experience and practices that make America so good at innovation and entrepreneurship. The halls of government development agencies are nearly devoid of entrepreneurship subject matter expertise (that is, people who have actually started or run a company). Subcontracting would appear to be a way around this problem (a workaround), but our government's procurement system is so deeply flawed that it excludes subject matter experts from winning contracts. In fact, the system is so opaque that those experts are reluctant to bid for government contracts anyway.

So, even if Washington wants to do entrepreneurship, and even if the government were to actually spend money on entrepreneurship, a serious problem remains: Good ideas are badly executed. Thanks to shortcomings in people and procurement, our government is turning a screw with a rubber screwdriver. This problem exists wherever government outsources tasks to contractors through arcane procurement processes, but it is especially obvious and harmful in economic development and entrepreneurship. Our government's policies, structures, and staffing kill any prospect of capitalizing on entrepreneurship's job-creating power, preventing us from employing a powerful tool for addressing the core foreign policy threat of our times: shaky economies loaded with frustrated, jobless young people.

We will discuss the two Ps in chapter 6 and specifically how to fix government so it can do entrepreneurship effectively in Part II. But first let us look closely at the funding problem. A little due diligence, if you will.

No Entrepreneurship in This Apple Pie

The federal budget of the United States of America is enormously complex. Obligated funds, disbursed funds, appropriated funds, mandatory spending, discretionary spending, receipts, outlays, debt, budget, off-budget, fiscal years, calendar years . . . This biggest of pies can be sliced many different ways. In fact, just knowing where to drop the knife and make any particular slice is no easy task given the multiple ways any particular expense might be categorized or defined.

But since the devil is so often in the details, I have found it worthwhile to try to understand something about the funding of foreign operations by the U.S. government. I repeat that I am no expert, but I do believe it is necessary to grasp the size of the total pie available for foreign affairs and, within that, to get an idea of what might be a reasonable budget for the kind of economic development work I think is so important: entrepreneurship promotion. So, in my simple way, I gathered together some numbers and calculated a few more. The results are not pretty in terms of our spending on entrepreneurship. I would call them shocking for a country reared on innovation and entrepreneurship.

Here is a good back-of-the-envelope figure to keep in mind. Going back a few years so that data is available across the board, in 2012, the U.S. government budget was roughly $3.5 trillion.[2] This covered everything from mandatory outlays for Social Security, Medicare, and Medicaid, to budgets for the whole gamut of agencies, like the Departments of Defense and Education, the Environmental Protection Agency, and the Small Business Administration. Everything. Amusingly, the average American estimates that 28 percent of this budget goes to foreign aid. That would be almost $1 trillion. 'Tis not so. We actually only spend about 1 percent—or $35 billion— on nonmilitary foreign assistance.[3]

One of the key points of this book is that that $35 billion—that 1 percent of our entire spending budget, that sliver of pie—contains almost no real entrepreneurship promotion spending. In fact, surprisingly little goes toward programs that target economic growth in any form, let alone via entrepreneurship promotion. The Congressional Research Service says that, in fiscal year 2012, USAID and the State Department spent less than $4.5 billion of that $35 billion on "economic growth activities." That is less than 15 percent. The bulk went to health, education, social welfare, security assistance, and humanitarian aid.[4] This came as a surprise, not just to me but to observers in the policy community, like the Center for Strategic and International Studies (CSIS), a nonpartisan think tank. In a recent report CSIS observed: "Despite the tremendous potential for broad-based growth to reduce poverty and further development, it plays a comparatively small part in the United States' development agenda."[5]

Important to understand, too, is that foreign assistance spending is spread over countless government offices. It is not just USAID and the State Department representing the American taxpayer abroad. Who else? Brace yourself. The African Development Foundation, Department of Agriculture, Department of Commerce, Department of Defense, Department of Energy, Department of Health and Human Services, Department of Homeland Security, Department of Interior, Department of Justice, Department of Labor, Department of the Treasury, Department of Transportation, Environmental Protection Agency, Export-Import Bank of the United States, Federal Trade Commission, Inter-American Foundation, Millennium Challenge Corporation, National Aeronautics and Space Administration, National Science Foundation, Open World Leadership Center, Overseas Private Investment Corporation, Peace Corps, Trade and Development Agency, and the U.S. Securities and Exchange Commission all fund foreign assistance projects.[6] Let us not forget that the United States contributes massively to multilateral organizations engaged in aid and development, as well, like the World Bank, Inter-American Development Bank, African Development Bank, Asian Development Bank, the U.N. Development Program, and various other specialized U.N. agencies. Of course USAID and State, along with Treasury, Agriculture, Health and Human Services, and the Millennium Challenge Corporation (more on MCC later), account for the great bulk of this spending, but you can bet the effective coordination between these agencies, and the dozens more distinct offices within these agencies that fund projects, is close to zero.[7]

Next step. Can we drill down and figure out exactly how much this scattered array of agencies actually spends on programs that bolster innovative, scalable entrepreneurship? I have tried to do this. Perhaps the best resource for the task—in part because it will let us compare our spending to that of, say, the Germans and Brits—is data published by the OECD, the Organization for Economic Cooperation and Development.[8] The OECD's Creditor Reporting System (CRS) provides a database of all aid projects implemented by OECD member (that is, rich) countries and publishes precise disbursement and commitment figures for each project. Moreover, each project is coded according to whether it relates to health, governance, energy, banking, fishing, forestry, and so on. The coding is fairly granular, and each entry contains a short description of the project. There is, however, no code specifically for "entrepreneurship." So I ran the data through a few filters to come up with some interesting results concerning our great question: Just how little does the U.S. government utilize entrepreneurship in its foreign assistance?

By my calculations, in 2012, the U.S. government probably spent less than 1 percent of its foreign assistance money on bolstering entrepreneurship. That would be 1 percent of 1 percent of all U.S. government spending, or 0.01 percent of the federal budget. By comparison, that same year, the United States spent over 300 times as much (about 3.29 percent of the federal budget) on military solutions to the political disasters of failed states, namely wars in Iraq and Afghanistan.[9] When you scour the OECD database and look at the 60,000 foreign assistance projects that the United States reported to the OECD in 2012 (60,000!), you find that very few have anything to do with entrepreneurship. (The Aspen Network of Development Entrepreneurs [ANDE] has also studied donor assistance to "entrepreneurship and SME-related projects" and arrived at the same 1 percent figure.[10])

And I am being generous. My methodology consisted of weighing whether a particular U.S. development project could in any way be construed as targeting entrepreneurship, not whether it met our desired definition of scalable, job-creating entrepreneurship. In doing the research, I cast three nets, looking progressively for project reports in the OECD data that contained the word "entrepreneurship;" or that contained the word "startup;" or that were labeled with an OECD category code that could potentially have something to do with entrepreneurship (for example, "vocational training," "SME development," "business support services").[11] If I am extremely loose with the definition of entrepreneurship, it is possible that more than 1 percent, perhaps around 3.5 percent, of America's 60,000 aid projects in 2012 somehow touched on entrepreneurship—at the very most.

But I can assure you that a tiny fraction of these projects, if any at all, are meant to help the high-growth, high-impact, job-creating firms we have been talking about. Instead, many of America's so-called "entrepreneurship" programs seek only to support the "expansion of self-employment and micro and small enterprises owned and operated by low-income people," or to "assist youth and adults in acquiring knowledge and developing skills beyond basic literacy and numeracy," or to "increase participation and establish networks among public and private civil society stakeholders to identify work force needs." I do not mean to belittle the objectives of these programs. They are important and there is a place for them. But these programs will not generate the massive number of jobs needed to address the tens of millions of unemployed young people in fragile and developing regions around the world. These are not the sorts of programs that my (very constrained) GEP envisaged, much less the bolder, leading-edge programs that I believe the United States should be modeling (and that we will discuss in chapter 8).

In any case, U.S. spending on entrepreneurship is *de minimis* and dwarfed not just by military spending but by spending in other major aid categories, as well (see figure 5-1).

Do other countries prioritize entrepreneurship more than the United States? The answer is likely yes. If you take a generous definition of "entrepreneurship," Germany, the Netherlands, Sweden, Canada, and the United Kingdom have all regularly spent a greater proportion of their recent development assistance budgets on entrepreneurship compared to the United States (see figure 5-2).

There are a few lessons here. First, the United States does not prioritize entrepreneurship in its foreign assistance. Altogether, based on my analysis of OECD data, we spend less than $250 million annually on entrepreneurship. We certainly spend less than $900 million (still only 3 to 4 percent of aid spending), and we only get close to that figure if you throw my definition of entrepreneurship (high-growth, job-creating) out the window and include projects like vocational training and microcredit. Government officials of course might present this differently. In July 2015, when President Obama attended the Global Entrepreneurship Summit in Kenya, the White

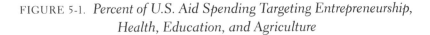

FIGURE 5-1. *Percent of U.S. Aid Spending Targeting Entrepreneurship, Health, Education, and Agriculture*

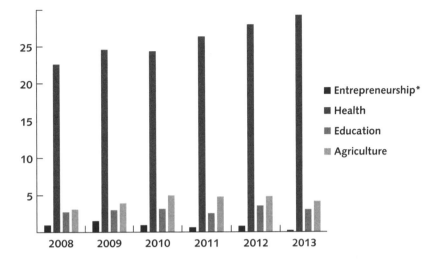

*Entrepreneurship defined as projects in the Organization for Economic Development CRS database that include the keyword "entrepreneurship."

House issued a press release summarizing "U.S. Investment in Entrepreneurship." But the laundry list presents no total dollar figure and instead offers a few funding commitments (some modified as "to explore" or "up to"); vaguely claims credit for private-sector initiatives; and boldfaces dollar figures that were "catalyzed" (not actually provided by the U.S. government) or were, in fact, raised by entrepreneurs themselves. It is true the U.S. government has recently rolled out new entrepreneurship programs, including the USAID PACE program (Partnering to Accelerate Entrepreneurship). Yet in addition to my skepticism as to their promise, discussed in chapter 6, there nonetheless remains the truth that the United States spends a paltry 1 percent of its foreign assistance money on bolstering entrepreneurship and programs are scattered like birdshot, a far cry from the coordinated ecosystem approach that this book advocates and describes in Part II.[12]

Next, we do not clearly define or track what we are doing around entrepreneurship. It is hard to get an aggregate number of how much we are spending to put angel investors in front of Jordanian startups, to help

FIGURE 5-2. *Percent of National Aid Spending Targeting Entrepreneurship**

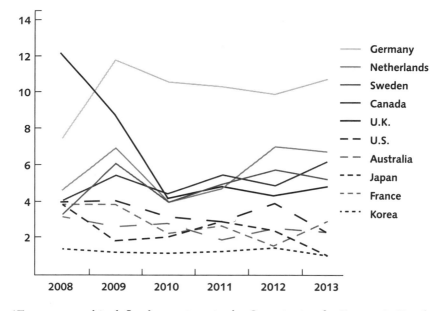

*Entrepreneurship defined as projects in the Organization for Economic Development (OECD) CRS database that include the keyword "entrepreneurship" or the keyword "startup" or that have an OECD "purpose code" potentially relevant to entrepreneurship.

Ghanaians export products, to network new hubs in Turkey with Silicon Valley mentors. Perhaps it is because we barely spend anything at all.

Third, other countries are doing more than we are. America may be the land of innovation and entrepreneurship, but our foreign development assistance bears no resemblance to this activity's importance in our own economy. As just one small example, the Netherlands and Sweden, countries that many Americans consider socialist, may well focus more on entrepreneurship in their foreign policy than the United States.

Not a Dime

I witnessed all of this firsthand at the State Department. My GEP program was strapped for cash. President Obama's Cairo Initiative may have been inspiring and Secretary Clinton may have given a rousing introduction of GEP at the first Presidential Summit on Entrepreneurship, but both State and USAID were unable to execute. There would be no direct funding for GEP. Amazingly, the $100 million that President Obama had planned to ask Congress for the Cairo Initiative would end up at a paltry $850,000 three years later.[13]

State's lack of prioritization of entrepreneurship initiatives ran all the way down to office space. GEP was relegated to State's annex building and a room where EEB stored unused furniture. We cleared some room to work, not that GEP had much in the way of staff. The GEP team was me (at that point as an unpaid volunteer), "Y tour" foreign service officers, a couple of Presidential Management Fellows on rotation (that is, fleeing) from other departments, an American Association for the Advancement of Science fellow, student interns, and people seconded—officially or otherwise—from other EEB offices because they had nothing to do all day. This was to run a program aimed at dealing with youth unemployment in the Arab world, the root cause of the political instability that was creating the greatest national security threat to Americans since the Cold War.

A shoddy office and no staff are obstacles, but easy enough to overcome. Much more harmful was the utter lack of funding for actual programming. I found that the only way for GEP to do real, programmatic work—to, for example, actually bring accomplished entrepreneurs and investors to the Middle East; to actually train high-net-worth Egyptians and Turks on structuring angel investments; to actually run a business plan competition in Jakarta—was for me to go cap-in-hand to parts of the U.S. government besides State and beg for funding to hire partners (that is, outside contractors) to run programs.

USAID seemed like an obvious place to start my search for funding. Naïvely, again, I assumed that because USAID reports to the State Department and because Secretary Clinton's picture hung in the USAID reception area, that a State Department policy idea might find a warm reception at USAID. This turned out to be wishful thinking. While some at USAID "talked the talk" in support of these programs, it was all but impossible to direct USAID funding to support GEP in a meaningful way. USAID was (and remains) so trapped by its own procurement and contracting mechanisms and pre-existing obligations that it had very little ability to shift money and respond to current priorities. Program implementation was a minimum two-year "time to market" exercise.

In addition I learned that the real budgetary power at USAID lies not in Washington but at the individual USAID country "missions" around the world. Most of the missions operate autonomously from each other, from the home office, and, very often, from the very embassy of which they are ostensibly a part. Persuading local USAID mission chiefs that it was a good idea to support entrepreneurship amounted to hand-to-hand combat. Some mission chiefs were very supportive and helpful. But overall, the process proved much more difficult than raising capital for my last startup, a process that required me to take a second mortgage on my house and make 200 pitches to investors in dozens of cities across the country (giving me an intimate familiarity with motels that "leave the light on for ya").

The GEP effort in Indonesia was particularly frustrating. In 2011, when I was getting GEP started there, I figured there was close to $1 billion in U.S. taxpayer money flowing to the country in various forms of economic assistance between USAID, the Millennium Challenge Corporation, and other U.S. government programs over the course of the immediate years.[14] None of that billion appeared to be spent on promoting high-impact, high-growth startups. In the end, with considerable—and needed—help from the U.S. ambassador to Indonesia, Cameron Hume (a huge supporter of entrepreneurship who understood the importance of job creation for youth, as did his successor, Ambassador Scot Marciel), we finally managed to secure $150,000.

But where exactly did our $150,000 come from? Despite the support of Ambassador Hume and his staff, Indonesia's USAID chief did not release a dime, arguing that basics like food security in rural areas had to be addressed before startups received support (thus discounting the idea that local entrepreneurs are precisely the kinds of people who devise solutions to food shortages and distribution). The U.S. government's Millennium Challenge Corporation, in the midst of negotiating what would soon become a $600 million compact with the Indonesian government, likewise could not find a penny for GEP, even though MCC projects purportedly aimed to "reduce poverty through economic growth [and] to increase household income." (The compact programs focus on child nutrition, modernizing government procurement, and reducing Indonesia's greenhouse gas emissions.[15])

In the end, our $150,000 to support job creation for unemployed youth in the fourth-largest country in the world, in the largest Muslim country in the world, came from that global development giant known as the Public Affairs Section of the U.S. embassy in Jakarta. Funding by the State Department for entrepreneurship very often comes from what is called the "public diplomacy" function (in the real world we would call this marketing and PR), not from economics or political sections, and certainly not from the military or security budgets that usually dwarf all other U.S. government expenditures combined. Not only is "public diplomacy" a very small pool of funds, but in relegating entrepreneurship on this local level, we limit its function to window dressing.

GEP-Indonesia was so grossly underfunded that we could not implement significant programming, despite the vocal support of Ambassador Hume and the vows of President Obama and Secretary Clinton to boost entrepreneurs in Muslim-majority countries.

GEP's biggest funding coup actually came in the country where President Obama first floated the idea of entrepreneurship in the service of foreign policy: Egypt. We had identified Egypt as the top focus country before the Arab Spring. After the events of Tahrir Square, the attention to and urgency in the country increased hundredfold, helping us land a sum of $2.3 million, but it wasn't pretty. The funds came from the USAID mission in Cairo, and for that I have Hilda "Bambi" Arellano to thank, one of the few people I encountered at USAID who understood how important it was for the U.S. government to fund job creation programs. A long-serving and widely respected USAID official, Arellano (like most veteran USAID staffers) is an expert in the arcane world of government contracting and procurement. In Egypt, she explained to me that there were really only two options for securing USAID funds; neither of them very good, she warned. One, I could start the USAID process afresh and apply to have USAID issue a unique contract for GEP work, which would take two to three years if it succeeded at all. Or, two, Arellano could tack our project on to an existing USAID contract in Egypt, which, though it had virtually nothing to do with our project, could help us implement faster. I chose immediate action, option two, and GEP was added to the Egypt Competitiveness Project (ECP), a roughly $30 million USAID contract implemented by behemoth American contractor Chemonics.

This turned into a "good news/bad news" scenario. While I was exuberant to get any funding, GEP's experience with Chemonics was a wreck.

We suffered as second-class citizens under the contract, and I had a hard time even getting a meeting with Chemonics' chief of party in Egypt. When I did finally convince him to meet with me, he wasn't particularly attentive, and it went downhill from there. My private-sector training told me that I (as program designer and representative of the contract-awarding government) was the client and Chemonics was the vendor, yet I was treated with none of the respect and customer service mentality that such a relationship would normally imply. I learned then and there that, through manipulation of the contracting and procurement system, large government contractors more often than not call the shots. As micro-level examples, Chemonics outright ignored my request that GEP's hire for "entrepreneur-in-residence" in Egypt be an actual entrepreneur and speak Arabic. Chemonics also insisted that our offices be in Port Said, 125 miles away from the entrepreneurship hub of Cairo.

Having said this, within the State Department and the U.S. government, GEP was nonetheless considered a successful program relative to other initiatives. Egypt was probably our most deeply implemented program. Yet even there, in the end, despite nurturing and finding investment for dozens of Egyptian entrepreneurs and startups, and despite representing a tiny glimmer of progress in the tortured United States-Egyptian relationship, GEP closed its doors in Egypt in 2014.[16] At the same time this funding for job creation in Egypt dried up, the U.S. government decided to send ten Apache military helicopters to a new Egyptian government heavily criticized for human rights abuses.[17] The cost of a single Apache helicopter, by the way, is about eight times greater than GEP-Egypt's entire three-year budget.[18] What has happened in Egypt since is not the subject of this book or a very happy story as regards America's support of regimes that are responsive (or not) to the needs of their people. Egypt's economic distress is even greater now than it was before Tahrir Square. The need for effective U.S. government support is even more desperate. Yet the billions of dollars we spend on Egyptian military supplies continues to bypass the core issue of addressing youth unemployment. (Only as this book went to publication in 2016 did USAID finally get a new Egypt program running. The Strengthening Entrepreneurship and Enterprise Development [SEED] project, however, is implemented by yet another classic, colossal USAID contractor without niche entrepreneurship specialization, AECOM, and initial program descriptions suggest SEED eschews the

GEP approach. Results may be TBD, but chapter 6 and Part II delve further into why this USAID approach to entrepreneurship is unlikely to succeed.[19])

For GEP as a whole, underfunding at this scale sent all the wrong messages, to both host-country entrepreneurs and investors and the Americans who participated in our programs. Well-known American entrepreneurs and investors were asked to pay their own way on "official" State Department delegations to Egypt, Indonesia, Lebanon, Jordan, and Turkey. For the local entrepreneurs themselves, equity funding, trips to U.S. incubator programs, or meetings with international firms operating in similar industries were completely out of the question. The prizes GEP gave to business plan competition winners in Tunisia and Indonesia were so small that the visiting delegates, mortified at the U.S. government's inability to put its money where its mouth was, actually opened their own wallets and donated a more substantial award for the winners.

GEP was not the only underfunded promise of the Cairo Initiative, it should be noted. A much ballyhooed "deliverable" was to come from the Overseas Private Investment Corporation (the U.S. government's development-finance wing, better known as OPIC) in the form of funds boosting MENA's telecommunications, media, and technology sectors. These promised to produce some $2 billion in capital.[20] To date, these vaunted funds are capitalized to barely a quarter of that amount and, five years after that promise, only a handful of deals with entrepreneurs are in the works.[21]

Good Ideas Badly Executed

Most frustrating in the matter of funding was Washington's tendency to overpromise and under-deliver. As a business guy, I aimed to do the opposite: under-promise to your investors, and then wow them when you over-deliver and exceed forecasted metrics. Instead, what I saw from the U.S. government on entrepreneurship (and a great many other things) were good ideas being badly executed.

Bad execution has much to do with people and procurement, the topics of the next chapter. But it relates to the funding issue, as well, because funding can get political (surprise, surprise) and the path from policy idea to funding to execution can prove impassable. I have no doubt that the State

Department and other government agencies are capable of coming up with good ideas. The problem is that government, at least in my narrow window of experience, often "doesn't walk the walk."

After the president's Cairo speech I thought people in the administration were really going to engage the Muslim world more broadly. I thought the people behind the first Presidential Global Entrepreneurship Summit were really going to develop serious entrepreneurship programming that leveraged America's innovation heritage. I thought a real budget would be established to get these ideas moving. Instead, the Cairo Initiative was mostly just a conference. All we did as organizers was decide where in the Ronald Reagan Building coffee breaks would be held and spend a great deal of time picking invitees. The summit became—and frankly, the annual Global Entrepreneurship Summits since then have all been—an exercise in marketing and public relations with a focus on getting the "brand message" right. There is virtually no concern for any substantive programming.

Vali Nasr has written: "Fixing America's broken foreign policy and correcting its jaded view of the Muslim world were the most important foreign policy tasks" facing the Obama administration.[22] Yet in the State Department there was very little trickle-down of mission and vision from the presidency and secretary through to the bureaucracy. Pulitzer Prize-winning journalist David Rohde noted that "Obama himself was disappointed by how few of his promises in Cairo had been turned into functioning programs."[23] Paul Brinkley, a businessman who served as deputy undersecretary of defense in both the George W. Bush and Obama administrations, has made the general observation that, "Even when an administration, regardless of the party in power, has a clear policy, there is too often little sense of alignment among the career staffers placed overseas."[24] Kori Schake, a foreign policy veteran with stints at the Pentagon, the National Security Council, and the State Department, says the top rarely get their policies through to the bottom:

> The president has both a right and a responsibility to shape America's foreign commitments and policies consistent with her or his campaign platform. Yet many of the professionals at Foggy Bottom really do consider themselves above the grubby confines of democratic politics where foreign policy is concerned. This attitude shocks the

sensibilities of people acclimatized to the American military, and would never be tolerated were it displayed by people wearing uniforms instead of suits.[25]

Ideas do not trickle down to execution for a variety of reasons. I have found that it is also political appointees—not just conventionally criticized civil bureaucrats, per Schake—who are implicated. For instance, in the Economic Bureau where I was housed at State, it was apparent to me that the bureau's management (headed by a political appointee) was not actually interested in the president or the secretary of state's policy agenda. They were interested in their own agenda. And if a program (like GEP) was not consistent with their own agenda, they were not on board, even if that program were an attempt to implement the president and secretary of state's agenda (like GEP). And, unlike in the private sector, since there is actually no "chain of command" in government (most people are not hired/fired by their immediate boss), there is no way to "discipline the troops," and inattention to the president and secretary's agenda is hardly a big deal. I witnessed a project for securitizing remittances from (primarily Central American) guest workers to leverage dollars for development get much attention from the bureau's brass, but never heard anything about it in Obama's Cairo speech or any other speech by any administration leader. It was never once mentioned as a priority by "senior management" yet seemed to be a priority of one of their "middle managers."

By the way, to be fair, an entrepreneurship program did emerge from State's Economic Bureau, though it was very different from what we at GEP envisaged. Originating in the Office of Multilateral Trade Affairs, the North Africa Partnership for Economic Opportunity (NAPEO) received a few hundred thousand dollars in funding and retained the D.C.-based Aspen Institute to act as its "secretariat."[26] I disagreed with the premise of NAPEO, namely that entrepreneurship promotion is a regional exercise, and that programs should span the whole Maghreb and treat thriving Morocco, socialist Algeria, chaotic Libya, Arab Spring cradle Tunisia, and dirt-poor Mauritania all alike. My view, and one of the key principles on which GEP is based, is that entrepreneurship is actually just the opposite of regional; it is hyper-local. Silicon Valley is different from Boston, and both are wildly different from mid-coast Maine and central Kansas. In fact, Silicon Valley is different from Stockton, California, which is less than

100 miles away! The five countries of the Maghreb are extremely different and undergoing considerable political change, verging on anarchy in the case of Libya. (Note, too, that Egypt, where the Cairo Initiative was born, did not get any attention from NAPEO.)

In the long run, the majority of U.S. ambassadors in the region shared my outlook on NAPEO, telling me they were against its programs in their countries. More objectively, a State Department Office of Inspections report was sharply critical of NAPEO:

> The bureau's work on the U.S.–North Africa Partnership for Economic Opportunity program over the last three years has consumed resources while yielding meager results and causing friction with the regional bureau and embassies. . . .
>
> The Bureau of Economic and Business Affairs should not engage in any new activities or grants under the U.S.–North Africa Partnership for Economic Opportunity.[27]

As Abraham Lincoln famously said, "You can fool all the people some of the time, and some of the people all the time, but you cannot fool all the people all the time." Few of the real, intended "consumers" (young Muslim entrepreneurs) of U.S. government programs have been fooled by what the U.S. government has done, or failed to do. Quite the contrary, they have been soundly disappointed by the Cairo Initiatives and other programs supposedly intended to improve United States–Muslim relations and bolster entrepreneurship.

Hosting a "presidential" summit on entrepreneurship that is in no way presidential and announcing programs for startups that will in no way be funded is more than a little disingenuous. "Convenings," public statements, marketing, branding, and optics are not the same as actual programs, and folks in the countries in which we work know this, particularly in the startup communities in the very countries we were trying to support. I actually believe that, as a government, we would probably have been better off not raising expectations and making any promises at all than creating the expectations we did and then failing to meet them.

Alas, even with ample and accessible funding, exporting American entrepreneurial prowess encounters another obstacle: our inability to effectively execute our policies even if we have made the necessary budgetary commitment. I call this the rubber screwdriver problem. The people and procurement issues around how we do development (and, therefore, how we do—or do not do—entrepreneurship) are at the heart of this problem. Understanding why a rubber screwdriver doesn't work is the essential first step. We will do that in chapter 6, and then in Part II turn to solutions.

SIX

Turning a Screw with a Rubber Screwdriver

HOW THINGS ARE DONE in America is different from how things are done at the State Department. This became increasingly clear to me during my time in Foggy Bottom, and nothing has changed my mind since I left to start an entrepreneurship consulting business that works with both public and private sector clients.

The America we explored in chapter 4 is not at all like Washington, D.C. This is an observation many have made, notably *New York Times* columnist Thomas Friedman when he toured Silicon Valley's most exciting tech companies in 2014 just as immigration reform and free-trade negotiations with Europe and Asia met their latest demise in Congress: "What a contrast. Silicon Valley: Where ideas come to launch. Washington, D.C.: Where ideas go to die. . . . Silicon Valley: Smart as we can be. Washington: Dumb as we wanna be."[1]

I will try to be less harsh but, frankly, I could be even harsher. As a business guy with little experience of Washington, I suffered "shock and awe" when I first arrived at the State Department. I was coming from a world chock-a-block with entrepreneurs, innovators, and commercializers with problem-solving attitudes, proactive types who relentlessly chased workarounds when the going got rough. The State Department and Washington were essentially the exact opposite. I soon coined a response to friends who asked how my work was going at State: "How should it be going? The State Department is the Antichrist of entrepreneurship!"

This was a (slight) exaggeration, of course, but even the language of Washington was imbued with dysfunction, overpromise-and-under-deliver, and faux execution; a focus on optics, not on output. Having been raised on my parents' dinner table stories of the horrors of Stalinism, it occurred to me that, in many ways, including architecturally, the State Department smacked of Soviet Russia. There was, for instance, "double speak" and long lists of almost Orwellian names and concepts. "Standing up" a new program meant doing events like lunches and conferences—more like propping up, and nothing like creating a real program with real elements. A close friend and exemplary foreign service officer told me the key to success at State was to "find a parade and get in front of it." Merit hardly figured in hiring, firing, or promotion. What mattered was "time in grade" and being a "team player." People would congratulate each other for "having moved paper," which meant getting it to the "front office." In the business world I knew, a deliverable was something I had to get done, something I was responsible for, and something a supervisor would check on for completion. In Washington, a deliverable was something to say in a speech—that everyone would forget as soon as it was said—so long as it sounded good. In other words, it didn't really matter.

Never Met a Payroll

Chapter 5 marveled at how ridiculously microscopic entrepreneurship's share of U.S. aid spending is. This chapter is about throwing good money after bad. Even if we did spend more dollars on entrepreneurship, we are not likely to see positive results if we don't change the process for how we spend. That is because our government turns screws with a rubber screwdriver. The people involved in development (and entrepreneurship) are, as a whole, not up to the task and, further, are beaten down by the system they work in. And the procurement process that dictates how our government contracts for goods and services (especially in the aid industry) is grossly broken, as likely to award contracts to those who know how to win contracts as to those who actually know how to execute the specific service required.

Let us start with the people problem. The main issue, as I see it, is simply a lack of private sector experience—not enough knowledge about what works in the real world—in the U.S. government. In my two years at the State Department, I did not encounter a single person who had ever met a payroll, delivered a product, or started a business. The "business people" at State all seemed to be lawyers, investment bankers, or heirs to industrial fortunes. These were not the people we met in chapter 4; these people had no experience creating and running businesses. I am sure there were some entrepreneurs somewhere in the vast bureaucracy, but I did not meet them, nor did I hear about them. And they were certainly not working on entrepreneurship promotion. The USAID team I liaised with for GEP had zero business experience, let alone an entrepreneurship background.

State was not oblivious to the problem. Private sector blood was added into the mix, but only feebly. In part, federal personnel regulations make it quite difficult to take on workers who have accumulated solid private sector experience.[2] Even the program that brought me to Washington, the Franklin Fellowship, amounted to a small (and totally unsupported) exercise. Despite herculean efforts by its single administrator, the wonderful, devoted thirty-plus-year foreign service officer Bill Pope, the fellowship was hardly a "program" in the sense that you or I would understand it. There was no training. There was no orientation. There were no seminars that brought all the fellows together (though we did once have our picture taken as a group with Secretary Clinton). And, of course, above all, true to State Department form, there was no funding. The Franklin Fellowship Program could, and should, have been so much more, a genuine effort to inject private sector expertise into government. I know that was Pope's vision. But the result was yet another example of a good policy idea sunk by miserable execution.

Kori Schake has noted that mid-career professionals are not readily integrated into the State Department mainly because they are expected to learn from the system, not the other way around:

An undersecretary for management once explained the absence of mid-career recruitment on the basis that no matter how skilled people from outside the Foreign Service might be, they didn't have the knowledge to work successfully in the Foreign Service. By this argument, the information management executive from Google would have nothing to contribute to American diplomacy because she had not apprenticed through the system.[3]

Not surprisingly, given the reluctance to import private sector experience, the State Department is also short on practices from the rest of America. For one, the information technology (IT) infrastructure at State is fresh out of 1992.[4] No Skype; no Macs; constrained web access and tools, and unimaginably inefficient travel systems in an organization where travel is crucial. No company in America could operate with the corseted and antiquated IT infrastructure that characterizes the State Department today. The default excuse for all of this backwardness is "security issues," a farcical answer to cover a multitude of inefficiencies.

Beyond the IT issues, the bureaucracy is mind numbing. Any document, even a cable (and, by the way, who ever heard of a "cable" in 2012?), requires dozens of signatures before it can go out. Even the lowliest intern "clearing" on a cable could indefinitely prevent a message from being sent. While at State, I attended a Foreign Service Institute training program for mid-level managers. No participant had less than fifteen years experience in government (except me), yet there was not a single person there who was not ready to quit if they had another job offer. During breaks in our training, my classmates would rush to have coffee with me to get advice on "transitioning to the private sector." In a well-run company, if the CEO heard that all mid-level managers were desperate to leave, a major shakeup would follow, likely starting with the head of HR getting fired. Instead, ironically, the career executive atop State's HR pyramid was brought in as the capstone speaker for our training group.

Though I encountered some amazing, dedicated, and largely unsung people at the State Department, most employees seemed exhausted by the system. In survey after survey, vast majorities of government workers say their superiors fail to motivate, and by large margins, they do not believe that promotions are based on merit.[5] "Morale across the federal government," says Max Stier of Partnership for Public Service, "is the lowest it has been since 2003."[6] Workers are unlikely to bring innovation to their jobs. Bureaucracy kills the hopeful, proactive "intrapreneur."[7] Schake says directly that the State Department could use an infusion of entrepreneurial spirit:

> The Department of State's need is not for more diplomats who can conform to existing institutional culture; it is for a burgeoning of diversity in skills that can transform State's institutional culture to be more entrepreneurial, more tech-savvy, more activist than

descriptive, and with a different balance of risk-tolerance inherent in how it does its job.[8]

There is a deeper problem, too. People and practices in government are increasingly not informed by the American experience. There is a growing disconnect between America and Washington. Nongovernment entities—here meaning not just businesses, but not-for-profits, cultural and educational institutions, and citizens acting on their own—are ever more disconnected from what is happening in government. One aspect of this trend is the increasing cynicism with which Americans, especially young Americans, view politicians and the political process.[9] But there is also the reality that nongovernment entities have a greater role in international affairs than ever before, reaching into a wide range of areas that have traditionally been the sole purview of government. Corporations form their own "foreign policies." Major organizations, aware of government's limitations, have stepped onto the world stage. Reviewing Vali Nasr's *The Dispensable Nation*, Steve Coll writes:

> The Gates Foundation, the Open Society Foundations, Google, Facebook, Apple, and (alas) even the Walt Disney Company have arguably projected more influence in the Middle East and Africa in recent years—including on the course of the Arab Spring—than the Department of State. These corporate and philanthropic actors have sometimes bigger budgets but also strategies that are better attuned to changes in technology, demography, and culture that are weakening states and empowering people and small groups worldwide.[10]

This is not to say that government bureaucracies responsible for managing hundreds of billions of taxpayer dollars and performing indispensible public services should be run like startups, or even large corporations. Governments and businesses have different mandates, goals, and bottom lines.

What I am saying, and what this book stresses, is that the wisdom that America's private sector has collected, and which has created our wealth and standing, is lost on Washington. This disconnect prohibits us from promoting entrepreneurship abroad. We are, as a result, greatly hindered in defending ourselves against twenty-first-century threats, which are about civil unrest and terrorism that breed in regions of the world afflicted with massive, chronic youth unemployment. In short, we are running a race with one leg. Our State Department in its current form cannot put America's best foot forward. As State's Office of the Inspector General says of the economic bureau I worked in, "structure and staffing reflect the missions and priorities of decades earlier." Our State Department, the body that represents America abroad, cannot "do entrepreneurship" even though startup culture is so quintessentially American.

A Mouse Dancing with a Hippo

Nowhere is government's inability to execute on entrepreneurship more obvious and damaging than the processes that govern how the State Department, USAID, and other agencies contract third parties to perform work. Procurement is a major problem. Remember that $3.5 trillion annual government spending figure? Here is another spending fact: Each year the U.S. government buys over $500 billion in goods and services from third-party vendors (with the Department of Defense responsible for two-thirds of those purchases).[11] The government makes these purchases poorly, and via mechanisms that most experts agree are grossly broken.

From HealthCare.gov to the reconstruction of Iraq, we have countless examples of shoddy outsourced projects and deep evidence that America's best are not hired to do America's important work. At $500 billion, the government is the biggest customer in the U.S. economy; its annual procurement spending is ten times greater than AT&T's[12] and exceeds Walmart's yearly revenues.[13] Government's approach to buying is completely different from that of private corporations. Despite its purchasing power, federal procurement personnel are outgunned and out-resourced by their vendors, with many of the "buyers" making a tiny fraction of the compensation of the "sellers."

The major issue is what I call a mouse-dancing-with-a-hippo situation. Our government's procurement process—and the paperwork that accompanies winning a contract—is so complicated and burdensome that, generally, only heavily resourced large firms can bid for and win work. The problem is, especially in the world of foreign economic assistance, these firms are less experts in economic assistance than they are experts in how to win a government contract. Smaller firms with real expertise in a sub-

FIGURE 6-1. *Top U.S. Agency for International Development Contractors for 2012 (percent of contracted spending won)*

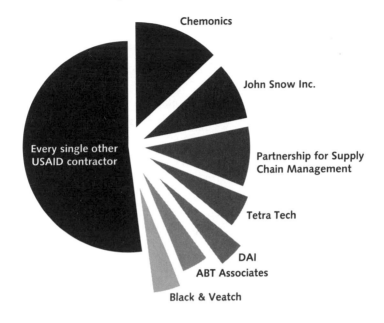

stantive field lack the administrative capacity to even bid for a government contract, let alone meet the reporting requirements that follow.[14] When a mouse dances with a hippo, it does not end well for the mouse. So the smart mice decline the invitation to dance.

A glance at the development "industry" reveals what I am talking about. In fiscal year 2012, 75 percent of all the money USAID awarded to contractors went to a mere twenty firms (see figure 6-1). Just three firms (Chemonics, John Snow Inc., and the beautifully named Partnership for Supply Chain Management) accounted for over 30 percent of the total haul.[15] Tellingly, many of the usual-suspect firms do virtually no private sector work, with USAID contracts (and similar donor work) comprising the majority of their gross revenues.

USAID works on projects in every conceivable sphere, from agriculture to governance to education to environment to women's empowerment to health to water and sanitation to trade . . . and it does this work in some forty sub-Saharan African countries, India, China, a dozen Southeast Asian counties, the troubled nations of Afghanistan and Pakistan, a handful of other -stans, up and down South and Central America, across the

Caribbean, in Eastern Europe and the former Soviet republics, and in the Middle East.[16] So much work and such variety. Yet so few contractors. I can understand that when you order up Abrams tanks, F-35 fighter jets, and nuclear-powered submarines there may be just a handful of vendors capable of delivering on a contract. But are the tens of thousands of very diverse development assistance projects we engage in every year best served by these mega-contractors?

USAID used to staff considerable subject matter expertise in-house, but budget cuts forced the agency to change its operating model.[17] Or, as Kori Schake says, "It was reduced from an agency that undertook development assistance to an agency that lets contracts for that assistance."[18] This change has made lots of people in the development industry very rich. Chemonics, USAID's favorite, raked in $650 million worth of contracts in 2012. The married couple leading International Relief and Development (IRD), another top-twenty firm and a nonprofit, no less, tallied nearly $1 million in annual salary as IRD ran (and botched) programs in Afghanistan and Iraq.[19,] Those top twenty contractors fare very well by the whole arrangement. One proxy indicator of the rise of contracting by USAID and other government agencies is the searing-hot Washington, D.C., metro area real estate market. The region gains wealthy "one percent" households like no other in the country, and personal fortunes are made on the backs of federal contracts.[20]

One reason that the usual suspects always win USAID contracts is that USAID prefers that only the usual suspects win contacts. To reduce procurement paperwork, USAID often purchases services with "indefinite quantity contracts," which essentially limit bidding to pre-selected, pre-approved firms, namely the USAID top twenty and friends.[21] USAID is trying to move away from this model[22] and former USAID Administrator Rajiv Shah has admitted that "writing big checks to contractors is not development."[23]

Still, as a practical matter, USAID's existing procedures tend to favor traditional vendors (aka beltway bandits) to win contracts because only these firms have the capacity to navigate USAID and federal procurement procedures. The process of government procurement and contracting—which, somewhat unfortunately, has often become the model for other public donors around the world, like the World Bank—virtually precludes any but the most experienced contractors from bidding and winning. Unlike in the private sector, selection for government contracts focuses on how well the rules of bidding are followed, not on ability to execute the actual contract.

The mouse-dancing-with-a-hippo problem is made worse by a barnacles-upon-barnacles problem. Many USAID (and other agency) contracts are hamstrung by congressionally mandated and politically motivated guidelines. Procurement rules are written to satisfy every little rule, old and new, so that in the end, as a crusty USAID veteran once said to me, procurement processes are laden with "barnacles upon barnacles," robbing the agency of virtually any flexibility or latitude in writing RFPs and contracts. USAID employees are often even more frustrated with the resulting procurement morass than outsiders. Indeed, the Federal Acquisition Regulation (FAR), which governs over $1 trillion in federal and state government procurement each year, comes bound neatly in a fifty-seven-volume set. Volume one is 2,000 tissue-thickness pages long. A representative of a mid-size European development contractor once told me that USAID's hoops and regulations make it the worst donor to work for, bar none, so they don't even try.

One of the acknowledged experts on government procurement and contracting law, and a frequent instructor in the field, Steven Tomanelli, began a class on the subject by urging all attendees who might have had any private business experience to "forget everything you know about private sector procurement as you take this course."[24] The idea that government contracting is completely different and, in fact, insulated from the lessons that the American marketplace has evolved over 200 years is troubling, to say the least.

Relying on a small slate of usual suspects who know how to win contracts but not how to deliver usually does not result in good work. How do we know? For one, reconstruction work in Iraq and Afghanistan has been a complete mess. Congress's Commission on Wartime Contracting in Iraq and Afghanistan has estimated that up to $60 billion of the $206 billion that the United States spent (to date) on contracts and grants in those countries was lost to waste and fraud.[25] Nancy Glaser, an experienced startup, venture capital, and operations advisor who worked on business projects for USAID in Afghanistan during 2012–13, was shocked and disheartened by what she saw:

Everyone would get there, start their project, hurry up, wham-bang, get it going, and then leave. Next person would come in, whether it was military or civilian, USAID, and say, oh, well, let's export nuts. But, wait a minute, someone tried last year. There was no coordination. There was tons of money and tons of programs, but they weren't coordinated to make a real impact. I'm sure there's been some impact, but not for all the resources we put there. And all the people we sent there.[26]

Glaser points a finger at the massive contractors that ran USAID's contracts. Flabbergasted by a lending program that set a minimum loan size far beyond the reach of most budding Afghan businesses, $100,000, Glaser and colleagues approached the highest in-country echelons of USAID and State to fix the problem. The reply, Glaser says, was simply:

"My hands are tied. That's how the contract's written." And that's what you hear over and over. Those big contractors have legions of lawyers, and you just don't want to try to change something. . . . The whole model just went bass ackward. We're not taking care of the client, we're taking care of what works for us as the government and the big contractor companies.[27]

In Iraq, Special Inspector General for Iraq Reconstruction Stuart Bowen found that senior Iraqi officials were unimpressed with U.S. efforts, noting especially a failure to solicit local input on programming and problems with widespread corruption. On page three of his final report, Bowen has a lovely photo of a PVC plumbing elbow. The caption notes that the contractor charged the U.S. government $80 for the piece, astronomically more than a competitor's price of $1.41. Iraqi officials told Bowen that the United States' $60 billion in spending and 90,000 contracting actions had resulted in few benefits for the country. The inspector general himself says, "Ultimately, we estimate that the Iraq program wasted at least $8 billion."[28]

Some might say that Afghanistan and Iraq are special cases, war zones and post-war zones where effective development is especially difficult. But that hardly matters; regardless of the scenery, the big boys get the contracts, and the big boys are nonspecialists, and nonspecialists do not do a good job. Unfortunately, not only is it extremely difficult for the true specialists to bid for and win a contract, most are not exactly eager to do so anyway. As Farhad Manjoo writes in *The Wall Street Journal*:

Today, any company looking to work with the government must navigate an obstacle course of niggling, outdated regulations and arbitrary-seeming requirements. For instance, your technology must be Y2K-compliant just to get in the door. The process locks out all but a tiny handful of full-time contractors, companies who also happen to be big federal lobbyists.[29]

Look at HealthCare.gov, a contracting disaster if there ever were one (and, more importantly, one that fueled cynicism about the entire health care policy debate just because the software was so bad). The health insurance exchange website has cost the government at least two to three times as much as Apple spent developing the iPhone.[30] That is crazy. We know there are people in America who can design websites for less than it costs to develop the iPhone, but those folks do not want to work for the government because, as political technologist Clay Johnson says, "It's a pain in the butt."[31] Thus, the contract to build the back end of HealthCare.gov went to conventional (and conventionally large) contractor CGI Federal. That did not go well, as we all know, and so the government hired another firm to fix the exchange, the conventional (and conventionally large) contractor Accenture, a firm with its own history of contract hiccups.[32]

Couldn't these big firms just hire, or sub-contract to, more specialized experts? They could and they often do. But that does not fix the mouse-dancing-with-a-hippo problem. The mouse still has to dance with a hippo, just a contractor hippo instead. Contractors are in the business of squeezing as much work from their subs for as little money as possible because they are in the business of ensuring contracts are lucrative, not in the business of providing expertise. They have an adversarial relationship with smaller contractors because their overall goal is to land the largest portion of the contract for themselves while doing as little of the work as they can. Unless the customer, the government, intervenes in the process to say, "Hey, where's the content here?" the customer will not get the content. Compounding the problem is that the guy selling stuff (the contractor) has more resources than the guy buying stuff (the government). In "America," procurement professionals receive training and pursue a career path. In "Washington," procurement is a dead end; in the military, the highest rank achievable in procurement is captain.[33]

The bottom line is that the U.S. procurement system ensures that the government does not have the right people to do a given job. As David Rohde says: "The use of contractors is a symptom—and a cause—of the decay in American civilian institutions."[34] And this is a huge obstacle to doing entrepreneurship abroad because, as we all know, entrepreneurship is about the nimble, the innovative, the two-person startup, the coffee-shop social media savvy, the young, and the restless. It is not about twenty large beltway bandits.

Entrepreneurship promotion is truly different from other categories of large government spending. Highways, airports, power stations, and weapons systems are projects with billions of dollars of capital costs that require lots of resources, especially person-hours. Most of the work of promoting entrepreneurship does not look like that. It is by definition more entrepreneurial, more innovative. But when you use the same clunky procurement mechanism to nurture startups as you use when hiring Lockheed Martin for fighter jets, you use the wrong tool. That is what happened with Health-Care.gov. The programmers who stay up all night coding are not the same people you hire to build a fighter jet. The project management and culture of hiring someone for a fighter jet is not the same as hiring someone to build a web portal or to do an innovative entrepreneurship promotion program. Our procurement process is unable to distinguish between these two.

It is no wonder that the Global Entrepreneurship Program that I started closed up shop in Egypt; that NAPEO was a sorry failure blasted by State's Inspector General; that there are barely any USAID projects genuinely focused on entrepreneurship development. It is no wonder that the United States does not and cannot promote entrepreneurship effectively. How could we? We do not spend money on entrepreneurship. We have precious little private sector expertise in Washington. Our procurement process energetically keeps entrepreneurial types out of the government contracting game.

We need to rebalance our economic assistance funding toward entrepreneurship and we need to fix the two Ps, people and procurement. Good ideas do not have to be executed badly. When it comes to government programs, I am a big believer in shades of gray. Even highly successful economic assistance initiatives like the Marshall Plan were not uniformly great when implemented. There are aspects of every government project that are not done as well as they could be, and, by the way, the same is true of any large-scale private sector project. Like the Marshall Plan, President Obama's Cairo speech and Hillary Clinton's QDDR ideas were consistent with some of the most enlightened American foreign policy initiatives. And GEP, despite the lack of support, did have its moments. These good ideas just need to be executed better.

Part II of this book is about how to execute better. The frustrations I encountered in Washington helped me think about and develop approaches to entrepreneurship promotion. They helped me think about how you actually do something. How do we find the bright spark in urban Cairo and set him or her on the path to starting a business? How do we ensure that Kenya's would-be entrepreneurs are learning problem-solving skills and the difference between debt, equity, quasi-equity, and convertible debt? How do we help techies in Jordan avoid mistakes we have seen in Silicon Valley? How do we encourage ease-of-doing-business factors in different cultures? How do we drive investor, customer, and media attention to Jakarta and Lagos?

The next chapters will dive into the ecosystem approach to entrepreneurship development and look closely at specific programs that are already helping startups grow, create jobs, and strengthen communities. We will explore making government better at doing the things it is supposed to do, how the U.S. government can truly engage entrepreneurship in the service of foreign policy. We can spend our money smarter. We can redirect funds from unsuccessful programs. We can change government staffing and contracting to reflect the hallmarks of entrepreneurialism: flexibility, innovation, boundary pushing. We can improve the efficiency of procurement processes and ensure that America's best are contracted to do America's most important work.

How will we do all this? Some fixes will be simple; others may require rethinking the structure and function of executive branch agencies and ultimately, require congressional action. These represent daunting obstacles, but that's exactly what the entrepreneurial spirit exists for. Let's start building the workarounds now.

PART II

The Solution

SEVEN

It Takes an Ecosystem

LIBERATION ROAD AND ALUGUNTUGUI Street don't intersect with U.S. Route 101 or Sand Hill Road in Silicon Valley. But if you find yourself in Accra, Ghana, take Liberation from the center of town and make your way to Aluguntugui. There, in the 'burbs of one of West Africa's important coastal cities, you will find the Meltwater Entrepreneurial School of Technology (MEST), nurturer of some of Africa's most promising tech startups.

In just a few years of operation, MEST and the entrepreneurs working behind its blue compound walls have launched a bevy of software startups that are attracting attention and markets beyond Ghana and beyond Africa. They include: Dropifi, a customer engagement platform that became the first African company to join angel investor Dave McClure's 500 Startups accelerator program; ClaimSync, an electronic health records service that was acquired by a Dutch biometrics firm in 2013; Saya, an instant messaging and Internet service for dumb phones that was the first African company to pitch at TechCrunch Disrupt Battlefield and was acquired by American mobile app company Kirusa in 2014; RetailTower, a preferred solutions provider for Amazon product ads; several other ventures that have won competitions and accolades from big entrepreneurship names like Google, Startup Weekend, and DEMO Africa. Media outlets like CNN, *The Guardian*, and *Forbes* have written about MEST, and—in that most ultimate of honors—the campus has hosted none other than Bono (and on a separate, less glamorous occasion, U.S. Secretary of Commerce Penny Pritzker).[1]

Before MEST's founding in 2008, Ghanaian tech entrepreneurs were not pitching in Brazil, making splashes in Silicon Valley, getting acquired by European and American companies, or garnering global headlines. Accra would never be considered a place to look for promising tech companies. Yes, Ghana as a whole is known as a standout in Africa on some measures: free-and-fair elections, a fast-growing economy, a strong soccer team known for eliminating the U.S. team from the World Cup in 2006 and 2010. But none of this added up to a reputation as the "Silicon Valley of Africa." Ghana is a poor country. Its university graduates have a terrible time finding work and are often resigned to the informal sector. By some estimates, only 2 percent of the quarter million young people entering Ghana's labor market each year find a job.[2] Electricity can be unreliable and bandwidth not always wide; these are nonstarters for the information and communications technology (ICT) crowd. Angel investors are practically nonexistent. Even if a bank gave you a loan for a startup, which they likely would not, that money would come with a 20 percent interest rate.[3]

Launching a startup is never easy. In Ghana the odds against success are stacked even higher. Steve Jobs or Mark Zuckerberg, products of ideal ecosystems, would have had a hard time launching Apple or Facebook in Accra. So what is it with these MEST entrepreneurs? How do they do it? Accra may not be a destination for techies, and it may not have Stanford or U.C.-Berkeley, venture capital (VC) firms, world-class national laboratories, or cool shared workspaces with blazing Wi-Fi. But MEST can replicate that environment on a small scale.

MEST is a training ground, an incubator, a seed fund, and a "center of gravity" for entrepreneurship wrapped into one. It is the brainchild of Jorn Lyseggen, born in Korea and adopted by a Norwegian family as an infant. Lyseggen grew up on a farm, became a successful repeat entrepreneur, and decided a way to give back—as well as find the next great thing—would be to search the developing world on a one-man mission to build a self-contained entrepreneurship ecosystem. Ghana, politically stable, English-speaking, and conveniently located in the GMT time zone, caught his eye and he founded MEST in 2008.

Each year MEST scours Ghana for twenty-five university graduates/aspiring entrepreneurs willing to devote two years to intensive software and business courses. At the end of that two-year training program, effectively a specialized MBA, these entrepreneurs-in-training (EITs) form startups and pitch the MEST brass for selection into the in-house incubator. In its first five years MEST invested over $1.5 million in sixteen companies founded by its students.

During training and after graduating to the incubator, MEST's EITs are exposed to a permanent staff and revolving cast of guest gurus. Venture capital experts, e-commerce veterans, experienced CEOs, successful entrepreneurs, and Oxford MBA students become teachers, mentors, and advisory board members. A rigorous application process ensures promising cohorts of EITs each year; the top-notch classroom training and close mentoring develops and pushes the EITs; visits from international players broaden their networks; a seed fund gets the most promising startups on their way; and meet-ups on campus, international press coverage, and photo-ops with U2's front man are the return on the sweat equity of EITs—and turn the entrepreneurs into role models for the next MEST class and Ghanaians at large.

So, notwithstanding the hazards of comparing apples and oranges, one nevertheless feels a little bit of the West Coast on Africa's west coast, a bit of the Bay Area in the Gulf of Guinea.

MEST is a great example of the ecosystem approach to entrepreneurship promotion (albeit a somewhat closed ecosystem serving only those admitted to its nurturing embrace). Entrepreneurs thrive in healthy ecosystems. Silicon Valley has not birthed the world's biggest names in tech—Apple, Google, Facebook, Instagram, Twitter, whatever the next big thing is—by coincidence. Entrepreneurs don't operate in a bubble. Even though personal ability to innovate and commercialize are crucial, there are many factors and many players that affect the probability of success. The fact is, you will see more successful startups more often in regions where it is easier for entrepreneurs to get in front of investors, where mentors and relevant training are accessible, where the regulatory environment is conducive to new businesses (and to investment in those businesses), and where startup kids are the cool kids.

The subject of this chapter is what you need to encourage scalable, job-creating entrepreneurship in an ecosystem. We will explore some of the world's most successful entrepreneurship ecosystems; Silicon Valley, yes, but also Israel, Rwanda, and university-anchored towns like Boulder, Colorado. The ecosystem concept is especially important when it comes to elevating entrepreneurship in the service of foreign policy. Why? Because ecosystems are influenceable. Not every region can (or should aspire to) become a Silicon Valley. But what MEST has accomplished in Ghana shows that there are specific things that can be done to bolster an entrepreneurship ecosystem and, thus, greatly improve the odds that new businesses will form and that those new businesses will create jobs. If MEST, a small investment by a single individual, can put a country like Ghana on the tech world map, then imagine what concerted, coordinated efforts by the U.S. government, perhaps acting in concert with private companies and individuals, could do in other countries suffering heavy youth unemployment.

My call for the U.S. government to elevate entrepreneurship in its foreign assistance programming is at its core a call to turbo-charge ecosystems. That is what it means for our government to "do entrepreneurship." We are not talking about picking winners or guaranteeing all startups succeed. Rather, we are talking about nurturing an environment, in a very targeted manner, that will convert a landscape of crabgrass into a victory garden, that will increase the odds that a region's entrepreneurs will meet with success. This is not a haphazard process. We are not talking about launching seed funds willy-nilly, or jetting Google's Eric Schmidt in for a guest lecture or two at a university or a fancy conference. Building ecosystems means more than designing tax-exempt categories for particular industries and waiting to see what happens. That is not what MEST has done, and that is not what works. Instead, ecosystem development combines several different specific, varied activities. It is a comprehensive approach, not a one-off contract for a beltway bandit firm looking to do the work as cheaply as possible.

To do this, we need a framework. Based on my experience as an entrepreneur, a State Department official, and a professional working in the space of entrepreneurship promotion, I have developed the Six + Six Entrepreneurship Ecosystem Model. The model highlights the six fundamental pillars of a successful ecosystem: *identify, train, connect and sustain, fund, enable* (through public policy), and *celebrate* entrepreneurs. Similarly, there are six categories of actors who must build these pillars: *NGOs, foundations, academia, investors, governments*, and *corporations*. These six pillars and six actors are the levers we have to work with when we think about influencing an ecosystem. I will not claim that my model is perfect or unique, but it is a constructive way to think about "doing entrepreneurship" and getting results.

Ecosystems and How to Influence Them

Steve Jobs and William Hewlett and David Packard may have started their legendary tech companies in garages, but it is important to note that those garages were not in Haiti. Innovative and high-impact startups are more likely to spawn in places with an infrastructure—physical, human, political— that amply supports entrepreneurs. The scale, duration, and quantity of viable launches are all greatly influenced by the nature of an entrepreneurship ecosystem.[4]

Los Altos and Palo Alto, both next door to Stanford University, are very good places to have a garage, and Silicon Valley is an obvious example of how ecosystems breed entrepreneurs. Actors go to Hollywood and so do many who are interested in the movie business—be they into lighting, costumes, set design, or the business of the business—because that is where the action is. Likewise with Silicon Valley and tech. There are countless factors that make the Bay Area a great place to be to launch a tech startup: a knowledgeable and skilled human resource pool; venture capitalists hunting for promising investments; universities performing cutting-edge research.

But Silicon Valley is not the only thriving entrepreneurial ecosystem. It is not even the only one with a high-tech bent. Take Israel. In 2014, in the second quarter alone, VC firms invested nearly $1 billion in Israeli private high-tech companies.[5] Israel, with a population of 8 million, trails only the United States (population approximately 316 million) and China (population approximately 1.36 billion) as one of the world's top three sources of NASDAQ-listed companies.[6] In 2008, venture capital investments in Israel were 2.5 times greater than in the United States on a per capita basis.[7] In the book *Start-Up Nation*, one of the best expositions of the entrepreneurship ecosystem concept, Dan Senor and Saul Singer ask, "Why Israel and not elsewhere?" The answer: a strong ecosystem. Senor and Singer survey a host of factors—some fortuitous, some encouraged by government— that account for the outsized success of Israeli startups. Among the reasons: a tradition of military service begets highly trained engineers whose unit mates become business partners down the road; a history of mass immigration, which takes advantage of the fact that, as an Israeli government advisor said, "a nation of immigrants is a nation of entrepreneurs;" and two government seed fund programs (BIRD and Yozma, about which more later) designed to help new companies get going and jumpstart the VC industry.[8]

There is a lot of buy-in around this concept of entrepreneurship ecosystems. From the World Economic Forum to development philanthropic groups like the Omidyar Network, from *The Economist* to the Kauffman Foundation entrepreneurship think thank, the notion of ecosystems pervades the language of entrepreneurship.[9] The current trend is to examine regions where startup activity thrives and study the factors that make for especially strong ecosystems, and then rank those regions. When my consulting firm works in a particular city or region, we start by turning to a growing array of sources for understanding entrepreneurial activity. The World Bank produces a useful *Doing Business* report that ranks countries according to how easy it is to (surprise!) "do business." The number of days to register a new firm and the enforceability of contracts factor into the rankings. (In 2015, Singapore was number one and Eritrea number 189.)[10] The Global Entrepreneurship Monitor (GEM) out of Babson College publishes "an annual assessment of the entrepreneurial activity, aspirations, and attitudes of individuals across a wide range of countries."[11] The Global Entrepreneurship and Development Institute (GEDI) runs an index "capturing the contextual nature of business formation, expansion, and growth."[12] Other prominent trackers of global entrepreneurship include the Legatum Institute, the Heritage Foundation, the World Economic Forum, Transparency International, the Mo Ibrahim Foundation, Cornell University's Global Innovation Index, and Startup Genome, which rates Silicon Valley the world's number one entrepreneurship ecosystem and Tel Aviv number two.[13]

These indices each have their own methodologies and focus on slightly different data. How to "measure" an ecosystem is not an exact science. In 2013, the Aspen Network for Development Entrepreneurs (ANDE) issued a report summarizing various methodologies for assessing ecosystems.[14] The Six + Six Model was among these, and while the Six + Six is not a ranking tool *per se*, it does offer a comprehensive analytical framework for understanding the strengths and weaknesses of ecosystems. We will get to my model in a moment, but first we need to consider a key point. We can grow ecosystems; they are amenable to cultivation.[15] Ecosystems are not black or white; present or absent. They can be improved and expanded. Boosting an ecosystem, influencing it, can greatly improve the odds of more success for more startups. That is exactly what is required in fragile, emerging, and developing markets burdened by huge numbers of unemployed young people.

Universities supply a skilled workforce, and tax holidays attract new companies. For eons, cities, states, and regions have used policy to attract business and create jobs. The idea of making a business climate more attractive is not new. But influencing an entrepreneurship ecosystem is a slightly different thing. The ways governments and citizens have gone about this to date is instructive, mainly to grasp that, yes, we can influence ecosystems; we can help startups grow into job-creating "gazelles"; there are specific things we can do to turbo-charge entrepreneurship.

One of the more famous recent attempts at influencing an entrepreneurship ecosystem comes from Chile. There, the government made (and still makes) an offer: Come to Chile, work on your fledgling startup here for six to twelve months, and we will give you a one-year resident visa, a desk, a Wi-Fi connection, and $40,000 in seed funding—without taking any equity stake. What a deal! The program is called Start-Up Chile, and since 2010 it has supported over 560 startups, selecting from a pool of 12,000 applications. The government's stated goal is to "position Chile as the leading innovation and entrepreneurial hub of Latin America." The strategy is very much about importing special sauce: get lots of cool startups together in one place, get them networking with each other and with mentors at Start-Up Chile HQ, and get Chileans drinking the entrepreneurship Kool-Aid.[16] Most of Start-Up Chile's resident companies come from the United States—participating startups need not focus on the Chilean or Latin American market—but Chile is the next most represented country. By many accounts the ecosystem is raising Chile's entrepreneurship profile.[17] It is impossible to say whether Start-Up Chile will rank a success in the long run, but the odds of ecosystem development have to be better with such a program in place.[18]

Israel's aforementioned high-tech entrepreneurship success drafted off many factors, but a few key contributors were premeditated efforts by the Israeli government to influence startup activity. For example, in the late 1970s, Israel and the United States established the BIRD Foundation (Binational Industrial Research and Development), an endowment that gave, and still gives, about twenty grants each year of $500,000 to $1 million for research and development aspects of joint ventures between Israeli and U.S. companies. Companies that win BIRD grants keep their equity, pay no service charges, and make repayments only in the event revenues from the project are realized. The joint venture angle helped Israel's fledgling tech companies learn about the vast U.S. market, and BIRD's $250 million worth of investments over the past decades has generated more than $8 billion in sales for recipient companies.[19] Then, in the 1990s, the Israeli government gave the VC industry a jumpstart that has led to the astonishing growth and development of Israel's tech sector that we see today. The Yozma program offered VC firms matching funds such that for every two dollars raised by a firm for a Yozma fund, the government would invest one dollar and offer extremely favorable buy-out terms after five years. The ten original Yozma funds raised $200 million and today, completely privatized, manage $3 billion of capital. Yozma was in effect a de-risking tool—not a small matter in the Middle East—and the leg-up to the VC industry soon led to widespread investing activity that had no need for Yozma crutches.[20]

Chile and Israel clearly feel that entrepreneurship ecosystems are influenceable. So does Brad Feld, a Boulder, Colorado-based early-stage venture capitalist and successful entrepreneur. His book, *Startup Communities: Building an Entrepreneurial Ecosystem in Your City*, calls on entrepreneurs themselves to take the lead in growing an ecosystem and for government, universities, and investors ("feeders") to play supporting roles. Feld's recipe, which he titles the Boulder Thesis, assigns a central role for entrepreneurs, but demands an inclusive atmosphere and open engagement with all kinds of members of a community. Importantly, his premise is hardly any different from Chile's and Israel's. There are ways to generate startup activity in almost any environment, including your own city.[21] Everyone is doing it. Wealthy Finland, which feared overreliance on communications giant Nokia, launched an innovation agency and VC fund; 300 former Nokia employees have founded startups.[22] Poor Rwanda, emerging from a genocide that killed hundreds of thousands, took steps to ease business formation, instituted policies to attract foreign investors and companies, and jumped 100 places in the World Bank's *Doing Business* rankings.[23] Michael Goldberg, of Case Western Reserve University in Cleveland, has taught a MOOC (massive open online course) called "Beyond Silicon Valley: Growing Entrepreneurship in Transitioning Economies" that examines a northeast Ohio program of seed funds, mentorship networks, and other ecosystem efforts as a case study.[24]

If we all agree that we can influence an entrepreneurship ecosystem, we still might not agree that we should. The big point to make here is this:

we should not be thinking about how to turn every village, province, and country into Silicon Valley. We often hear things like "Bangalore is the Silicon Valley of India" or "Nairobi is the Silicon Valley of Africa." Government officials often vow to "turn City X into the Silicon Valley of Region Y." That is great, but only in the aspirational sense. Aspirational goals can be enormously powerful forces, and using "Silicon Valley" as shorthand for "energizing an innovation sector and spurring young people and investors to invest in startups" is a worthy sentiment. But using "Silicon Valley" as an actual blueprint often leads to failure and frustration, especially in developing and emerging markets, and even in the West and the United States. As Goldberg's MOOC notes: "Most markets around the world do not look like Silicon Valley, and they never will."[25] You cannot turn City X into the Silicon Valley of Region Y because the conditions required to produce Silicon Valley were so unique. Setting out to photocopy Silicon Valley in your hometown is so completely unrealistic that it invites discouragement and frustration; it sets the bar too high.

What's more, when we talk about Silicon Valley as a role model, we are talking primarily about tech entrepreneurship. It is important to remember that entrepreneurship is hyper-local and, thus, conditions vary widely by geography. Different strokes is the name of the game. As mentioned earlier, entrepreneurship promotion means helping low-tech and no-tech startups as well as high-tech startups, particularly in developing countries. Indeed, if one's primary goal in sponsoring entrepreneurship is job creation, then tech entrepreneurship may be the least likely to achieve that objective. You need to tailor efforts to the given situation. (The Six + Six Model helps you figure out what those appropriate efforts are.) This is not to say that lower-skill, lower-wage jobs should be the goal of job creation and entrepreneurship. But because entrepreneurship is hyper-local, what works in Silicon Valley may not work in Oakland, let alone Beirut. E-commerce may be important in one part of a country while agribusiness is a better target industry in another. Rather than chasing Silicon Valley—which has grown so organically and benefited from a unique confluence of private sector, academic, and government activity—ecosystems should be looking to their own strengths. One of the sectors Rwanda has focused on in its pro-business efforts is coffee; Boston leverages its area universities in the bio-tech and health fields. Entrepreneurship promotion is not one size fits all.

What about the idea that some places simply are not "ready" for entrepreneurship? This is an argument I came across frequently while developing

GEP for the State Department. One senior, highly experienced (in government, not business) American official suggested to me that Egypt was not "ready" for entrepreneurship promotion programs because the enabling environment—regulatory regimes and such—were too weak for entrepreneurship to take off. To boot, corruption, one of the biggest (and least discussed) obstacles for entrepreneurs in developing countries, was especially severe in Egypt, the official observed. But I found this point of view frustrating because improving the enabling environment is a part of proper entrepreneurship development. (It is the enable parameter in the Six + Six Model.) It is not a signpost we need to pass before work can begin. It is a road we build. In fact, as we saw in chapter 3, one of the reasons entrepreneurship is good for you is precisely because it increases the constituency in a country for sensible business regulatory reforms. Improving the regulatory environment is a simultaneous event with entrepreneurship promotion, not sequential. The line of argument this government official was pursuing is dangerous. What are the millions of unemployed Egyptians supposed to do while an enabling environment slowly comes into being? Egypt is an ancient country where time is measured in millennia, so I suppose we could wait another 1,000 years for a ripe enabling environment. But while aid policy sits in waiting mode, uprisings and discontentment will continue and the core problem driving chronic instability—youth unemployment—will remain unaddressed. Fixing a country's enabling environment is a long process. In fact, as the 2012 JOBS Act demonstrates, we are still working on it in America. If, since 1776, the U.S. government had waited for some fabled perfect conditions to support entrepreneurs, the course of U.S. economic development would have been very different.

GEP's work in Indonesia faced different concerns. USAID felt that lackluster entrepreneurship was the least of Indonesia's woes. Indonesia's problems, the argument went, were much further down the pyramid of needs. More important were consistent access to food, water, shelter, and medicine, all of which are huge challenges for large portions of the population. Until these basic needs were addressed, what good would it do to focus on entrepreneurship? While I saw the point, I disagreed. Is it not possible, I countered, that there are different rates of development in different parts of a country, particularly one as large as Indonesia? Couldn't we work on entrepreneurship in Jakarta and tend to basic needs in the more rural parts of the country? Couldn't entrepreneurial ventures drive the sort of basic development that those rural areas need? In fact, social enterprise, a subset of entrepreneurship, is very much about private sector solutions to basic human needs. A large nation like Indonesia (the fourth most populous country in the world, with 250 million people) is far from monolithic. Different strategies work for different regions.

I believe strongly that entrepreneurship ecosystem building happens simultaneously with other development efforts. There is nothing sequential about entrepreneurship. You do not have to wait till a country is "ready" in terms of business climate, or until everyone enjoys 2,000 calories per day and access to electricity, hot and cold running water, and first world sanitation systems. Entrepreneurship is ready to help now, tailored to the particular region or country.

The Six + Six Model

If we want to influence entrepreneurship ecosystems, we need a framework to organize our analysis and plan our attack. My approach to ecosystems is the Six + Six Entrepreneurship Ecosystem Model (see figure 7-1). Six + Six presumes that no single factor alone can move the needle on entrepreneurship: not funding, not regulatory reforms. Rather, entrepreneurs thrive when multiple sectors and actors consciously work together to develop a supportive environment. NGOs, foundations, academia, investors, governments, and corporations all need to play some role in identifying, training, connecting and sustaining, funding, enabling (through public policy), and celebrating entrepreneurs.

Let us look at the six pillars that capture what an ecosystem is about. First, identify. Entrepreneurs need to get on an investor's radar screen, whether that investor is a Sand Hill Road VC, a low-profile angel investor, or a captain of industry in a poor country. A robust ecosystem will do a good and efficient job of bringing investors to Hewlett and Packard's garage. MEST actively runs an intensive recruitment and application process to identify promising entrepreneurs for its two-year program, and then invests (both money and mentorship) in a select few that develop a good idea and make a good pitch. Business plan competitions are a great way to cast a wide net. The next chapter discusses the best ways to run business plan competitions, but generally speaking, aggregating a large number of startup teams and enabling them to pitch their companies is a good way to shake the tree and find a community's entrepreneurs.

FIGURE 7-1. *The Six+Six Entrepreneurship Ecosystem Model*

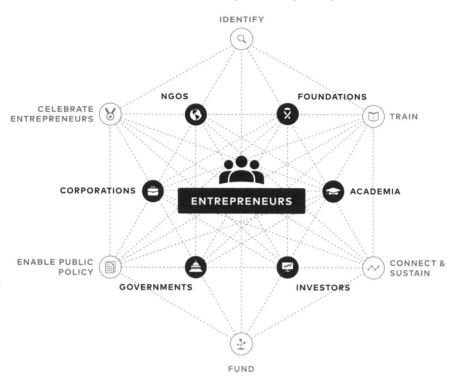

But many potential entrepreneurs do not have the training and skills needed to operate a business, even those (sometimes especially those) who win business plan competitions. They may be good at the pitch but not so good at the execution. A successful ecosystem, thus, requires educational resources that transfer knowledge and build real skills. This might come from world-class universities, but training comes in many forms and at different ages. Entrepreneurs in poor countries often don't learn much in the way of accounting and bookkeeping from their under-resourced school systems, let alone master product piloting, types of financing vehicles, intellectual property protection, customer segmentation, or market research. Entrepreneurship hubs, aid programs, mentors, friends, foreign investors—these might all become sources of training. Some programs focus on early learning, teaching entrepreneurship concepts and how to think creatively to teenagers and even children age ten and younger. Entrepreneurship pedagogy is a major academic field. One of the discipline's leaders,

Babson College (and its affiliate Babson Global), runs programs worldwide, including training for community college faculty, on how to work with existing, local small businesses.[26]

Entrepreneurs also need to be connected to other entrepreneurs and veteran business leaders to develop business acumen. This is very much the idea behind the mixing bowl of Start-Up Chile, MEST's campus-based program, and the inclusive spirit of the Boulder Thesis that Brad Feld talks about in his book *Startup Communities*. Connecting a new entrepreneur to someone who has "been there and done that" is vital to the newbie's success. In fact, I believe that mentoring—not funding—is the single most critical determinant of success or failure for a startup. In the long term, and often in more formal programs, connecting is about sustaining progress. Incubator programs and extended mentorship arrangements are key here. Be it 500 Startups, the Unreasonable Institute, MEST, or the Demeter Network's mentor matchmaking service, mechanisms that deliver experience and encouragement to startup founders are a key presence in strong ecosystems.

Funding is the lifeblood of any business, of course. It ensures entrepreneurs have the financial means to build upon ideas. No access to finance means (very likely) no startup. But financing means different things at different stages of growth. Only the strongest ecosystems supply options at each stage. For instance, in almost any economy, an entrepreneur's own resources (and access to credit) are very likely to be the first source of funds. This is important. An entrepreneur's first dollars are almost always their own; not the money of angel investors, venture capitalists, the bank, or even friends and family. (Friends and family, though, are very often the next source of funding: a rich uncle, the savings of university classmates, the contributions of a tight knit church congregation.) This is true in the United States and Nicaragua and Niger . . . everywhere.

In developed economies (and in some poor economies) angel investors may well emerge to provide early-stage support. Further down the line comes venture capital, and then debt (for example, bank loans and mortgages), strategic partnerships with larger firms, and private equity. (By the way, despite the hype, less than 1 percent of American companies have ever received venture capital financing.[27] And banks never loan to a true startup; the goal of banks is to lend money to people who do not need it and avoid lending to those who do, because the latter are almost always a poor credit risk.) The earlier in this progression a startup is, the more risk it presents for potential investors. Thus, whether you are in Ghana or Silicon Valley, the seed stage is usually the trickiest; the leap from friends and family money to VC or debt backing is often called the "financing gap." Where can a startup get the $25,000 or $500,000 needed to prove a concept and run with an idea? The strongest ecosystems do not just dish out seed money for everyone, but they do have multiple mechanisms for funding the best ideas and a mature financial apparatus for companies further along.

Public policy must be conducive to entrepreneurship. Startups should be enabled rather than hindered by the regulatory environment. This is the catchall ecosystem parameter regarding red tape, tax incentives, rule of law, and all the political and institutional factors that can help or hurt a startup. One-stop-shop filing for new businesses, clear pathways for foreign investors to get money in and out of a country; these are among the myriad issues that determine whether an ecosystem is friendly toward entrepreneurship. A crucial, related factor here is corruption. It is difficult to measure the burden this places on startups, both in cost and time. Suffice to say that, in my experience, corruption is often one of the most decisive reasons why startups fail. An infant firm's bottom line breaks under the extra weight of "facilitation" expenses; a young entrepreneur lacks access to the "big man" who *de facto* decides whether or not a business goes ahead on his turf.

Finally, entrepreneurship must be celebrated as a desirable, worthy, and viable career path. I believe that celebration rivals mentoring and funding in importance to a successful ecosystem. Silicon Valley is full of entrepreneurs. Everyone there thinks it is cool to be an entrepreneur, even (and especially) if you turned down a job with Goldman Sachs to pursue your own dream. In Ghana, if you have a university degree, you may well be considered an idiot, or at least irresponsible, if you do not take a job with a bank, an international NGO, or the government. Result: far fewer entrepreneurs.

A culture that belittles rather than extols entrepreneurs must change. In my view, one of the best ways to accomplish that change is precisely to celebrate those local entrepreneurs who do succeed. When you open the business section of a local newspaper, are you reading about a startup founded by college kids, or the latest sales figures for Coca-Cola? Do MEST's latest graduates appear on the radio and TV talk shows, or is it just the CEOs of multinationals and parastatals? Celebrating entrepreneurship is about rewarding successful entrepreneurs and introducing them to a community as role models.

These six parameters—identify, train, connect and sustain, fund, enable, and celebrate—are the key pillars to a strong ecosystem. If all of these activities are in evidence, then you will see more garages occupied by entrepreneurs and more of those entrepreneurs finding success.

But who exactly is responsible for erecting these pillars? Naming those builders is the other half of the Six+Six Model: NGOs, foundations, academia, investors, governments, and corporations. Each of these actors can contribute to one or more of the six pillars. There are no hard and fast rules about who does what, but in a healthy ecosystem you might see something like this: an NGO running a bookkeeping training program for startup founders; a foundation sponsoring a business plan competition with a seed grant for top prize; a university engineering department building a prototyping and testing facility; multiple angel investors and VC firms looking for deals; town hall encouraging business formation by subsidizing workspace on Main Street and a key minister championing entrepreneurship nationally; a major corporation sponsoring an incubator to house new firms that could become customers or suppliers.

The concept for the Six+Six has its roots in my days in Foggy Bottom, when I was trying to walk through the raindrops at the State Department and figuring out what was possible in a rigid, noninnovative environment, without funding or staffing but with a relentless need to show that the U.S. government was "doing" something big. In fact, if you had a clean piece of paper and were to approach developing an ecosystem framework completely *de novo* and with no constraints and unlimited resources, you might design something different from the Six+Six. ANDE has researched nine different frameworks, and there are doubtless dozens more out there.[28] (Nevertheless, there are not likely to be any "perfect" environments anywhere in the world, so the business of entrepreneurship promotion is always one of adjusting to local circumstances.)

GEP had no money. At least not at the outset. Whatever work GEP was to do had to involve something other than giving money (much to the surprise of many of our foreign partners). We were not USAID or MCC devising grant schemes and managing staffs. A second constraint: State and the U.S. government broadly were (and still are) focused on the idea of "public–private partnerships," a major buzzword in Washington. In large measure this means getting nongovernment organizations to fund programs that the government then can take credit for. So GEP had to include a substantial "public–private" element. It could not be a government-only operation. My search for private sector partners led to the realization that there were several types of partners, several types of actors.

The idea of "ecosystems of partners" gained further traction in my mind because, as I have pointed out, State is heavy on policy and light on implementation. I am a big supporter of practice over theory, but State was the other way around. So there was a necessity to couch much of GEP's work in theory and policy terms, and talk less about implementation and actual practice. The concept of pillars and partners lent themselves perfectly to this need. (In a classic display of misplaced priorities, during my tenure at State, USAID was able to find money to contract a consulting firm to produce a 120-page document describing the ecosystem approach to entrepreneurship development[29] but not a dime to actually implement entrepreneurship development programming.)

In a sense, the idea of a medley of partners working together within an ecosystem resembles one of my favorite old Yiddish tales, the "stone soup" story. A poor traveller goes from village to village, arriving at each one with nothing but a small stone. But he tells villagers he is a gourmet cook, chicken soup is his specialty, and that his secret ingredient is his magic stone. To make his brew, he asks the villagers for contributions: a pot, a fire to boil the water, chicken, vegetables, salt and pepper, an accompaniment of bread and butter, and more. He cooks up a storm and drops in his special (that is, ordinary) stone. Everyone loves the soup, and the poor traveller has gotten himself a meal. If you are clever, you can get yourself almost anything, even a meal, from just a stone in the field.

Constrained as it was, GEP was a bit like the poor traveller in the stone soup story. Greg Behrman, who was State's point person on Obama's Cairo Initiative, was very much a partner in developing an ecosystem approach for GEP's work (as well as various deliverables for the Presidential Summit on Entrepreneurship). Sue Saarnio was an expert in mechanics, process, and telling the story, all of which were of enormous service in helping develop what became GEP.

The stone-soup trick with GEP—the way we dealt with our constraints— was to use partners. Since we had no money, we could not pay them. But we could crown them "official GEP partners" and encourage them to do what they did naturally and try to coordinate that with GEP and its other partners.

GEP might have been staff-less, but we soon cobbled together a list of some 150 for-profit and nonprofit groups that were specialists in entrepreneurship ecosystem building. They were startup incubator advisors, angel investor trainers, business plan competition gurus, and more. We would use them to deliver programming. After I left State, I formalized this approach into the categories of actors in the Six+Six Model.

What does Six+Six look like in practice? Today, my consulting firm works with clients to strengthen ecosystems through a three-step process of 1) diagnostic, 2) design, and 3) implementation. The Six+Six paradigm governs all three stages. The first step in entrepreneurship development is to understand the ecosystem at hand, and the Six+Six Model guides the research as we conduct this initial diagnostic.

My firm did such an exercise in Ghana for the United Kingdom's Department for International Development. (You can download the report on Koltai & Co.'s website.[30]) We walked through the model, investigating how entrepreneurs are identified (StartUp Cup was running a business plan competition while we were researching in-country), what their options for training are (Stanford had just launched their SEED program matching mentors with rising businesses), what funding sources are available (an angel investor platform was struggling to make its first deals), and so on. We looked to see what NGOs are doing (Enablis does trainings and business plan competitions), what government programs are in place (the Kofi Annan Centre runs solid IT courses), and who the investors are (beyond MEST, there were very few seed-stage players). Using the Six+Six Model in this way produces a comprehensive survey of a particular ecosystem's landscape.

With the diagnostic in hand, we are in a good position to identify which pillars of an ecosystem need bolstering. It becomes clear which pillars are weak, which are especially active, and what kinds of programs might be especially useful for the specific ecosystem under study. We can design programs that address particular weaknesses and then implement them. In Ghana, among other ideas, noting a wide and deep financing gap, we recommended a seed fund and an entrepreneurship delegation of American, British, and West African angel investors (like the ones GEP took to Turkey and Egypt). We also thought a journalism prize for entrepreneurship reporting might get Ghana's rising startups in the news more and inspire a new generation of entrepreneurs.

Would programs like these be successful? I think so. Indeed, the whole argument of this book—that the U.S. government should far more heavily promote entrepreneurship to combat the joblessness underlying strife and threats to America today—relies on our ability to see results from the ecosystem approach to entrepreneurship development, results like new business formation and job creation. Fortunately, if the success of MEST graduates proves anything, it is that we have an executable solution at the ready. And MEST is not the only evidence. Endeavor, a United States-based organization that mentors high-growth startups in Latin America, the Middle East, and elsewhere, makes a point of its ecosystem approach and has seen the companies it supports create jobs at a rate five times faster than comparable firms.[31]

Chapter 8 will examine groups like Endeavor that are already running programs that turbo-charge entrepreneurship. Some are particularly good at training entrepreneurs or stimulating funding or connecting founders with experienced mentors. Others touch several of the Six+Six Model's ecosystem pillars at once. After we learn more about these programs and how they work, we will turn to our ultimate goal: coming up with a business plan to get the U.S. government more involved in entrepreneurship ecosystem building and on the path to world peace.

EIGHT

How It Works and Who Does It

IN EXPLORING THE MAKEUP of entrepreneurship ecosystems via the Six + Six Model, we have seen that new businesses rarely "go it alone." Startup founders rely on helping hands, be it pro-entrepreneurship government policies, an angel investment, or just a chance to pitch an idea. Did even Mark Zuckerberg or Bill Gates (both college dropouts) need a hand? Yes, of course. Remember, their companies grew not in the Central African Republic— where angel and venture investors, sage mentorship, and legal protections are practically nonexistent—but in what is almost universally considered to be a nurturing, enabling ecosystem.

All startups, even the ones that grow to be successful in America, need help overcoming obstacles. Entrepreneurship is no cakewalk. In fact, starting a business is just about the hardest thing one can do professionally. In emerging and developing economies, the places this book is most concerned with, the constraints are often more obvious and easier to pinpoint. An Omidyar Network-sponsored Monitor Group report titled *Accelerating Entrepreneurship in Africa* makes no bones about the truth that startups and their founders need help. The report identified a "prohibitive" cost of capital, a dearth of professional and managerial skills, and a lack of quality business support services as real barriers to entrepreneurialism on the African continent.[1] Ramez Mohammad, CEO of the Egypt-based Flat-6Labs accelerator, says MENA entrepreneurs have difficulty accessing startup capital, too, and that they operate "in closed markets in terms of data and information" about competition and regulations unless they can afford a high-flying consultant to conduct market studies and legal analyses.[2]

It follows that the more startups that have access to a helping hand, the more startups we will see succeed, grow, and create jobs. The nature of those helping hands is the focus of this chapter. Government is an obvious player, but there are many other so-called "intermediaries,"[3] as captured by the players in the Six+Six Model: NGOs, foundations, academia, investors, governments, and corporations. The previous chapter mentioned Endeavor, a nonprofit that supports promising startups in certain ecosystems with close mentorship. Endeavor has seen its mentee companies create jobs five times faster than comparable companies and grow 2.4 percent faster.[4] Their programming appears to produce real results.

But ecosystem building and entrepreneurship programming are new enough concepts that the jury is still out about what works, and to what extent. Stepping up entrepreneurship programming will require commensurately stepping up monitoring and evaluation to improve programming and determine the very best practices. Indeed, even in the case of Endeavor, one of the gold standards of entrepreneurship support organizations, it is difficult to prove a direct causation between participation in the program and accelerated success. Some critics point out that supporting high-performing "winners" proves very little since these founders may well have been successful no matter what, with or without programming like Endeavor's. Nevertheless, Endeavor's success over nearly twenty years in twenty countries suggests there is something to their model, and there are many indications that similar programs have had positive effects. Indeed, all my championing of entrepreneurship would be for naught if we did not have evidence of programs that can, in fact, turbo-charge ecosystems. The good news is that such programs do exist and the U.S. government can and should support them to better promote entrepreneurship in fragile, developing, and emerging economies around the world. There really are ways to implement the Six+Six Model and actually do something about the 30-plus percent youth unemployment rates that undermine Middle East stability, that render jihad a decent career choice, and that threaten America. This chapter discusses specific programs under each of the Six+Six Model's ecosystem parameters and examines exactly how ecosystems can do a better job of *identifying, training, connecting and sustaining, funding, enabling,* and *celebrating* entrepreneurs.

Before we start, in self-defense and indemnification, I want to make clear that the programs, organizations, and people mentioned in this chapter (and throughout this book) are far from the only practitioners of entrepreneurship promotion. These choices might not always be the best, but they are a sampling of notable groups I have come across during my work as creator and manager of the State Department's Global Entrepreneurship Program, as an advisor to startups, and as a consultant in the entrepreneurship space thereafter. The organizations I mention seem to be doing a good job and, as such, are illustrative of the actors working in various aspects of entrepreneurship ecosystems. My goal is not to present an exhaustive list, but to cite some real-world examples of organizations that are doing good work (often profitably) in the name of entrepreneurship. I want to note, also, that as a practitioner in entrepreneurship, I am directly involved as a consultant, an investor, and/or a member of an advisory or directors board with several organizations and firms that work within entrepreneurship ecosystems. Several of these groups are mentioned in this chapter and elsewhere in the book, including: Artha Networks Inc., Babson College and Babson Global, the Demeter Network, and the Startup Institute.

One reason this exercise is especially important hearkens back to one of the takeaways from chapter 6: The U.S. government's shortcomings in contracting, its failure to use American best practices, and its lack of entrepreneurs among civil and foreign service ranks mean that our government needs real-world examples of how to "do entrepreneurship." This also holds true for foreign governments, both developed and developing. Consider this analogy: Imagine if USAID's humanitarian aid staffers were unaware of improved designs in disaster relief tents and pre-fab refugee housing. USAID would, obviously, fail to procure the new designs. The next time a typhoon hit Southeast Asia or an earthquake rocked Haiti, USAID's performance in providing temporary housing would suffer. Likewise with entrepreneurship. If our government does not know that ecosystem-building programs exist, or who does them and that they work, our government will be hopeless at promoting entrepreneurship.

 IDENTIFY

As we discussed in chapter 7, bolstering an entrepreneurship ecosystem in a holistic way, rather than engaging in one-off programs, is the best way to increase the quantity and quality of high-growth, job-creating startups in a particular geography. We bolster an ecosystem by strengthening each of the six pillars of the Six+Six Model: identify, train, connect and sustain, fund, enable, and celebrate.

So, first, what are the ways we can "identify" entrepreneurs? What programs exist that shake the tree, find people with really good ideas, and help them take the first step? Whom, for instance, could one turn to in Saudi Arabia to identify the most creative minds toying with desalinization or renewable energy technologies?

One tried-and-true way to identify entrepreneurs is through business plan competitions. These events—like the GEP competitions in Egypt and Turkey, or the dramatized made-for-TV *Shark Tank* version—offer entrepreneurs an opportunity to pitch their startup ideas to investors (not to mention potential mentors and board members, the media, future customers, future suppliers, and a whole lot of people who could be interested in their startup's success). In addition to exposure and affirmation, business plan competitions frequently award prizes in the form of grants, mentorship, office space, pro bono legal services, and so forth.

Business plan competitions have proliferated far and wide, but not all competitions are created equal. I think the best competitions recognize that entrants come in different shapes and sizes, from different sectors and at different stages of gestation. For example, dividing a competition into categories for tech versus non-tech and early-stage versus growth-stage companies levels the playing field for entrepreneurs and curates the pool of startups for investors. It is not useful to pit a university student looking to develop a product he conjured up in his engineering program against a going-concern entrepreneur with real customers seeking Series-A financing. Some competitions might be only for women entrepreneurs (often underrepresented in open competitions), or for startups in a particular industry.

So who does this stuff? Startup Weekend is a program with a grassroots approach and a focus on early-stage ideation. Anyone—really and truly anyone—can apply to Startup Weekend for support and materials to put on a high-speed brainstorming event. Upon arriving at a Startup Weekend, attendees network among themselves and Startup Weekend facilitators before an open microphone session. Participants give one-minute pitches of their ideas, teams form around the standout ideas, and business development begins. Teams work into (or through) the night and all day Saturday, with occasional breaks for speakers or discussions. On Sunday, teams finalize prototypes and presentations for an afternoon of five-minute pitches and questioning from judges (typically local business rock stars). Winners take home prizes (often donated and often in the form of cash, IT gear, or services like website design or legal consulting).

Since its inception in 2007 with a competition in Boulder, Colorado, Startup Weekend has supported more than 1,500 events in 700 cities around the globe, tallying 123,000 entrepreneurs who have spawned 13,000 startups. Startup Weekend, which tends to yield web- or mobile-based businesses, says that over half of the teams formed at its events stay intact after the event's end and pursue the ideas generated during the weekend.[5] The format is especially conducive to newbie entrepreneurs in the countries we are concerned about, as they typically have little experience pitching in front of an audience or writing anything that looks like a business plan.

The Artha Venture Challenge (AVC) is an entirely different kettle of fish. Targeting Indian-based social enterprises (and started by the extremely successful, low-key diaspora entrepreneur, Anglo-Indian retail tycoon Tom Singh), AVC showcases non-tech companies that have a proven concept and are looking to scale. For each competition, the organization identifies entrepreneurs working to positively disrupt the water, agriculture, energy, or livelihoods sectors and awards the top firms roughly $50,000. There is a catch, though. To be eligible for a $50,000 prize, companies must identify matching outside investment in the form of loans or equity; grants do not qualify. In a nod to the multi-pillar complexity of growing healthy ecosystems, AVC explicitly aims to identify not only entrepreneurs but investors, too. As their website notes, "We also aim to strengthen the social investment market by using the Artha Venture Challenge to attract new impact investors who are willing to bring much needed early stage, patient capital to the market."[6]

Universities are frequent hosts of business plan competitions. Laying claim to the title of "largest and richest graduate intercollegiate business plan competition in the world" is Rice University in Houston, Texas. Rallying sponsors from the private (for example, Ernst & Young) and public (for example, NASA) sectors, the Rice Business Plan Competition (RBPC) awarded nearly $3 million to companies at its 2014 competition, including over $500,000 to the top winner. RBPC has historically focused on early-stage tech companies, though it has added a track for social ventures in recent years. Notable RBCP "graduates" include Auditude, purchased by Adobe in 2011. In less than fifteen years, 138 past competitors have raised over $600 million in funding, with four companies raising over $30 million each.[7]

While business plan competitions can unearth promising entrepreneurs in a particular ecosystem, merely identifying—like all of the Six + Six Model's pillars—is insufficient in and of itself if the goal is to see those entrepreneurs succeed. Competitions, however, are especially well suited to add-on activities that touch other pillars. Funding, for example, is an obvious add-on to a competition (via prizes). GEP often built entire entrepreneurship delegations around a capstone business competition. In Turkey we brought together fifteen American and eight Turkish angel investors who judged a competition, conducted speed mentoring sessions (connect and sustain), and met with government officials about entrepreneurship policies (enable). Congregating entrepreneurs at a competition also creates golden opportunities for a bright, shiny media event (celebrate).

 **TRAIN**

The "train" pillar is about skills development. Microfinance programs the world over recognize that a microloan often does little good if it is not accompanied by, say, training in basic accounting skills. The same is true with entrepreneurship. While some skills are more teachable than others (some people are born with marketing swagger, while almost anyone can learn basic accounting), all entrepreneurs can benefit from training across a "core curriculum" of business ABCs: basic finance and accounting; competitive analysis; marketing; human resources and organizational development; selling and pitching; and so forth.

There is little doubt that USAID and other donor institutions have deep experience funding contractors who conduct workshops, courses, and seminars across countless sectors but, like business plan competitions, some methods of training are better than others. The trick is to figure out what works in spurring different categories of entrepreneurship, a question that is not settled. And train is a layered pillar. There is the training of entrepreneurs and their teams, and then there is the training of trainers, also known as entrepreneurship pedagogy.

In terms of the former, we have already discussed the exemplar MEST program in Ghana. MEST's "entrepreneurs in training"—selected through a rigorous, highly competitive process—pursue a two-year curriculum of coding and business courses designed to equip them with the tools to become leading ICT entrepreneurs. It may not be surprising that poor countries like Ghana have school systems that fall short in teaching critical business skills, but the same problem exists in the United States of America.

To address that issue, General Assembly was founded in New York in 2011 by four twenty- and thirty-somethings to be, as *Fast Company* magazine has said, "a stopgap for the startup economy. It's an intermediary that gives the post-collegiate crowd real-world skills they didn't get at their alma mater, exposure to the way business is done on the ground."[8] General Assembly does this by offering workshops, classes on entrepreneurship basics, and eight- to twelve-week full-time immersive programs covering everything "from web development and user experience design, to business fundamentals, to data science, to product management and digital marketing." Now operating ten campuses (in the United States and other rich countries), General Assembly says that its 70,000 students have access to a network of over 2,300 potential employers and that 97 percent of job-seeking graduates from its immersive programs have found jobs within three months of graduation.[9]

There is also a growing number of alternative training programs that do not require full-time attendance, designed to fit the needs of working entrepreneurs. One great example is Startup Institute, headed by legendary entrepreneur (and close friend) Diane Hessan, which provides part-time courses on specific skills (like programming and web design) in the United States and Europe.[10] Programs like Startup Institute are entrepreneurial answers to problems in entrepreneurship development. They recognize that traditional business schools, even shortened "executive education" programs, are not always sufficient or practical for entrepreneurs in the midst of their startups.

Universities themselves remain a critical training (and proving) ground for entrepreneurs. The last decade has seen a massive proliferation of courses and degree programs worldwide. In the United States, *The Princeton Review* ranks Babson College's undergraduate entrepreneurship program as the country's best and its graduate program second best. One hundred percent of Babson's entrepreneurship faculty have "started, bought, or run a successful business," and the suburban Boston school's alumni have launched 300 companies over the last five years.[11] From Harvard University's Innovation Lab to Rensselaer Polytechnic Institute's university-wide program to Santa Clara University's Global Social Benefit Institute, it is hard to find a school in any region of the United States and at any level of selectivity that is not elevating entrepreneurship within its curriculum (and extra-curricular opportunities).

Effective programming under the train pillar is by no means limited to universities and entrepreneurs. Especially important to ecosystem building is learning about and experimenting with entrepreneurship early and often. Many organizations specifically focus on empowering children as young as elementary school age with entrepreneurial skills. One Hen, a Boston-based nonprofit, uses a children's book about a successful Ghanaian chicken farmer (who built his empire from, yes, a single hen) to teach young students about microfinance and starting a business. Having worked in American schools, One Hen is now applying its curriculum to projects in Ethiopia and has made its materials available on the web. The organization estimates it has reached over 17,300 students in 142 countries.[12] One particularly well-known program for youngsters is Lemonade Day, founded in 2007 by Michael Holthouse in Houston, Texas, which aims to empower "today's youth to become tomorrow's entrepreneurs." The classic lemonade stand serves as an experiential learning tool to build self-confidence in children, teaching them to launch and grow a company in fourteen steps. Lemonade Day has grown from its initial reach of 2,700 children in Houston to 200,000 in cities across the globe.[13]

And then there is entrepreneurship pedagogy—training the trainers. Bolstering an ecosystem involves spreading the gospel and ensuring teachers and trainers are equipped with tools and methods for helping entrepreneurs. Babson is a leader on this front, as well. Its subsidiary, Babson Global, collaborates with other institutions and shares its "proven methodologies for teaching entrepreneurship" with universities around the world through initiatives like the Global Consortium of Entrepreneurship Education.[14] Babson College itself contributes heavily to the literature on entrepreneurship and entrepreneurship pedagogy, among other things cofounding the Global Entrepreneurship Monitor project, which measures entrepreneurial activity in

countries worldwide.[15] Serial entrepreneur and startup guru Steve Blank in-
novates in this space, as well. His two-and-a-half-day Lean LaunchPad
Educator Seminars train instructors how to get their students out of the
classroom and incorporate real-world market research into the class
experience.[16]

CONNECT & SUSTAIN

Ask the person on the street what it means to support entrepreneurs, and
he or she is likely to come back with something about funding, like venture
capital or seed funds. Ask an entrepreneurship enthusiast, and you'll get a
very different answer. The most important support is not investment but
shared workspaces, meetups, and incubator and accelerator programs.
These are the bread and butter of the "connect and sustain" pillar. This is
the pillar of mentorship, of networking entrepreneurs with one another, of
feeding startups with hands-on advice and diverse programming. In fact,
the guts of connect and sustain—mentorship of entrepreneurs by people
who have been there and done that—is the single most important factor for
entrepreneurial success.

The "connect" portion of connect and sustain recognizes that entrepreneurs learn a lot from one another, motivate one another, and make
breakthroughs and deals with one another. They even bond over their shared
difficulties. It cannot be overemphasized how important critical mass is to
an ecosystem and its entrepreneurs. Encounters and discussions with like-
minded folks are integral to this.

Luckily, there are many ways of connecting entrepreneurs, some more
formal than others. Connection can be as simple as a gathering at a coffee
shop. A quick Google search for "entrepreneurship meetups" will yield
countless results for meetup groups all around the world. A particular city
might have a strong tradition of PechaKucha nights at a popular bar, where
anyone can present twenty slides for twenty seconds each on any topic they
want, then everyone mingles.[17] Coworking spaces—long popular in cities
of all shapes and sizes—exist not just because entrepreneurs need a cheap
desk and Internet connection, but because people want to connect and
share stories of their hard work. A good social bump helps deal with the
slog. Impact Hub runs coworking spaces in seventy cities around the world

and says it provides "a physical space that offers a flexible and highly functional infrastructure to work, meet, learn, and connect."[18] You will find that in every successful ecosystem something like this exists, and pizza night at a coworking spot doesn't blow anyone's budget.

More formally, professional networking groups like Entrepreneurs' Organization (EO) and Young Presidents' Organization (YPO) exist specifically to link entrepreneurs; they are the startup world's answer to Rotary Club or Lions Club. EO's network connects over 10,000 entrepreneurs from forty-six countries,[19] while YPO's more exclusive (but larger) membership includes 22,000 chief executives under the age of forty-five from 125 countries. There are plenty of others. TiE—The Indus Entrepreneurs—started in Silicon Valley's Indian community, but now claims sixty-one chapters in eighteen countries.[20] The Organization of Pakistani Entrepreneurs of North America (OPEN) has chapters across the United States to connect Pakistani Americans. The Washington chapter has a specific interest in networking high-tech entrepreneurs.[21]

Joining one of these professional networks is a very good way for entrepreneurs to stay motivated, get leads for sourcing staff, and develop business relationships—and mentorship relationships. Mentorship is also the specific *raison d'être* of several outfits seeking to help entrepreneurs in a range of economies. The Stanford SEED program launched in Ghana in 2013. It matches rising West African businesses with seasoned American entrepreneurs and businessmen with deep professional connections. The mentors travel to Ghana and regularly meet with a cohort of businesses for several months.[22] The Demeter Network, a new group with roots at MIT, aims to provide businesses operating in "low-income countries" with ongoing mentorship for at least three years. Member businesses are assigned a "personal advocate" and enjoy access to industry experts and "Global Neighborhoods" of like-minded startup founders.[23] The Gerson Lehrman Group (GLG) also seeks to link entrepreneurs to C-level types (chief executive officers, chief marketing officers, and other "chiefs") and strategic advisors. One of their programs, GLG Share, targets startups already on the rise and, as their brass says, "connects them with professionals—throughout the world—who've actually solved [business] challenges, helping the founders increase their chances of getting to the right answer and accelerating growth."[24] Both Demeter and GLG are piloting interesting business models and charge for admission: Demeter requires a $500 per month fee and a

2 percent option in a member company (or a straight 3.5 percent option), and GLG Share asks not for equity but $25,000 per year for unlimited services.

Connect and sustain tilts very much toward "sustain" when it comes to the incubator and accelerator programs that are springing up nation- and worldwide. (The National Business Incubator Association says that there were twelve incubators in the United States in 1980 and 1,250 by 2012, with a further 6,000 to 7,000 around the globe.) I distinguish between the two types of programs. An incubator is usually (but not always) a physical space that provides temporary premises for an entrepreneur (or small team) at the early stage to develop a concept or refine a product or service or develop a business plan or pitch. Incubators usually have additional resources like courses (such as those offered by General Assembly) and basic administrative support. Accelerator programs, on the other hand, are more often "virtual" (or run only short-term in physical residence) and are for startups that are further along. These businesses need more specific mentoring and are fine-tuning their products or services, perhaps preparing for an angel or first round of investment. For the purposes of sustain, however, incubators and accelerators do the same thing. They provide startups with mentorship and support that will help them grow.

In the United States, Y Combinator in Silicon Valley has gained particular fame. Named the top incubator of 2012 by *Forbes*, Y Combinator invests $120,000 in several dozen startups twice a year. The investees give up a 7 percent equity stake in their startup, move to Y Combinator's campus for three months, and receive training on investor pitches, deals, legal issues, and other important key topics. By Demo Day, held ten weeks after a cycle begins, companies generally have a prototype to unveil or are even ready to launch (or be acquired). Over 700 companies have been funded by the outfit since 2005, with the total combined valuation across these companies in excess of $30 billion. The best known include Airbnb, Dropbox, and reddit.[25]

MassChallenge in Boston runs a different business model. A nonprofit backed by corporate sponsors like Microsoft as well as the Massachusetts government, MassChallenge eschews equity, yet still offers a three-month cycle and $1 million in prize money to roughly 125 startups each year. Incubated startups have raised $554.2 million, and though the accelerator receives thousands of applications each year, every single applicant receives written feedback from mentors and judges.[26] Miami's Venture Hive likewise benefits from public sponsorship and private-sector partnerships, offering startups $25,000 grants, a three-month program, and one-year residency without taking equity. Launched in 2013, Venture Hive was one of just fifty companies to win a $50,000 grant from the U.S. Small Business Administration's first Growth Accelerator Fund competition, and one of its first participants, Everypost, has raised $850,000 in seed funding.[27]

Exceptional incubators and accelerators proliferate in developing and emerging economies, as well. In Africa, in addition to Ghana's MEST, iHub in Nairobi stands out as a continental leader in the IT industry. Running a tiered membership system that offers more services for more established and/or paying entrepreneurs, iHub estimates it has amassed 16,000 members, worked with 150 companies (several of which have gone on to receive outside investment), and helped create 1,300 jobs. Spawned from successful Kenyan tech startup Ushahidi (a crowdsourcing crisis-mapping service that won praise for its utility in the aftermath of 2007 election violence in Kenya and Haiti's 2010 earthquake), iHub and its founders say they aim to "create a petri dish where people engage and collaborate."[28] Unreasonable East Africa is a spinoff of the leading social enterprise Unreasonable Institute accelerator program in Boulder, Colorado. Unreasonable East Africa, based in Kampala, Uganda, brings together each year a dozen or so startups developing solutions around health care, sanitation, and poverty. Unreasonable has experimented with its business model, from charging tuition to entering revenue-sharing agreements with its participants.[29]

In the Middle East and North Africa, one of the standard bearers is Flat-6Labs, the Sawari Ventures-backed spin-off whose early days included partnership with GEP-Egypt. If there is a poster child for the promise of "peace through entrepreneurship," Cairo-based Flat6Labs might be it. Since its inception in 2011, Flat6Labs has employed a Y Combinator-esque model ($15,000 of seed funding in exchange for 15 percent equity) to incubate over seventy-five companies in three- to four-month cycles. These companies have generated 400 jobs, opened offices in Silicon Valley, attracted follow-on funding, and drawn highly respected angel investors, venture capitalists, and even finance ministers to Flat6Labs Demo Days. The Cairo program's success prompted Flat6Labs to open accelerators in Saudi Arabia in 2013 and Abu Dhabi in 2014; a Beirut program will open in 2015–16.[30] Despite operating in a region wracked by 30 percent-plus youth unemployment rates and a general instability that fosters terror and threats to America, Flat6Labs sees entrepreneurship taking root. As Flat6Labs' managing director in Abu Dhabi, Nina Curley, says, "Accelerators have proven to be one of the most effective vehicles today for helping to build scalable, investment-ready companies . . . [We] intend to seed a culture of entrepreneurship . . . that supports youth to transform their talent into economic opportunity."[31]

Flat6Labs is the product of tireless work by Egyptian American diaspora entrepreneur Ahmed El Alfi. Among the many lessons to be learned from Flat6Labs is the power and importance of diaspora entrepreneurs. You would be hard pressed to find a single country in the world that does not have a son or daughter who has made it in America. These diaspora innovators are among the first line of those with knowledge and experience to help their countries of origin get a leg up.

 **FUND**

I believe that mentorship (the key element of connect and sustain) is the primary determinant of startup success. Funding alone does not a startup make. But in the end (or in the beginning if there is a large up-front capital cost), you will need money. Lack of capital is the lament not only of entrepreneurs in Kenya and Egypt, but also in Palo Alto and Boston. Without startup capital—be it via debt, equity, grant, or otherwise—how would founders develop and test their products? How would they pay employees? How would they become household names and multi-million (or billion) dollar companies? Some entrepreneurs will bootstrap their startups, but that is a difficult path, particularly for entrepreneurs in emerging markets and low-income communities (who tend to lack resources or have only informal resources that can't be leveraged in the formal world of banking and finance).

So, just how do ecosystems fund startups? The stock answers are venture capital and seed funds. This is both interesting and not interesting for our conversation. We must acknowledge the role private seed funds play, particularly when attached to incubators and accelerators, which are very much implementable programs. But we should also remember that outside of the United States and Israel, venture capital is barely a blip on the financing radar. Even in the United States, it is only a blip. Less than 1 percent of American companies have raised capital through the VC process.[32]

So, when it comes to funding the startups we want to grow in chaotic neighborhoods of the world, different mechanisms are more likely to prove most useful. This would include strategies like angel investing, impact investing, U.S. government enterprise funds, and tools to leverage "dead capital."

Before we turn to these, however, let us tip our hat to programs that function like VCs or seed funds. Several of the incubators we talked about above—Flat6Labs, Y Combinator, MassChallenge, MEST—not only sustain startups but also fund them. Y Combinator participants currently receive $120,000 in exchange for 7 percent of the startup. Flat6Labs companies give up 15 percent for $15,000. MEST is founded on philanthropic money, and its "entrepreneurs in training" receive two years of free training. But the students whose startups are eventually selected for incubation in the MEST incubator also make an equity deal. According to *Forbes* and *CB Insights*, accelerator 500 Startups was the top/most active seed funder in 2013.[33] Founded by renowned entrepreneur and investor Dave McClure, 500 Startups provides seed investments of $25,000 to $250,000, backing over 800 companies in over forty countries (including MEST alum Dropifi and Flat6Labs participant ElWafeyat). 500 Startups also partners with SeedInvest, an online "platform that enables equity-based crowdfunding" to raise money for its four currently open funds, which, in addition to its flagship fund, includes a Latin America-focused fund and a Southeast Asia-focused fund.[34]

Incubator-cum-seed-fund programs tend to lean toward the exclusive and high-tech. This may not be the best approach for certain ecosystems, especially those in developing or emerging markets where low- and no-tech innovations in agriculture and energy hold promise. In lieu of incubators that turn into funding, there are many gap-filling options—including angel investors, family offices, and impact investors—that typically operate in the $10,000 to $100,000 range.

Angels and family offices are, generally speaking, in the business of investing personal wealth into very early-stage, high-risk businesses. While individual angel investors are essentially startup investors by definition, family offices are newer to the entrepreneurship game. Family offices have traditionally been in the business of preserving dynastic wealth through investment in blue-chip stocks, real estate, and other safe "parking spots," but the younger generation of heirs has become interested in startups and impact investing. Angels are certainly a major feature of the U.S. startup world, but they are increasingly important abroad. Angels are vital to a successful ecosystem, since early-stage capital is always the hardest to find. In an interesting blend of the train and fund pillars, Golden Seeds, an angel investor group whose members have made $70 million in investments in companies with women in leadership roles, conducts structured training for angels themselves.[35] Investors need to be trained to invest in startups as much as entrepreneurs need to be trained to run startups. Even the poorest, most fragile nations on Earth have a class of wealthy individuals. Urging local elites to invest in local startups (as opposed to stowing money away in London or Switzerland) can activate local money and bolster the "fund" pillar of an ecosystem. Investor training is a program GEP ran several times (including with Golden Seeds) and is a recommendation my consulting firm frequently makes in developing-country contexts.

The growing field of impact investing—typically, investment in firms that have social as well as financial objectives (that is, social enterprises)—holds obvious potential for fragile, developing, and emerging markets. The Aspen Network of Development Entrepreneurs is an organization with a specific interest in what it calls "small and growing businesses" (SGBs), especially those whose products, services, and jobs will bring environmental, health, and other social benefits. Impact investors include angels, but also foundations, institutions, and even run-of-the-mill fund managers interested in SGBs. J.P. Morgan and the Global Impact Investing Network estimate that nearly $50 billion in impact investments are currently under management.[36]

On the other end of the wealth spectrum from angels and family offices are the 99 percent. Crowdfunding—drawing financing in small chunks from many people—is on the rise. Kickstarter and Indiegogo, founded in 2009 and 2008 respectively, are among the biggest online portals for crowdfunding, with Kickstarter claiming its platform has delivered $1.28 billion to over 77,000 projects from more than 7.7 million backers.[37] Though these two portals work strictly via donations, the JOBS Act of 2013 legalized equity crowdfunding. There is an expectation that, globally, crowdfunding could be double the size of today's global venture capital industry by 2025, peaking $90 billion.[38] Says Wayne Kimmel of SeventySix Capital, "I believe that the democratization of fundraising through crowdfunding is an incredible breakthrough for entrepreneurs and nonprofits."[39]

Governments, donor institutions, and aid organizations have created funds of varying size, objective, and geographic focus that are relevant to entrepreneurship in the context we care about. Small Enterprise Assistance Funds (SEAF) and its Center for Entrepreneurship and Executive Development (CEED) trace their origins from programs run by CARE (an international NGO) and USAID. Today SEAF and CEED are independent operations that target low-income countries for their investments. SEAF "provides growth capital and business assistance to small and medium enterprises . . . in emerging and transition markets underserved by traditional sources of capital." SEAF has put $378 million in 338 investments throughout twenty-two emerging markets; CEED trains entrepreneurs through accelerator programs, mentorship, and networking.[40]

An interesting historical example of U.S. government funding abroad has relevance to entrepreneurship promotion today. After the Cold War, Congress passed the Support for East European Democracy (SEED) Act and the Freedom Support Act (FSA). SEED, introduced in 1989, initially called for enterprise funds for Poland and Hungary but, after the addition of FSA, soon grew to ten funds in eighteen countries. Combined, the funds invested over $1.5 billion in over 500 companies and made loans to a further 100,000-plus. More than 250,000 jobs were created, and over $70 million was put toward technical assistance for entrepreneurs and their businesses.

A final funding consideration is the "dead capital" and property rights problems highlighted by Hernando de Soto. The Peruvian economist has estimated that the total amount of "dead capital," unleverageable assets, in the developing world nears $10 trillion.[41] Dead capital, in fact, frequently resides in assets commonly used in the United States for funding entrepreneurship: an entrepreneur's own resources, like credit card debt, mortgages, and second mortgages. As we have already noted, venture capital is not only a tiny source of American startup capital, it also tends to be relevant only in certain sectors and only to more mature businesses. To get started you need cash, credit, and leverage. But as de Soto points out, people operating in informal economies—that is, many of the entrepreneurs we would love to help in the MENA region—do not have clean title to property and cannot leverage their assets for credit. If you do not have title to your land, you can't take out a loan against it. In the end, this is an issue to be dealt with via reform of legal and financial regimes (a topic under the "enable" pillar), but there are, nonetheless, programs that attempt workarounds. For example, First Access, based in New York City, assists borrowers in informal markets by helping their lenders make better credit rating assessments. Absent the formal credit agencies, mortgage records, and credit card data of rich countries, First Access, instead, gathers demographic, geographic, financial, and social data from mobile phones to assess the credit risk of a borrower (for example, using payment records as a sign of creditworthiness), thereby greatly lowering risks for lenders operating in informal markets.[42]

First Access may seem to be a far cry from Y Combinator and a $120,000-for-7-percent-equity deal. But it typifies the innovations needed to overcome the obstacles faced by entrepreneurs in countries with 40 percent unemployment rates—not San Francisco, California. To build a robust ecosystem, we must think beyond the standard venture capital and incubator-cum-seed-fund models.

ENABLE PUBLIC POLICY

The Six+Six Model's "enable" pillar is where "ease of doing business" happens in an entrepreneurship ecosystem. Programming under this pillar is less about "programs" *per se* than government (and working with government) and best practices. In chapter 4 we talked about all the ways the U.S. government enables and invests in entrepreneurship. Favorable (but not too loose) tax and regulatory regimes, the balance of which government hardly gets right all the time, stimulate entrepreneurship. So do our government's judicial institutions and our systems around intellectual property rights, shareholder protection, and other rule-of-law issues that ensure being an American entrepreneur is worth the blood, sweat, and tears. The United States has further enabled entrepreneurship with investment vehicles—grants via the National Institutes of Health and the Small Business Administration, for example—and through foundational R&D, major research universities, and DARPA, for instance.

In chapter 7 we noted examples of specific actions by governments geared toward turbo-charging entrepreneurship. Chile entices startups to work in Latin America through the Start-Up Chile program. Israel's government has long bolstered its ecosystem, specifically the high-tech sector, through grant-making programs like BIRD and schemes to prime the venture capital pump, like Yozma. Start-Up Chile, BIRD, and Yozma are great examples of government action under the enable pillar. We will look at other actionable policies here, but first we will consider a *sine qua non* truth about entrepreneurship ecosystem building. You need a government champion.

One of the first things my GEP programs sought to do when working in a particular country was identify a local government official who was waving the entrepreneurship flag. You will not get far with regulatory matters, let alone encourage the creation of government-backed seed funds, if there is not someone somewhere in government who buys into the importance of entrepreneurship and sticks his or her head out for the cause. GEP-Turkey was regularly able to engage with government on numerous projects. High-level ministers in Turkey's government, including the prime minister, hosted the second Global Entrepreneurship Summit and attended conferences on pro-entrepreneurship regulatory policy. In 2014, in Egypt, another GEP country, Minister of Communications and Information Technology Atef Helmy appeared at a Flat6Labs Demo Day to say entrepreneurship is "Egypt's best [tool] for a brighter future."[43]

Prime Minister Najib Razak of Malaysia is often held out as an example of a leader who has truly embraced entrepreneurship. Opening the 2013 Global Entrepreneurship Summit in Kuala Lumpur, Razak said:

> I believe that greater opportunity for our entrepreneurs will not only drive national progress, but also help us address the great global problems of our age: poverty, sustainability, and development. . . . an enabling environment is necessary to convert [a business] opportunity into a successful and profitable venture.[44]

With backing like Razak's, Malaysia is catalyzing startups through policy, physical infrastructure, access to credit, and government grants, among other measures.[45] Malaysia even earned a shout-out from President Obama, who, in his 2014 speech at the United Nations, said the country's "vibrant entrepreneurship is propelling a former colony into the ranks of advanced economies."[46] My consulting firm is reluctant to work in a particular geography if we cannot identify a government representative willing to give his or her backing, in word and deed, to entrepreneurship promotion programs.

Chile, Israel, and Malaysia (and the United States) are examples of governments in the entrepreneur's corner. (That support is not universal in these countries, but certainly to the extent that there are clear examples of champions and policies that ripen the enabling environment for startups.) At home and abroad we can find other instances of specific actions governments take to turbo-charge entrepreneurship.

In the United States, the state of Ohio launched the Ohio Third Frontier program over a decade ago to shake off post-industrial rust by specifically supporting entrepreneurs with funding and the sourcing of promising, investable ideas. Ohio Third Frontier programs include grants to seed funds that target startups; subsidized debt financing for mature companies to develop "next-generation products"; and a mentorship network linking high-tech startup founders with experienced entrepreneurs. According to a 2009 mid-program report by SRI International (a well-known economic consultancy and research institute begun at Stanford University and now operating as an independent, private firm), public "expenditures of $681 million generated $6.6 billion of economic activity, 41,300 jobs, and $2.4 billion in employee wages and benefits as a result of the Ohio Third Frontier. This represents a nearly $10 return on every dollar of the State's investment."[47] These results, SRI reports, blow away what might have happened if that same $681 million had simply been returned to taxpayers as rebates:

> [T]he Ohio Third Frontier investments resulted in follow-on federal and private sector investments and increased R&D activity, products sales, and construction, generating more than seven times the level of economic activity, more than six times the employment growth, and eleven times the wage growth for Ohio's economy compared to that of a hypothetical tax refund.[48]

Not all government initiatives are this successful, but Ohio Third Frontier points to the dramatic role government can play in enabling entrepreneurship. In 2010 Ohioans voted to extend the program through 2015.

As the mentorship elements of the Ohio Third Frontier program suggest, enable pillar activities need not always connect with the funding pillar. Rwanda's investment law grants permanent residence to foreign investors who deposit $500,000 into a Rwandan commercial bank, thereby eliminating an immigration hurdle that is often the bane of the ex-pat businessman in Africa.[49] Singapore similarly offers an Entrepreneur Pass, commonly known as the EntrePass, that provides visas and residency for "technopreneurs" and their immediate family members, provided certain business ownership requirements are met.[50] Spain, sufferer of unemployment rates exceeding 20 percent for several years, passed *la Ley de Emprendedores*—the Entrepreneurship Law—in 2013 in an effort to make starting a company easier. Though the law has its critics, the government claims that all necessary documentation and permits should be able to be completed and obtained in one place within twenty-four hours. New visa categories, one especially for entrepreneurs, aim to assuage worries for foreigners, and the government promises to make decisions about visas within ten days and residency permits within twenty days.[51]

Is there room for nongovernment actors under the enable pillar? Yes. Especially as a source of pressure. The World Bank's *Doing Business report* provides a comprehensive quantitative account of business regulations in over 180 economies, aimed at encouraging governments to adopt more entrepreneurship-friendly regulations. By charting a country's regulatory performance against a host of metrics (including starting a business, registering property, getting credit, and protecting investors), *Doing Business* rates how effectively a country is enabling entrepreneurship and gives it a world ranking. Because no one ever wants to be last at anything, *Doing Business* can provide a real kick in the pants. As mentioned in the last chapter, Rwanda's pro-entrepreneurship measures have seen it jump 100 places in the rankings.[52] Other useful tools for pressuring governments on entrepreneurship (that is, other rankings) include the Global Entrepreneurship Monitor (cofounded by Babson College), the Global Entrepreneurship and Development Institute Index (GEDI), and the Legatum Prosperity Index. Finally, Transparency International's Corruption Perceptions Index turns a spotlight on what might be one of the biggest hindrances to entrepreneurship in fragile, developing, and emerging markets: corruption.

In short, strengthening the enable pillar of an ecosystem is about best tax and regulatory practices, but also, and consequently, about securing a government champion and pressuring governments to think about "ease of doing business."

CELEBRATE ENTREPRENEURS

In the United States, someone who turns down a Wall Street job offer to launch a startup is a hero. Someone who drops out of Stanford or Harvard to take up a Thiel Fellowship to pursue a new venture (as required by sponsor and PayPal cofounder Peter Thiel) might be exalted as the Second Coming. In many other countries those same people would be considered fools. Entrepreneurship simply does not have the same reputation overseas, especially in the Middle East and North Africa region and other countries where joblessness pervades. The MEST entrepreneurs my firm spoke with in Ghana repeatedly described the doubt, bafflement, disappointment, and even anger of friends and family when they enrolled at the incubator. For many bright, capable young people in fragile, developing, and emerging markets, it is better to take a government job or a gig with a big international firm or NGO; after all, what the heck does an entrepreneur do?

Programs under the "celebrate" pillar are all about changing that perception. In a healthy ecosystem, entrepreneurs are respected (or at least accepted as sane), entrepreneurship is considered a viable career, and words like "exit" and "convertible debt" are exciting and sexy. To accomplish this, success stories must be told and local entrepreneurs celebrated. It is not enough to talk about Mark Zuckerberg or Steve Jobs, who are generally unrelatable to entrepreneurs in, say, Indonesia or Tanzania. One must talk about the less spectacular but far more relevant stories of local entrepreneurs, who, despite the odds, have managed to succeed like crabgrass growing up through cracks in broken pavement.

Today in the United States and other countries where high-impact entrepreneurship flourishes, media coverage of startups and their founders is bountiful. Gone are the days when only *Forbes* or *Fortune* might devote a 'graph or two to an innovative startup inside Massachusetts Route 128 or the peninsula south of San Francisco. Along came *Wired*, and then *Inc.* and *Fast Company*, and now *TechCrunch*, *PandoDaily*, and loads of other media covering entrepreneurship. *The Wall Street Journal*, the *New York Times*, and popular websites like reddit all have sections devoted to entrepreneurship. The robustness of an entrepreneurship ecosystem is reflected in how much ink is spent on the subject. So programming under the celebrate pillar must aim to increase the quantity and quality of startup coverage.

One way to do this is through journalist training. While any country's leading newspaper will cover business, the vast majority of stories will concern the giants of the local economy: the parastatal mining company, the president's brother's construction firm, the agricultural giant, the foreign oil company. Reporters simply do not have experience with, or know what questions to ask, a fledgling startup. In Turkey, GEP approached this problem by running a series of workshops for Turkish media led by experienced entrepreneurship journalists. Scott Kirsner, a technology and innovation columnist from the *Boston Globe*, and *Inc.* contributing editor and author Donna Fenn both traveled to Turkey and met with leading local journalists. Their workshops reviewed stories published in the United States related to entrepreneurship and brainstormed story ideas in Turkey.[53] In some instances, my firm has recommended that clients (such as donor institutions or private corporations) launch a journalism prize to acknowledge and incentivize consistent, high-quality coverage of a local startup scene.

Encouraging the entrepreneur or startup directly is, of course, a good tactic, as well. Business plan competitions simultaneously identify and celebrate entrepreneurs, but there are plenty of "lifetime" or "good job with your early efforts" awards, too. EY (formerly Ernst & Young) runs an Entrepreneur of the Year award managed by Maria Pinelli; the overall winners in 2015 were Andreas Bechtolsheim and Jayshree Ullal of Arista Networks, a network switching technology company in Santa Clara, California. But EY salutes leading entrepreneurs with regional awards, too.[54] Babson College created "the world's first entrepreneurship hall of fame" in 1978. Its Academy of Distinguished Entrepreneurs "has recognized and honored entrepreneurs who have contributed significantly to the development of free enterprise throughout the world."[55] Long before the entrepreneur can contemplate such achievement awards, he or she might pursue appetite-whetters like Peter Thiel's abovementioned fellowship, which grants $100,000 and mentorship for two years to chosen Fellows to forgo college and give entrepreneurship a try. With Mark Twain's proclamation that "I have never let my schooling interfere with my education" stretching across the fellowship's website, Thiel writes: "We hope the . . . Thiel Fellows inspire people of all ages as they demonstrate that intellectual curiosity, grit, and determination are more important than credentials for improving civilization."[56]

Making entrepreneurship cool can be done the old-fashioned way, too: with a flashy, over-dramatized reality television show. Even though they're not to everyone's taste, programs like *Shark Tank* and its foreign inspiration, *Dragons' Den*, are a great way to generate interest in (and celebrate) entrepreneurs and angel investing. *Shark Tank* has aired over 100 episodes and features budding entrepreneurs pitching to multi-millionaire and billionaire investors who have varying doses of attitude. *Shark Tank* "shark" Mark Cuban, owner of the Dallas Mavericks basketball team and a hugely successful investor and entrepreneur, has articulated the show's power of celebration:

> I do *Shark Tank*, the deals are good and I enjoy it, but to me, the importance of doing *Shark Tank* is more sending the message that the American Dream is alive and well. . . . [T]here's absolutely no other platform where you can go out and reach kids, families, and entrepreneurs, and encourage them, support them, train them, really fire them up, and give them some guidance to go ahead and really start that business.[57]

In fact, it is not hard to find people who will tell you that "everything I know about business, startups, and investing I learned from *Shark Tank*."

To be sure, entrepreneurs and entrepreneurship are already celebrated around the world. With offices in Beirut, Dubai, and Amman, online outlet Wamda ("inspiring, empowering, and connecting entrepreneurs") does a great job of covering startups in the Middle East and North Africa region with extensive multimedia content and a strong social media presence. Wamda also invests in startups through the Wamda Capital Fund.[58] And Global Entrepreneurship Week, whose founders and supporters include the Kauffman Foundation (a celebrator-cum-researcher of entrepreneurship itself), is an annual November event linking tens of thousands of local organizations and events in some 140 countries. It is billed as "the world's largest celebration of the innovators and job creators who launch startups that bring ideas to life, drive economic growth, and expand human welfare."[59]

Analyses by Matrices

If we did some picking, choosing, and condensing of the programs in this chapter, we could put together a comprehensive package of entrepreneurship promotion programs. Consider the chart (at right), structured around the Six+Six Model, and what might be rolled out in a developing country with a high rate of youth unemployment called Country X.

To paraphrase a popular chant, "This is what entrepreneurship ecosystem development looks like!" Doing entrepreneurship does not mean picking a winner and dropping a grant on its books. It does not mean creating a stand-alone seed fund or running a single one-day accounting workshop. It does not mean one size fits all. Promoting entrepreneurship means deeply researching and engaging all six actors across all six pillars of the Six+Six Model and implementing tailored programming to strengthen the entire entrepreneurship ecosystem. Only this kind of comprehensive approach will move the needle on entrepreneurship in Country X, or anywhere else.

Three further things are worth pointing out about this matrix. First, a real plan would be populated with many more programs. A new, formal mentorship network like Demeter might organize in Country X (connect and sustain); a government-backed seed fund resembling Ohio Third Frontier could be launched (fund). Note that many programs hit more than one pillar. I have siloed programs for the sake of explaining the model, but, for example, the incubator-cum-seed-fund really does represent two pillars. Give the incubator a marketing or communications staffer and it could surely support the celebrate pillar as well.

Second, these programs can and should repeat in cycles. One Hen could institutionalize its curriculum at particular schools and deliver it each year; the One Hen project becomes an eagerly anticipated fifth-grade activity, a tradition at select schools. The angel investor trip becomes an annual event, perhaps marketed to wealthy diaspora and timed to holidays that frequently bring them home. Good programming must not only reflect intimate understanding of an ecosystem, but ongoing engagement as well.

Third, and most important, we must return to a lesson from chapter 7: "Different strokes for different folks." This example chart really is for Country X; not Egypt, not Detroit, not Buenos Aires. Not every ecosystem needs another business plan competition or an overhaul of capital gains taxation policies for foreign shareholders. The design of programs for boosting an entrepreneurship ecosystem greatly depends on the balance of no-, low-, or high-tech industries. A traditional business incubator consists primarily of a lot of people working at computers in a big room. This is great for mobile

	Identify	Train	Connect and Sustain	Fund	Enable	Celebrate
NGOs		One Hen teaches curriculum in five schools in Country X's capital				
Foundations			U.S. foundation backs incubator-cum-seed-fund in Country X	U.S. foundation backs incubator-cum-seed-fund in Country X		
Academia		Country X's flagship university joins Babson's Global Consortium of Entrepreneurship Education				
Investors	Angel investors tour Country X and judge business plan competition					
Governments					X's investment promotion agency convenes startups and foreign investors	
Corporations						U.S. corporation operating in Country X sponsors "Shark Tank"-type TV show

app or e-commerce businesses, but far less appropriate for someone creating a new textile or housewares product. Designing a package of entrepreneurship programs resembles an architect's role in building a house; walls, roof, kitchen, and bathroom are all required (just as all ecosystem pillars are required), but the materials, brands, craftspeople, costs, and more all greatly depend on the local circumstances and goals. Country Y's chart will look much different from Country X's.

So we have a working ecosystem model and examples of successful ecosystem development programs. But what's the next step? How do we put this model to work toward fixing troubled economies? How do we move the needle on world peace? What is the U.S. government's role in all this? This is the topic of our next and final chapter. Coordinating, funding, and—at times—implementing effective entrepreneurship ecosystem development is something our government can and should do. Rolling out comprehensive packages of entrepreneurship promotion programs for Countries X and Y around the world is our best tool for securing America from twenty-first-century threats, threats grounded in the rampant jobless rates that destabilize societies and leave young people idle, angry, hopeless, and vulnerable to extremism. Government's job is to prime the pump and be the first investor in (and the first one out). Getting involved in the kinds of programs discussed in this chapter is government's route to doing just that.

Entrepreneurship in the service of foreign policy is not just our best tool, but one of our most underutilized. And, as we will see, it is not expensive. We can be more efficient with our existing economic development spending; we can shift funds from underperforming USAID projects to the job-creating programs of entrepreneurship. If that does not fit the bill, and I argue that it does, we could turn a single AH-64 Apache attack helicopter for Egypt into years of funding for programming across North Africa. This is, after all, about national security.

NINE

A Business Plan

IN MY PREVIOUS LIFE, when I worked as a senior executive for Warner Bros. in Los Angeles, I occasionally gave talks titled "The Business of the Entertainment Business." I often began such a session with the following thought: Warner Bros. is the largest film and television studio in the world. It releases blockbusters and Emmy-award winning TV shows. It employs several thousand people. It finances, distributes, markets, and holds the copyright for many of your favorite movies and television shows. It has done so for decades. *Dirty Harry, Buffy the Vampire Slayer, Batman, The Matrix*, and the list goes on. It owns and exploits ancillary rights, as well, selling themed toys, t-shirts, and video games that spin off the biggest hits. In fact, Warner Bros. does everything in movies and television except make movies and television shows.

Warner Bros. may be the biggest studio in Hollywood, but it does not actually make movies and shows. No studio does. Rather, it is small production companies that actually make all the content we enjoy on our screens. Sometimes a small production company is a single writer, or a director, or a producer, or a combination of those people (who pitch ideas by the hundreds each week). What Warner Bros. does do, like all major studios, is finance these small production companies—with the studio assigning support staff like accountants, line producers, legal and subcontractor personnel— and, just as important, sell (that is, distribute) the final content. But studios like Warner Bros. do not come up with the guts of a creative product—the story, characters, setting, and so on.

The point? Even in a creative industry, it is not the large corporation that delivers creativity and innovation. Rather, creativity and innovation come from small, often sole-proprietor creators, artists, and innovators who are then organized by the corporate players.

Asking the government of the United States of America to develop and implement innovative entrepreneurship development programs is a lot like asking Warner Bros. Entertainment Inc. to have its own employees pen classics like *A Clockwork Orange, All the President's Men,* or *Harry Potter.* That does not work. When the U.S. government does creativity and innovation it does so with all the grace of a hippo dancing with a mouse. It does not end well for the mouse. In fact, the hippo can be left without a partner.

By contrast, in the private sector, especially in the über-creative world of Hollywood, hippos do dance with mice. The creativity and nuance of those aforementioned Warner Bros. films were enjoyed far and wide. The Warner Bros. bureaucracy found a way to efficiently scale and distribute the genius of individuals like Stanley Kubrick and Anthony Burgess, Carl Bernstein and Bob Woodward, and J.K. Rowling.

This chapter is a dancing lesson for the clumsiest hippo of them all, the U.S. government. It explains how our government can learn to execute on entrepreneurship and promote this truly American value (one rivaled perhaps only by Hollywood itself in terms of worldwide admiration). It explains how the government can actually turn the ecosystem approach to entrepreneurship development discussed in chapters 7 and 8 into a functional program.

It is important to review why we are signing up the hippo for dancing lessons. Though some might prefer that government stay far away from entrepreneurship, and though we have documented throughout this book the government's missteps in doing this work, there remains an indisputable truth. The U.S. government must elevate entrepreneurship in its foreign policy and it is the only American entity truly able to harness this critical tool.

We find ourselves in a day and age when our government needs to use entrepreneurship to confront twenty-first-century threats to American security and prosperity. The root cause of ISIS's terrifying beheadings, of shoot-ups in Paris, of meat-cleaver attacks in Israeli synagogues, of school-girl kidnappings in Nigeria, of all the anti-American rhetoric that feels closer and closer to home is lack of economic hope. And entrepreneurship, by creating jobs, delivers that economic hope.

Make no mistake. Extremists turn extreme not because of ancient tribal slights or a desire for religious domination or even because of political disappointment but, rather, because so many young people face lives of horrific economic darkness. Rebel movements, extremism, and terrorists stew and thrive in failed, fragile, and developing countries, the kind of countries that often suffer 30 to 40 percent youth unemployment rates. Of course, none of this is to say that there are not bona fide religious fanatics, nationalist fanatics, and just plain crazy people out there. (We have plenty of them in the United States, too. Remember the Branch Davidians?) But the vast majority of extremist operatives are simply people put in a corner economically, with no recourse but the extreme. For proof, one need look no further than Mohamed Bouazizi, whose suicidal protest at the confiscation of his wares by Tunisian authorities, out of economic hopelessness, launched the Arab Spring, or the young Kenyan man who told BBC he joined al-Shabaab in Somalia not out of ideology but because he was offered a one-off $1,000 payment. "If I had had a job," he said, "I would not have gone there."[1]

Let us not re-make the same mistake. No amount of U.S. military might will protect America or preserve world order unless this underlying economic hopelessness is addressed. The rise of ISIS in the ashes of our failed Iraq reconstruction efforts is a case in point. A Hellfire missile delivered by a Predator drone will not change the heart and mind of a Pakistani teenager (at least, not in a good way). An opportunity to launch a business, or a job with a Karachi startup, just might. Hernando de Soto is among those trying to shake the powers-that-be from traditional, failing, responses:

[P]olicy makers are missing the real stakes. If ordinary people in the Middle East and North Africa cannot play the [economic] game legally—despite their heroic sacrifices—they will be far less able to resist a terrorist offensive, and the most desperate among them may even be recruited to the jihadist cause. . . . The radical leaders whom I encountered in Peru were generally murderous, coldblooded, tactical planners with unwavering ambitions to seize control of the government. Most of their sympathizers and would-be recruits, by contrast, would rather have been legal economic agents, creating better lives for themselves and their families.[2]

The entrepreneurial heroes of the Middle East and North Africa region agree that economic hope is ultimately crucial. Says Fadi Ghandour, Aramex founder and board member of Middle East entrepreneurship players Wamda and Oasis 500, "The stability and future of the region is going to depend on our teaching our young people how to go out and create companies."[3] MENA, as we have discussed, has both the world's highest youth unemployment rate and one of its youngest populations. The consequence, says the International Labor Organization, is that "political tensions and social instability are expected to increase across the MENA region well into the 2020s."[4]

In other words, unless we change our behavior, it's gonna get worse before it gets better. The disorder that threatens America will continue until we learn to address the causes of despair. As we say in the entertainment business: Don't tell the market what it wants; listen to what the market is telling you. If the market does not like what you are selling, then you, not the market, have to change. Or, as Albert Einstein supposedly said, "Insanity is doing the same thing over and over again and expecting a different result." So let's try entrepreneurship.

We have seen throughout this book, especially in chapters 2 and 3, that entrepreneurship poses a truly viable and untapped solution to threats to America. Entrepreneurship is a wellspring for jobs. It transcends religious, political, and ideological differences. It efficiently grows economies. It emphasizes the importance of education and innovation. It provides opportunity and hope for the underprivileged and disadvantaged. It stabilizes societies. It does so without guns and bombs. In a million different ways, entrepreneurship is good for us. So how can the U.S. government use entrepreneurship more effectively as foreign policy tool?

Rubber Screwdriver Redux

As discussed in chapters 5 and 6, several shortcomings hobble government's attempts at using entrepreneurship promotion as a tool of foreign economic policy. Even when we talk wisely and proudly about supporting foreign entrepreneurs, we do not follow through. Case in point: the Global

Entrepreneurship Program that I ran, one of the few practical expressions of President Obama's widely touted first-term initiative to "change the conversation with the Muslim world," and announced by Secretary of State Clinton at the first Presidential Summit on Entrepreneurship, never received a dime of State Department funding. U.S. government spending on entrepreneurship amounts to less than 1 percent of total U.S. foreign aid. This is not just a money question, either. Foreign economic development projects are scattered across so many government agencies and offices that they defy cataloging. Coordination is practically nonexistent. We do not spend enough on bottling and exporting America's special sauce, and when we do spend, we don't spend efficiently. Good ideas are executed badly.

One of the reasons our good ideas are executed badly is that Washington is a very different place from the America that runs on innovation and entrepreneurship. The halls of the agencies most directly related to foreign economic activity are generally filled with people who lack private sector experience and who are unfamiliar with "practices from America," even the people who work in economic development and entrepreneurship. People who have never sweated to meet a payroll or deliver a product on time and on budget are often the ones running our economic development and entrepreneurship programs. How can we expect such (otherwise often devoted) staffers to do something that is as foreign to them as performing open-heart surgery is to me?

The government's ultimate bureaucratic shortcoming is its broken contracting and procurement system. Among other outsourcing failings, like the website rollout of HealthCare.gov, this ongoing fiasco has run up at least $10 billion in wasted funds across Afghanistan and Iraq reconstruction and economic development efforts.[5] It's fair and accurate to say that this is what turning a screw with a billion-dollar rubber screwdriver looks like.

But lamenting that the system does not work and concluding that government should stay out of the entrepreneurship space is not the answer. For all the reasons we have described in this book, we must make it work. There is no other player that has the responsibility, the resources, and the imperative to make it work. The bottom line is this: the U.S. government needs to up its entrepreneurship game for the sake of national security and prosperity. We need to rebalance economic development budgets toward entrepreneurship and refresh the two Ps, people and procurement, if we are to use that great American asset—entrepreneurship—to create jobs and build peaceful societies abroad. No one else is going to do this. Google won't;

Starbucks won't; Instagram won't. Only the U.S. government has the where-withal and the ability (and obligation) to be the "first in" when it comes to promoting entrepreneurship in shaky states.

We've seen that promoting entrepreneurship is not a simple, one-stop solution. It requires building an ecosystem, encouraging a diverse cast of actors to collaborate across pillars. We see in the Six + Six Model a clear framework for planning an ecosystem approach and a pathway to forging interactions. Entrepreneurs are identified at business plan competitions, trained at schools and incubators, connected and sustained through mentorship programs, funded by angel investors, enabled with friendly public policies and regulations, and celebrated in media and society broadly.

So what do we do with a rubber screwdriver? We put it down and get a better one. Programs already exist around the world that succeed at the ecosystem functions that the Six + Six model lays out. So how do we reproduce those successful programs at scale, and adapt them for the unique geographies of troubled economies? Here are four areas we need to focus on:

Smarter Spending

The U.S. government must spend its economic development money smarter by redirecting existing funds to entrepreneurship promotion programs. Entrepreneurship spending currently amounts to less than 1 percent of our annual economic development assistance expenditures. This should be at least doubled as a first step, from a scattered $250 million to a focused $500 million per year. I suspect that all of the additional money, and more, can come from improving procurement efficiency and redirecting existing funds that are ineffectively being spent on development and defense. If we begin to treat entrepreneurship development as a key national security issue, then allocating a portion of our gargantuan defense budget makes perfect sense.

Consolidated Efforts

The U.S. government must consolidate entrepreneurship development efforts under a single office or agency or, at the very least, centralize intra-government coordination. This could entail creating a small office within an existing agency; expanding the remit or powers of an existing agency; or launching a brand-new "E-Agency" that specializes in private-sector solutions to development and entrepreneurship programming.

Improved Participation

The U.S. government must create mechanisms for small- and medium-size, especially entrepreneurial, companies to participate in U.S. government contracts. The procurement and contracting process must be refreshed to ensure America's best performs America's important work.

Improved Recruitment

The U.S. government must recruit more people with private-sector experience into development agencies, especially those involved in entrepreneurship programming. This could entail, in part, establishing new programs that inject people from "America" into "Washington" on temporary assignments as part of a career path that combines public and private-sector work.

In short, it is about funding, organization, and fixing the two Ps: procurement and people. This is the draft business plan for moving forward.

A New Marshall Plan

One can view the overarching story of twentieth-century foreign policy as the settling of the political turbulence born in Europe that embroiled much of the world.

The aftermath of World War I taught the Western powers a lesson: It is better to invest in your enemies than to punish and humble them. This may not provide the same immediate psychic high, but in the long run, the more measured, mature approach serves all far more effectively. After World War II, the United States heeded the lesson of Versailles and implemented the Marshall Plan to strengthen the economy of defeated Germany (and of Western Europe, broadly). Since then, Germany has become a job-creating global economic power, leading Europe's economic integration, reunifying with and absorbing its decrepit communist east, and posting the lowest unemployment rates of any industrialized nation during the world's recent financial crises. Germany has not started any world wars or devolved into a bedlam that spawns murderous terrorist organizations.

American support for entrepreneurship in certain fragile, developing, and emerging economies is the twenty-first century's version of the Marshall

Plan, and responds to what seems to be the twenty-first century's key political turbulence so far. While the Marshall Plan cost the United States something in the vicinity of $125 billion in current dollars, a new entrepreneurial version need not add a single cent to the federal budget. Much can be done with very little when it comes to entrepreneurship promotion, and because the waste and inefficiencies of our current economic development apparatus are so great, even modest improvements could yield many times the funds needed to implement effective entrepreneurship programming.

The low-hanging fruit is the U.S. government's "currently unworkable" procurement and contracting system (to quote expert Steven Tomanelli).[6] I suspect that the entirety of funds required for an effective U.S. government entrepreneurship promotion program could be found merely by cleaning up our archaic and broken procurement and contracting, within international economic development budgets alone. Waste and inefficiency are currently hallmarks of our economic development work. Recall that our nine-year $60 billion reconstruction effort in Iraq—our "Marshall Plan" to put Iraqis on a stable footing and ensure prosperity and peace—earned this damning appraisal from Special Inspector General Stuart Bowen: "Ultimately, we estimate that the Iraq program wasted at least $8 billion."[7] This was development work done by both Department of Defense and State Department entities (including USAID). And we know how prosperous and peaceful Iraq is today. That other war? In its first five years reviewing economic development work in Afghanistan, the Special Inspector General for Afghanistan Reconstruction "identified $1.8 billion in questioned costs, funds that can be put to better use, and funds identified for potential recovery."[8]

We will talk about how to tighten up the procurement and contracting mess that leads to these ridiculous figures, but the point is that mere efficiency gains could likely fund increased entrepreneurship programming. At nearly $1 billion per year, Iraq reconstruction waste alone would support the greatest job-creating entrepreneurship program mankind has ever seen. The admittedly difficult working environments in Iraq and Afghanistan aren't the only places to find systemic waste. USAID's own inspector general office routinely uncovers procurement and contracting waste and fraud around the world.[9] In the ultimate sign of a broken bureaucracy, even that USAID office has been accused of hiding from the public especially ugly agency fails and alleged transgressions.[10]

But suppose procurement and contracting efficiency gains do not, in fact, yield sufficient entrepreneurship funds. Suppose reform is politically or practically impossible (for example, the mighty beltway bandits cry foul). There is some slightly higher but still low-hanging fruit. We could reallocate international economic assistance funds to prioritize entrepreneurship promotion. Today, we spend less than 1 percent of our economic development assistance on entrepreneurship (across a ramshackle collection of agencies). We do not need to crank up entrepreneurship's portion to 40 percent. What I am talking about is a modest bump to 2 percent. This is reallocation, not budget increase.

If we identify significant job creation as the most important objective of economic development, and we agree that entrepreneurship is the best job creator of all, then we should adjust our priorities to ensure more than 1 percent of our foreign aid spending goes to entrepreneurship promotion. Some negotiation and compromise might be needed if entrepreneurship nibbled into the huge swaths of American development assistance devoted to, say, health (29 percent),[11] but that haggling may not even be necessary. Let us, instead, first shutter the many economic development projects and policies that have proven fruitless.

I am talking here about schemes peddled vaguely as "private-sector development" or "competitiveness" or "vocational skills" programs. For example, a four-year, $90 million USAID project in Pakistan, implemented by Chemonics, that sought to help local SMEs increase sales and employment achieved, according to USAID's inspector general, "no measureable increases in sales or employment" after two years.[12] A $24 million "Biz Plus" program in Sri Lanka, per the inspector general, "achieved less than 2 percent of its performance targets for job creation and income generation."[13] A $62 million program in the Sahel pointedly sought to address unemployment and the consequent recruitment to violent extremism, but as of "the end of March 2013, more than $10.4 million had been spent with few results."[14] Anecdotally, I found the strategies of the $34 million USAID/Chemonics Egypt Competiveness Project to which my GEP program was attached to be bizarre, unbusinesslike, and useless in terms of creating jobs.

In short, many of our so-called economic development programs lack the proven job-creating power of entrepreneurship and the programs we talked about in chapter 8. So let us move some money to entrepreneurship programs that actually stimulate job production for the millions of jobless youth in the Middle East.

A final and potentially huge source of existing funds rests within the Department of Defense. Throughout this book we have discussed why job creation is the best countermeasure to the radicalization of unemployed Arab youth. Entrepreneurship is a security move, not a charity move, just like the Marshall Plan. We are investing in jobs to keep terrorists off the streets. Yet our current military-heavy solution to terror involves shipping AH-64 Apache attack helicopters to Egypt and dispatching MQ-1 Predator drones on sorties over Afghanistan and the Middle East. Amazing but true, the budget of the GEP program I oversaw in Egypt could have been increased nine-fold merely by foregoing the purchase of a single Apache and a single Predator.[15] In other words entrepreneurship promotion programming amounts to a Defense Department rounding error. Remember, the Hellfire missiles carried by Apaches and Predators kill people; entrepreneurship gives them jobs.

This is not a call to cut into traditional defense spending, but the point I want to emphasize is that it makes perfect sense to call on Defense Department funds to bolster programs that help ensure American security. If we recognize entrepreneurship as a security play, then the Defense Department's $600 billion annual budget is very much part of this discussion; entrepreneurship should not be shunted off to USAID.

In addition to tilting spending toward entrepreneurship promotion, the United States should also encourage multilateral development finance institutions like the World Bank to join in on entrepreneurship. The famous Ronald Reagan line, "I am paying for this microphone," comes to mind here. The United States is the largest shareholder of the World Bank (boasting more than twice the shares and voting power of the next two largest shareholders put together).[16] In fiscal year 2012 our government appropriated nearly $2.5 billion to the Bank and similar development finance institutions, like the Asian Development Bank, African Development Bank, and Inter-American Development Bank.[17] As the World Bank itself says, "the United States plays a unique role in influencing and shaping development priorities."[18] We should do more influencing and shaping around entrepreneurship. The World Bank Group in 2014 committed $65.6 billion to poor countries and private businesses via loans, grants, equity investments, and guarantees.[19] That is a big pool of money already earmarked for development. Groups like the World Bank's small infoDev program and other development banks do very much consider entrepreneurship and SMEs key funding targets, but let us make sure that they truly understand the importance of entrepreneurship promotion as a "must have" rather than a "nice to have" component of economic development and fund it accordingly.

The U.S. government needs to consider entrepreneurship promotion a true stand-alone category of spending. We need to keep better track of what we spend on entrepreneurship and ensure that funding for the entrepreneurship we care about is not lumped in with microfinance or self-employment or small-scale vegetable plots. Scalable, job-creating entrepreneurship that strengthens and builds peaceful societies deserves the detailed tracking with which we follow "agriculture" and "health" projects. I do not pretend that aid data and tracking spending are simple topics,[20] but I do believe this would be far easier if our entrepreneurship promotion activities were housed under one roof instead of several dozen.

Five hundred million dollars per year is a decent yearly budget for a modest entrepreneurship program in several key countries. That would be the equivalent of less than 7 percent of all the wasted reconstruction funds in Iraq, or just half the Millennium Development Corporation's (MCC) annual appropriation, discussed later. But there really is no right number, just a right relative number. Our foreign assistance spending should both be effective and reflect our values. If we recognize that broken societies abroad are the root cause of threats to American security and prosperity, and that job creation is a huge part of the solution, then we should implement economic development policies that reflect this. Entrepreneurship is both the most significant creator of jobs and an all-American attribute respected the world over. It must figure much more prominently in our foreign assistance budget.

Blow the Whole Thing Up and Start Over Again?

Bumping up entrepreneurship spending means practically nothing if the dollars are sliced, diced, and scattered across the State Department, USAID (and its countless missions and programs), Overseas Private Investment Corporation (OPIC), the Defense Department, Peace Corps, the Trade and Development Agency, and who knows where else. The United States needs a consolidated agency devoted to bolstering entrepreneurship ecosystems in fragile, developing, and emerging economies. This cuts to the heart of our rubber screwdriver problem. Our spending will actually achieve some torque if we know who within the government "has the lead" on entrepreneurship.

I have three ideas for how the U.S. government might go about this. Some solutions may sound more bureaucratically scary than others, but all have precedent and amount to trimming fat from the agencies that have no business or competence in doing entrepreneurship and, instead, create one tight, focused program. Additional pro-entrepreneurship funds would reside with this program. We must put the money and "the lead" in the same place, where the entrepreneurship programming is happening.

So, three ways we might re-envision the delivery of entrepreneurship promotion programs are:

1. Create a small office within an existing department (such as the Department of State), thus establishing a central command for entrepreneurship as an add-on function to that department.
2. Expand the remit or powers of an existing agency, assigning (and re-assigning) all aspects of entrepreneurship ecosystem development to a single agency that already pursues private-sector solutions to development in some form or another. Candidates for this include the OPIC.
3. Launch a new, large E-Agency that consolidates all foreign economic activities (sometimes called "economic statecraft"), including private-sector solutions to development like entrepreneurship, but that leaves other traditional aid programming (for example, humanitarian aid, health) to existing agencies (such as USAID).

Option 1, starting a brand-new office within an agency, is essentially what I had hoped to do with the Global Entrepreneurship Program at the State Department. GEP managed to attract a whopping zero dollars from State. Had it thrived, GEP's ideal path would have led to a permanent office within State charged with coordinating international entrepreneurship promotion programs across several (preferably not many) U.S. government agencies. The strategy here is to anoint a single office the master controller of entrepreneurship promotion, policy, and coordination across agencies.

Such specialized (and often relatively low profile) government offices actually have a decent track record. A prime example is PEPFAR, the President's Emergency Plan for AIDS Relief, which was launched by President George W. Bush in 2003. The original legislation authorized $15 billion in spending on HIV/AIDS treatment, prevention, and care in fifteen countries for five years. It created the Office of the U.S. Global AIDS Coordinator (OGAC) within the State Department to manage the whole show. The OGAC staff is small in number, and implementation and project management are largely handled by HIV/AIDS offices at USAID, the Centers for Disease Control, and other agencies, including Defense, Commerce, and the Peace Corps.[21] This may sound like a repeat of the whole everything-is-scattered-across-a-million-agencies mess I have been railing about but, importantly, OGAC retains control of funding and policy and strategy. Its authority is clear and it does a great job. As of September 2013, PEPFAR was supporting antiretroviral treatment for 6.7 million people and provided testing and counseling for 57.7 million people in fiscal year 2013.[22] PEPFAR is one of the few Bush-era initiatives, martial or otherwise, that has received high, widespread, and across-the-aisle praise.[23]

Note, however, that merely making an announcement does not cause everything to just fall into place. Actual legislation and strong support by a president and secretary of state are what enabled PEPFAR to take proper, effective command of HIV/AIDS programming. The same should be quite possible for entrepreneurship: Just substitute "entrepreneurship" for "HIV/AIDS."

Here is another example of effective specialized government management: the Office to Monitor and Combat Trafficking in Persons (known as J/TIP), also in the State Department. Charged with diplomacy and assistance around human trafficking and slavery issues, J/TIP supports programs run by nongovernmental organizations and foreign governments around the world on an international programs budget of roughly $20 million per year.[24] It produces an annual report that has been called "our country's greatest diplomatic resource for fighting modern day slavery" by International Justice Mission, a U.S. nonprofit.[25]

Option 2, re-institutionalizing entrepreneurship programming, would expand the authority and capabilities of an existing agency. For this approach, one popular candidate agency is OPIC. Currently our government's only true development finance institution, OPIC offers loans and investment guaranties to businesses and projects around the world provided the business or project "meaningfully involves" a U.S. citizen or company via equity share, long-term debt, or other participation (for example, a construction contract). OPIC has backed microfinance institutions all over Latin America and Africa, and given loans to projects like private schools in Kenya, a hotel in Armenia, and health-care facilities in Pakistan.[26]

OPIC is self-sustaining and actually makes money for the U.S. government, having earned profits from its financial products for decades. But OPIC is still hamstrung by red tape and, as yet, largely targets projects that do not really fall under this book's understanding of entrepreneurship. This can change. For starters, Todd Moss, Benjamin Leo, and Beth Schwanke of the Center for Global Development, a nonprofit think tank, have advocated for an "OPIC Plus" that would enjoy flexibility and tools that are currently standard at equivalent government-backed institutions in the United Kingdom, the Netherlands, Germany, and elsewhere in the rich donor world. In particular, Moss and crew echo OPIC's own call for "equity authority," the right to take a minority equity share in funds and projects. Today, OPIC can only do debt. But for entrepreneurs, the hardest financing is the relatively small amounts (under $250,000) of seed capital (equity, not debt) that are the obligatory firestarter for any new business. OPIC, and all other U.S. government agencies, have zero ability to contribute to these key, first dollars.

Perhaps just as important to our entrepreneurship agenda, the OPIC Plus advocates would also like to see OPIC's financial services supplemented with "technical assistance" like project management services and training so that the agency can ensure the undertakings it backs actually work. For now, OPIC is stuck trying to coordinate with USAID, MCC, or USTDA (and stuck with their budgets) if it wants to add technical assistance onto its loans and guaranties.[27] The calls for a bigger and better OPIC are quite widespread. The U.S. National Advisory Board on Impact Investing has also advocated loosening the reins on OPIC, closely echoing the OPIC Plus recommendations.[28] George Ingram of the Brookings Institution, likewise, frequently outlines how OPIC and other elements of U.S. development policy that engage the private sector might be reformed.[29]

An expanded OPIC, free to be a full player in the funding and training pillars of my Six+Six Model, would be well positioned to take on entrepreneurship-specific programming and startup-specific levels of funding. Importantly, as we will discuss below, OPIC (and a few other stand-alone agencies) enjoy certain freedoms concerning staffing, hiring and firing, and procurement that other executive branch agencies do not.

In other words, it can be more innovative and entrepreneurial in its programming.

Option 3, a new E-Agency, is an idea that grew from conversations with several State Department "intrapreneurs," like former Deputy Secretary of State Tom Nides and former Under Secretaries of State Bob Hormats and Tara Sonenshine. This may sound like a "blow it all up and start all over again" solution, but it really amounts to a blend of the first two options: new office and consolidated authority. The best way for the U.S. government to do entrepreneurship may be to simply launch a new agency that aggregates purely economic development projects—as opposed to humanitarian aid and basic needs programs like food aid or clean drinking water or malaria bed nets—under a single roof. This E-Agency would lean heavily on private-sector solutions to development (the realm of OPIC's loans and guaranties, for example), with entrepreneurship promotion comprising one of its major pillars of activity. What would set an E-Agency apart from an OPIC Plus concept is that the new agency would take on several other additional functions, touching on international economic relations as well, such as export promotion (for example, marketing U.S. goods and services abroad and buoying foreign industries interested in those goods and services) and investment promotion (for example, marketing the United States to foreign investors, corporations, tourists, etc.). The E-Agency would, in other words, take charge of "economic statecraft" broadly.

A brand-spanking-new development agency is discussed in Washington often and has been successfully pulled off before. The Center for Global Development's Moss and Leo, before advocating for an OPIC Plus, had already imagined a brand new "U.S. Development Bank" not unlike the E-Agency idea, and did so for reasons that will sound familiar to us:

> Promoting the private sector in low-income and fragile countries clearly supports U.S. national security. . . . The U.S. government currently has a large number of existing tools, policy options, and institutions to encourage entrepreneurship and commercial activity abroad. To date, these tools—technical assistance, credit lines, seed capital, and other mechanisms—have not been deployed in an efficient or strategic manner. The fragmentation of effort and lack of cohesion across multiple agencies means that the sum of these parts is far less than optimal. . . . While the Obama Administration

currently is focused on consolidating the various export promotion agencies, an equally compelling case applies to the USG's various international agencies and programs focused on promoting private sector-based development abroad.[30]

The substance of Moss and Leo's U.S. Development Bank closely resembles that of their OPIC Plus idea, and I agree with their premise: Let us unite the private-sector development programs scattered across USAID, OPIC, USTDA, State, and elsewhere. President Obama's Global Development Council, which produced its first report (all of seven pages) nearly four years after the president announced its creation,[31] has also recommended the creation of a "U.S. Development Finance Bank" that mimics OPIC Plus, but has additionally called for OPIC to do more lending to SMEs.[32] These types of ideas are circulating around Washington. A new agency devoted to private-sector solutions to development would be the best place to house entrepreneurship promotion. A new agency might also be the best way to ensure that "the lead" on entrepreneurship also has the control of both programming and strategy, and the money.

Carving a whole new development agency out of the U.S. government beast is not without precedent and not without examples of success. The best recent example is the Millennium Challenge Corporation (like PEPFAR, established under President George W. Bush). The MCC is a U.S. government aid agency, and its projects tend to focus on infrastructure and income-generation activities with a prime interest in economic growth and poverty reduction. But MCC stands entirely separate from USAID and the State Department. It works only with countries that have met strict criteria pertaining to governance, business and regulatory climate, and social indicators like education, health, and environment. The agency forms five-year "compacts" with recipient countries. These compacts are negotiated with the recipient governments, spell out target sectors and desired projects, and lead to the formation of a local Millennium Challenge Account that actually manages implementation. Full compacts range in size from $66 million (Vanuatu) to $698 million (Tanzania), and from 2004 to 2014 MCC's annual appropriation has averaged about $1 billion per year.[33] As we will discuss, MCC's unique structure and its detachment from USAID confers a flexibility, in hiring and contracting, for example, that a new E-Agency would almost certainly require.

Working Around the Two Ps

Whichever option is picked—new coordinating office, expanded agency, or new E-Agency—changes to contracting, procurement, and human resources policies are vital to the success of entrepreneurship promotion programming. I shorthand the solution reforms required as "the two Ps": procurement and people.

In chapter 6 we talked extensively about the hippo-dancing-with-the-mouse problem. The U.S. government (the hippo) purchases over half a trillion dollars worth of goods and services from private-sector vendors each year. Winning contracts from the federal government is a very big business played by very big boys (other hippos). Foreign assistance is exemplary. Nearly a third of the money USAID dishes out goes to three firms, just three, and 75 percent goes to only twenty firms, even though USAID's work spans five continents and everything from clean water to microfinance.[34] There is little place for small, innovative firms or firms with true niche expertise (the mice). Just the process of signing up to become eligible to bid on government contracts brought my business partner and me, with four graduate degrees between us, to our knees. The result? Project failures of the sort routinely uncovered by USAID's inspector general and billions wasted in Iraq and Afghanistan reconstruction. And, maybe worse, fewer and fewer Americans want to even bother bidding to work for the American government.[35]

In short, our procurement system is no longer effective. We cannot get the best people to do important work. This is lethal to entrepreneurship development. The same mechanics used to procure a nuclear submarine or a section of interstate highway cannot be used to contract a successful American entrepreneur to mentor a virtually-zero-starting-value startup in Beirut or to hire experienced angel or venture capital investors to design a social enterprise seed fund in West Africa. USAID's system of "indefinite quantity contracts" and huge deals for huge beltway bandits is simply not built for entrepreneurship promotion. And we can be sure those nuclear submarines, highways, and other government works are not products of some kind of contracting nirvana, either. The Department of Energy's inspector general alone pursues well over 200 criminal investigations at any given time, 60 percent of which concern contract fraud.[36]

While substandard procurement and contracting must be addressed government-wide, a good first step would be to fix procurement and contracting as it pertains to economic development broadly and entrepreneurship specifically. There is no need to boil the ocean. After all, what better area to try an entrepreneurial and innovative approach than entrepreneurship programming itself? Since entrepreneurship by definition invites new approaches, and since many of the best contractors are going to be small firms or individuals (as opposed to beltway bandits who somehow claim expertise in both drip irrigation and mobile-ready software-as-a-service products); and since entrepreneurship promotion implicates just hundreds of millions of dollars, not tens of billions, I would suggest entrepreneurship as an ideal area for testing new models of contracting and procurement. The field is circumscribed and inherently open to new ways of doing things.

I am absolutely not a government procurement expert (itself a highly complicated field, sort of like open-heart surgery). I have, however, learned a bit about procurement and contracting from some true experts. One, Steven Tomanelli, the Federal Acquisition Regulation (FAR) guru, describes the FAR process as "currently unworkable."[37] To borrow a page from the private sector, the answer to an unworkable situation has to be a workaround. And I do know a thing or two about workarounds. Drawing on my own experience of State Department and USAID procurement policies as well as interviews with economic development practitioners, regulatory experts, and development policy wonks, I have cobbled together ideas on how to change contracting and procurement in entrepreneurship promotion's favor.

One, we need to create a channel for small- and medium-size companies to interact with the U.S. government and win contracts. These companies will be the ones with expertise in entrepreneurship ecosystem development, not the twenty usual suspects who currently do practically all of USAID's work. At the very least, involving more bidders will both bring diversity to the procurement pool (an excellent way to uncover innovative programming) and increase competition for contracts (an excellent way to uncover value for money).[38]

One way to do this could be through aggregation. A hippo capable of managing the onerous bid preparation, M&E (monitoring and evaluation), and accounting tasks required under government procurement would bid for a contract and then pull together mice (who have the expertise but lack legions of accountants and lawyers) to implement the contract. This might sound like the current prime-and-subcontractor arrangement we see today.

As noted in chapter 6, primes are in the business of squeezing subs, not helping them get work. So what I have in mind is a "rent-a-prime" arrangement.

This is somewhat akin to what VEGA does today. The Volunteers for Economic Growth Alliance (now an independent nonprofit, but originally birthed by none other than USAID) helps its twenty-three members compete for USAID contracts. VEGA's members include what might be termed the "mid-majors" of the international development league, the likes of Winrock and Land O'Lakes, as well as a few smaller organizations, and they are expected to be nonprofit firms with an emphasis on incorporating volunteers in their work.[39] Entrepreneurship development needs a similar aggregator that can help the for-profit and nonprofit firms and programs we talked about in chapter 8 win government contracts (and collaborate with one another). Think of the Hollywood studio model discussed at the outset of this chapter, but with a slight twist. Hippos like Warner Bros. are quite adept at working with mice like creative directors, writers, and producers—often through intermediaries like talent agencies, lawyers, and managers—without squeezing the creative life out of them.

Two, the requests for proposals (RFPs), terms of reference (TORs), and statements of work (SOWs) for entrepreneurship development projects should be written (or cowritten) by subject matter experts. Government economic development staffs are short on people with experience running a business, let alone a startup. That should change, but just for a start, people experienced in building entrepreneurship ecosystems must participate in RFPs for ecosystem development projects. This much is obvious. And rather than relying largely on government staffing, we might consider mechanisms that provide for third-party oversight from the private sector. Experts from business might work alongside a government official during the RFP writing process, during the bidding process, and during oversight. (The United Kingdom's DFID has, in fact, adopted this very accessing of private-sector expertise in its new Smart Rules program.[40])

This third-party advisor might also help ensure that subject matter expertise and ability to execute are the foremost qualifications for securing a contract, not a beltway address or bandit-size compliance staff. As procurement law expert Steve Schooner told me, "Oversight has hijacked public procurement today." Government procurement is moving away from a "service function model" to a "third world model." It is no longer about value for money, efficient supply chain management, and winning at the margins (as it is in the private sector); it is about avoiding fraud at all costs (including the cost of decent execution).[41] This is why the usual suspects always win USAID contracts. Even if a capable small firm cannot fill out all of the ten thousand reporting forms USAID requires for a particular contract, that firm could still win the job with the help of a third-party advisor with private-sector mojo.

Three, we should professionalize procurement within the government. Let us make procurement a real and respected career track. In the private sector, procurement is a recognized field and companies provide their procurement officers with extensive training and motivate them with clear paths to promotion. That is not the case in government, where captain is the highest rank for procurement roles in the military[42] and, as Schooner says, "Most people end up in procurement because, as they were rising, at some point, they didn't get the big job—and they got bumped over to procurement."[43] That is, procurement brings neither prestige nor respect, so top-shelf talent is rarely found in government procurement positions. Make procurement important—by offering training, deep career tracks, and good pay—and you will see better procurement work. Another argument for boosting procurement as a career: outsourcing the work of government is a rapidly growing business. Since 2000, government spending on contracts has increased by nearly 90 percent (outpacing inflation), so that we are today procuring goods and services in excess of $500 billion each year. That spending makes up an ever-greater portion of U.S. federal spending (15 percent in 2012, up from 11 percent in 2000).[44] Increasingly, government agencies are, in effect, contracting offices disbursing money to private-sector implementers. The people who handle that disbursement are procurement officials. If their role has become such a crucial one, they should be correspondingly trained, honored, and promoted.

Four, maybe the professionalized procurement officer and the agency the officer represents could be held to the same level of discipline they require of contractors. In my own limited experience bidding for projects sponsored by bilateral and multilateral donors, I have endured countless timetable postponements, rescheduled meetings, retracted RFPs, tardy communications, and other arbitrary actions that quite clearly would have eliminated my firm from a bid competition had we been the offending party. This is another reason only twenty firms do USAID's work; they are the only ones large enough to smooth cash flow over the whimsical behavior of donor agencies.

There are doubtless more contracting fixes out there, and I urge the contracting and procurement experts to come forward. There could be outside-of-the-box solutions. Perhaps government, in procuring entrepreneurship projects from entrepreneurial types, could rely less on contracts and more on grants (which usually come with fewer strings attached), "challenges" (which pay upon result[45]), or even surprisingly flexible but less-discussed OTAs (Other Transaction Authorities). Contracting and procurement are not sexy, but they are important.

Finally, there is one certainty about contracting and procurement. Much more flexibility awaits an entrepreneurship program run outside the purview of the traditional executive branch agencies, especially USAID and State. This is what makes a new E-Agency or expanding and amending OPIC's mission so attractive. In fact, this is very much what the creation of the Millennium Challenge Corporation was about. MCC, when first created, was empowered and structured with a number of procurement and contracting workarounds that have enabled it to, simply, do good work. For example, an MCC compact with a foreign government entails the formation of a local Millennium Challenge Account. This local MCA entity is the actual implementer of MCC projects. As holder and manager of the purse strings, the local (that is, foreign) MCA is not beholden to the bureaucratic barnacles of the United States and can hire and procure more freely, and can circumvent "buy America" and earmark straight-jackets. The fixes that effective entrepreneurship ecosystem development requires may only come after entrepreneurship is re-institutionalized in government.

And what about people? A not-too-distant cousin of the U.S. government's broken procurement system is our people problem. Government bureaucrats do not do entrepreneurship, almost by definition. Do they need to? Contracting out entrepreneurship ecosystem development to the experts is a good workaround, and that is part of the answer. But those procuring—and writing the RFPs, the TORs, and the SOWs—need to know what they are talking about, as do those designing programs and, indeed, those devising strategies and policies.

Let me return to the 1990s Hollywood example. One of the major Warner Bros. projects I was involved with was the construction of a new state-of-the-art film preservation and archive building. Back then, the studio had acres of nitrate vaults, but the entire industry, including Warner

Bros., really was technologically backward; *Looney Tunes* and decades of celluloid greats were decomposing into vinegar. I was far from a trained archivist, and I did not know the first thing about the chemistry of preserving different types of film and tape. But I did know that having the biggest asset on our books turn to salad dressing was a problem. Working with our procurement people, we contracted experts in the preservation and restoration of the physical elements of film, tape, and animation cells. We knew our needs and our business well enough to know what kind of expertise to look for. And with the underlying primary asset of the business at stake, we did not just outsource the entire job to a single, generalist contractor, nor was our goal to spend the maximum amount of money in the minimum amount of time so we could be reauthorized at the same or greater level (which is how beltway bandits think). Our goal was to preserve our elements in the fastest, most cost-effective, and most reliable way. In other words, the goal of the procurement was more important than the process of procurement itself.

My experience inside the State Department and engaging with USAID was not the same. The people in charge of the often weak entrepreneurship programs had no entrepreneurship experience and, usually, little to no business experience in general. Instead, they were contracting and procurement experts; "subject matter expertise" was usually regarded with practical disdain and considered not very important. Washington is not the real world. It has its own gravity. Innovation, business skills and entrepreneurship, and the best practices of America were nowhere to be found in government. Of course I know the government plays a different role in society than the private sector and that the Executive Branch has many masters in the 535 members of Congress (imagine a corporate board with 535 directors!). But the unique terrain of government work doesn't stop other programs from staffing up with experts long on real-world experience. Imagine if the CDC were staffed with people who had never worked in a hospital, or if an RFP for a PEPFAR antiretrovirals contract were written by someone who did not know the difference between protease inhibitors and fusion inhibitors. What if Pentagon personnel did not know about the latest military equipment or surveillance technologies? If we are to do entrepreneurship properly, we need people from the private sector in government. We need their experience with the practices that make America great and we need them to inform government on where and how to spend on entrepreneurship. Whether on a rotating (which I strongly recommend) or permanent basis, we need to find ways to infuse government with more of America's number one asset: qualified people.

The rubber screwdriver problem could be partly solved if we tapped people with private-sector experience more often and more consistently. A re-envisioned OPIC or a new E-Agency might well come with authority to hire middle managers (or consultants on a project basis) from the private sector at competitive salaries. It is also important that these imports follow a viable career path that returns them back to the private sector after a specified term or after their assignment is complete so as to keep both them and the agency's advisors to the public sector fresh and current. (The Peace Corps does, in fact, have a five-year rule "to ensure that Peace Corps' staff remain as fresh and innovative as its Volunteers."[46]) Entrepreneurship is not a field for career bureaucrats. Intimate knowledge of what the private sector is doing is critical, and there's only one place to learn.

The government, to its credit, does have a mishmash of programs to woo real-worlders to Washington. These include things like the AAAS Science & Technology Policy Fellowships for math and science Ph.D.s and M.D.s, the White House Fellows Program for accomplished young professionals, the Presidential Management Fellows Program for recent graduates, and the Franklin Fellowship for old people like me (that is, mid- and upper-level business and nonprofit professionals). But what we really need are new programs that structure government stints less as career tourism and more as real work with immediate responsibilities.

There is room for improvement in existing programs. One of their main problems is that they are "front-end loaded." That is, the programs seem to focus more on who gets selected and how, not on what they do once they are in the building. The Franklin Fellowship had no orientation, no training, and no guidelines for the offices that receive fellows; no spelling out examples of worthwhile and interesting projects (or counter-examples). That is quite easy to rectify, and the result would likely see more than a small minority of Franklin Fellows actually serving their full one-year term. The Presidential Management Fellows (PMF) Program is similarly under fire of late for not showing fellows the ropes. According to the *Washington Post*, PMFs so often find supervision lacking and assignments lame that one veteran federal executive says "we are turning them off from government service early in their careers."[47] Like so many government policies, this is another example of "great in theory, not so great in implementation." So let us make sure these programs orient the newcomers, that they do a better job of mentor matching, that they get "America" excited about "Washington." This does not require money; it requires the same processes executed every day in private-sector America.

Government: A Work in Progress

Tilting spending priorities toward entrepreneurship; re-envisioning our economic development agencies; improving contracting and procurement; and injecting private-sector experience into the government. It sounds like a lot, but the lifts really are not that heavy. These reforms are practically without new spending, and they are geared toward dealing with an imminent threat to America: the masses of unemployed young people in unstable and developing parts of the world.

One reason I remain optimistic about elevating entrepreneurship as a foreign policy tool, despite my firsthand disappointments in government work, is that our government is not entirely about inaction. There are also nongovernment actors fighting the good fight to improve our bureaucracy. There are many examples of government success, and I am far from the only one beating the drum for continuous improvement to government operations.

For example, look at information technology, where the government has taken steps to upgrade its stone tablets by hiring former Google stalwarts. One, a site-reliability expert, is the first administrator of the U.S. Digital Service, which aims to improve the online experience of Americans visiting government websites.[48] Another, Megan Smith, who served in several executive roles at Google, became the country's third Chief Technology Officer in September 2014. She urged a more upbeat outlook for those considering working in government:

> So many kids at the top schools apply for Teach for America. I'd like to talk to those young people and say: Consider government. It's real service, and you can affect hundreds of millions of people. And if you're working for USAID and the State Department, you can affect billions of people. . . . If you come, you can bring your own methods. The American government will be whatever we all make of it.[49]

Elsewhere, Health and Human Services runs an "entrepreneurs-in-residence" program that brings startup founders into the agency to help with IT-related health projects. Tom Kalil of the Office of Technology and Policy describes the program as the Obama administration's effort to "encourage agencies to use a broad range of approaches to solving problems."[50]

Outside of government, the Partnership for Public Service, a nonprofit whose mission is "to revitalize our federal government by transforming the way government works and inspiring a new generation to serve," advocates for policies and management structures to improve government's human resources and make government work better.[51] The organization has worked with IDEO, a design consultancy, on research into "innovation in government."[52] The Center for Global Development routinely publishes papers on improving the government's work in economic development. I even know a particularly entrepreneurial former National Security Council staffer, Quintan Wiktorowicz, who started a blog "for anyone who believes we need to design a smarter, agile government . . . dedicated to the thousands of government intrapreneurs and partnership-builders, whose daily, unseen and dedicated struggles against ossified bureaucracy are truly humbling."[53]

Though USAID has been late to the private-sector-solutions-to-poverty party, and though its programs remain scattered and ill-defined, it deserves credit for acknowledging that the great ship's bearing needs to be drastically altered. The agency's former administrator, Rajiv Shah, has said that "writing big checks to contractors is not development,"[54] and the agency launched the USAID Forward program, declaring on its website an interest in data-driven results, partnerships with the private sector, and "innovative, breakthrough solutions to intractable development problems."[55] In 2014 USAID announced a Global Development Lab intended to tap expertise across the private sector, NGOs, and academia to "lead our efforts in applying science, technology, innovation, and partnerships to solve global development challenges and improve our development impact."[56] The agency's other efforts include PACE (Partnering to Accelerate Entrepreneurship), which aims to catalyze private-sector investment for early-stage startups, and the Development Innovation Ventures and Grand Challenges for Development initiatives.[57] Grand Challenges, in fact, to use a verb that rings of the cutting edge, crowdsources solutions to specific development problems by issuing grants to promising approaches. The Saving Lives at Birth challenge, for instance, awards seed grants and expansion funds to private enterprises, nonprofits, and universities that develop high-impact, groundbreaking goods and services to prevent maternal and newborn deaths in poor countries.[58]

While I have little faith that USAID as an institution can actually break through its (often Congressionally imposed) constraints to really do entrepreneurship, I do have faith that there are people who know a better way is possible. Be they at USAID, on the President's Global Development Council, or at nonprofits like the Partnership for Public Service, there are, in fact, real people thinking about how to improve our government's ability to execute policy and programs.

Moreover, I remain confident that government can execute on one long-held attribute vital to innovation and entrepreneurship: its convening power. Even if government cannot build a health-care website, and even if it wastes $10 billion in economic development funds, the state nonetheless retains a unique power to bring people together. I saw this firsthand while running the Global Entrepreneurship Program at the State Department. Consider the entrepreneurship delegations I led to Egypt and Turkey. Even though our government barely funded GEP; and even though our government did not buy plane tickets for investors and mentors; and even though our government did not fund the Flat6Labs incubator in Cairo; and even though it was private-sector people who really made things happen in Egypt and Turkey, our government did put up a tent bearing the words "entrepreneurship" and "innovation." Lo and behold, people came and people got excited about entrepreneurship in the Middle East and North Africa. An A-list slate of angel investors and rock star entrepreneurs paid their own way to the region and mentored and invested in a lot of startups. Flat6Labs did take off, and Ussal Sahbaz did go ahead and found the Garaj incubator and a new seed fund for Turkish startups. Even the mere act of convening a crowd can catalyze entrepreneurship, even in places where the American government is not everyone's best buddy.

Peace through Entrepreneurship

Entrepreneurship creates jobs, and jobs are the foundation of a stable, civil society. Entrepreneurship is also a quintessentially American value, a founding, characteristic value of the United States alongside democracy and human rights. Yet, when it comes to American foreign aid and foreign policy, the American specialty of entrepreneurship is nowhere to be found.

The minimal, scattered, and ineffective entrepreneurship programming the U.S. government has implemented falls far short of what we need: a robust entrepreneurship program that supports startup firms in fragile, developing, and emerging markets around the world.

El Alfi, the founder of Egypt's Sawari Ventures and Flat6Labs incubator starkly captures what is at stake:

> We have a massive population problem in Egypt. Six years ago the birth rate was 1.9 million newborns per year. It's gone up every year by 100,000 to 150,000. Last year it was 2.6 million. I can't imagine a model where these people will have jobs, or that the economy will be able to absorb these waves of people coming in, other than entrepreneurship.[59]

These circumstances, which are not limited to Egypt, are at the core of the global changes that today frighten us, threaten us, and, at times, harm us. There will be no peace when huge swaths of the world—especially the Middle East and North Africa—cannot find work for 40 percent of its young working-age people. Likewise, there will be no peace when we only treat the symptoms of this unemployment affliction with war, drones, torture, and detention. No entrepreneurship, no jobs, no peace. As El Alfi says, "We have to give people something to live for, instead of the guys that pitch them something to die for."[60]

Now, government is not a businessman, and government does not pick winners. But, as we have seen, even in America, government does enable and it does invest. It can create a regulatory environment that allows entrepreneurs to succeed, and it can seed the industries and the learning institutions that yield high-impact, job-creating companies and business leaders. It can also support the organizations that are already making entrepreneurship happen and that strengthen entrepreneurship ecosystems: the business plan competitions, the incubators, the mentorship networks, the seed funds.

In fact, it is only government that has the wherewithal, mandate, and obligation to do entrepreneurship at the large, highly coordinated scale required. It is government that stimulates investment in failing and fragile states, and it is government that can turn sectors safe as a first-in investor. And, most important, it is government that is responsible for the security of its citizens. A government that allows the source of its threats to fester and spread unchecked is negligent, and especially so when a solution to those threats presents itself in the expertise of that government's citizens. The U.S. government must elevate entrepreneurship as a foreign policy tool.

This book is meant as a springboard, a call to action. I have seen entrepreneurship work. I have seen jobs created, to my benefit and to the benefit of thousands of others. Government can play a vital role in this area. I have firsthand experience with the obstacles that must be overcome: our through-the-looking-glass government culture and our ineffectual processes. Those versed in the ways of "Washington" and those versed in the ways of "America" can certainly, together, manufacture a better screwdriver.

They can ensure our government rebalances aid spending to better reflect the reality that entrepreneurship is the engine of our prosperity. They can re-envision our institutions to better deliver entrepreneurship programming, install improved procurement and contracting models, and tap the best private-sector talent and practices. They can build the best entrepreneurship programs on Earth.

The United States, for all its faults, has a great tradition of pursuing freedom and prosperity for its citizens while also standing for freedom and prosperity for others around the planet. Our foreign policy has always enlisted our military to defend what we believe is right, and our diplomats to negotiate for the welfare of Americans. It is time that we enlist entrepreneurship in the service of foreign policy and put America's best foot forward.

Notes

Preface

1. *Treaty of Rome,* 1957, http://ec.europa.eu/archives/emu_history/documents /treaties/rometreaty2.pdf.

2. Claire Suddath, "Why Did World War I Just End?," *Time,* October 4, 2010, http:// content.time.com/time/world/article/0,8599,2023140,00.html.

3. SES S.A., *New Horizons: Annual Report 2014,* 2015, http://read.uberflip.com/ i/488134-annual-report-2014-english.

4. Joseph A. Schumpeter, *Capitalism, Socialism and Democracy (1947)* (Kessinger Publishing, 2010).

5. International Labor Office, *Global Employment Trends for Youth 2013,* May 2013, www.ilo.org/wcmsp5/groups/public/—dgreports/—dcomm/documents/publication /wcms_212423.pdf; World Economic Forum, *Addressing the 100 Million Youth Challenge Perspectives on Youth Employment in the Arab World in 2012,* 2012, www3 .weforum.org/docs/WEF_YouthEmployment_ArabWorld_Report_2012.pdf.

6. e4e, *Education for Employment: Realizing Arab Youth Potential,* April 2011, www .e4earabyouth.com.

7. Barack Obama, "Remarks by the President on a New Beginning at Cairo University," 2009, www.whitehouse.gov/the_press_office/Remarks-by-the-President-at-Cairo -University-6-04-09.

Chapter One

1. Sources providing youth unemployment data typically define "youth" as ages fifteen to twenty-four or twenty-nine.

2. Precise unemployment rates vary by source. The figures provided here come from: The World Bank Group, "Unemployment, Youth Total (% of Total Labor Force Ages 15–24) (modeled ILO Estimate) | Data | Table," http://data.worldbank.org/indicator /SL.UEM.1524.ZS; International Labor Office, Global Employment Trends for Youth 2013, May 2013, www.ilo.org/wcmsp5/groups/public/—dgreports/—dcomm/documents /publication/wcms_212423.pdf; World Economic Forum, Addressing the 100 Million Youth Challenge Perspectives on Youth Employment in the Arab World in 2012, 2012, www3.weforum.org/docs/WEF_YouthEmployment_ArabWorld_Report_2012.pdf.

3. UNESCO, "World Arabic Language Day | United Nations Educational, Scientific and Cultural Organization," www.unesco.org/new/en/unesco/events/prizes-and -celebrations/celebrations/international-days/world-arabic-language-day/; e4e, Education for Employment: Realizing Arab Youth Potential, April 2011, www.e4earabyouth .com.

4. Robert D. Kaplan, The Revenge of Geography: What the Map Tells Us about Coming Conflicts and the Battle Against Fate (Random House, 2012).

5. Vali Nasr, Forces of Fortune: The Rise of the New Muslim Middle Class and What It Will Mean for Our World (Free Press, 2009), p. 201.

6. Hernando de Soto, "The Capitalist Cure for Terrorism," Wall Street Journal, October 10, 2014, http://online.wsj.com/articles/the-capitalist-cure-for-terrorism -1412973796.

7. Dane Stangler and Robert E. Litan, Where Will the Jobs Come From? (Ewing Marion Kauffman Foundation, November 31, 2009), http://papers.ssrn.com/abstract =1580139; Chiara Criscuolo, Peter N. Gal, and Carlo Menon, "DynEmp: New Evidence on Young Firms' Role in the Economy," Vox: CEPR's Policy Portal, May 26, 2014, www.voxeu.org/article/dynemp-new-evidence-young-firms-role-economy.

8. McKinsey & Company, The Power of Many: Realizing the Socioeconomic Potential of Entrepreneurs in the 21st Century, October 2011, www.g20yea.com/en/wp -content/uploads/The_Power_of_Many-_McKinsey_Report.pdf.

9. Rory Stewart, "Afghanistan: 'A Shocking Indictment,'" New York Review of Books, November 6, 2014, www.nybooks.com/articles/archives/2014/nov/06/afghanistan -shocking-indictment.

10. Siri Roland Xavier, and others, Global Entrepreneurship Monitor 2012 Global Report (Global Entrepreneurship Research Association, 2013), www.gemconsortium.org /report/48545; Omidyar Network, Accelerating Entrepreneurship in Africa: Understanding Africa's Challenges to Creating Opportunity-Driven Entrepreneurship, 2013, www .omidyar.com/news/omidyar-network-releases-report-challenges-faced-african -entrepreneurs-and-recommendations.

11. See Mariana Mazzucato, The Entrepreneurial State: Debunking Public vs. Private Sector Myths (Anthem Press, 2013).

12. "Global Heroes," The Economist, March 12, 2009, www.economist.com/node /13216025.

13. William J. Baumol, Robert E. Litan, and Carl J. Schramm, Good Capitalism, Bad Capitalism, and the Economics of Growth and Prosperity (Yale University Press, 2009).

14. See, for example, Michael E. Gerber, *The E-Myth Revisited* (HarperCollins, 2009).

15. Major research universities, in fact, often employ staff devoted to identifying commercialization and market opportunities for products and processes developed on campus. See, for example, Caitlin Kelly, "Inventions that Will Help Save the World (if We Let Them)," *Yale Alumni Magazine*, 2013, www.yalealumnimagazine.com/articles /3664?page=1.

16. Michael Kimmelman, "Refugee Camp for Syrians in Jordan Evolves as a Do-It-Yourself City," *New York Times*, July 4, 2014, www.nytimes.com/2014/07/05/world /middleeast/zaatari-refugee-camp-in-jordan-evolves-as-a-do-it-yourself-city.html.

17. Erik Hersman and Ken Banks, "Africa's Innovation Generation: Dynamos and Mobile Wiz Kids," *National Geographic Digital Diversity*, February 8, 2011, http:// newswatch.nationalgeographic.com/2011/02/08/africas_innovation_generation.

18. "Tech Entrepreneurs in the Middle East: Start-Up Spring," *The Economist*, July 13, 2013, www.economist.com/news/business/21581737-clusters-internet-firms-are -popping-up-all-over-region-start-up-spring.

19. "Arab Women Entrepreneurs: Untraditional Choice," *The Economist*, July 13, 2013, www.economist.com/news/business/21581740-middle-east-beats-west-female-tech -founders-untraditional-choice.

20. Vivek Wadhwa, "The Truth about Entrepreneurs: Twice as Many Are Over 50 as Are Under 25," *PBS NewsHour Business Desk with Paul Solman*, 2013.

21. Jaron Lanier, *Who Owns the Future?* (Simon & Schuster, 2013); Joe Nocera, "Innovation, Optimism and Jobs," *New York Times*, February 14, 2014, www.nytimes .com/2014/02/15/opinion/nocera-innovation-optimism-and-jobs.html.

22. Starbucks Corporation, "U.S. Securities and Exchange Commission Filing: Form 10-K for the Fiscal Year Ended September 29, 2013," November 18, 2013, www .sec.gov/Archives/edgar/data/829224/000082922413000044/sbux-9292013x10k.htm.

23. Facebook Inc., "U.S Securities and Exchange Commission Filing: Form 10-K for the Fiscal Year Ended December 31, 2013," January 31, 2014, www.sec.gov/Archives /edgar/data/1326801/000132680114000007/fb-12312013x10k.htm.

24. Google Inc., "U.S. Securities and Exchange Commission Filing: Form 10-K for the Fiscal Year Ended December 31, 2013," February 11, 2014, www.sec.gov/Archives /edgar/data/1288776/000128877614000020/goog2013123110-k.htm.

25. Apple Inc., "U.S. Securities and Exchange Commission Filing: Form 10-K for the Fiscal Year Ended September 28, 2013," October 30, 2013, www.sec.gov/Archives /edgar/data/320193/000119312513416534/d590790d10k.htm.

26. Ha-Joon Chang, 23 *Things They Don't Tell You about Capitalism* (Bloomsbury Press; Reprint edition, 2011).

27. Koko King, "KOKO KING: Purveyors of Fine Foods," www.kokoking.com.gh /history; Kofi Mangesi, "Koko King," *Business World Magazine*, September 27, 2012, www.businessworldghana.com/koko-king.

28. Jim Y. Kim, "How Bolivian Farmers Made the World Crave Quinoa," *Bloomberg View*, October 13, 2013, www.bloombergview.com/articles/2013-10-13/how-bolivian -farmers-made-the-world-crave-quinoa; Franz Chavez, "Bolivian Entrepreneur Helps

Quinoa Shine in U.S.," *Inter Press Service News Agency*, April 2013, www.ipsnews.net /2013/04/bolivian-entrepreneur-helps-quinoa-shine-in-u-s.

29. Kngine, "Kngine Announces New Round of Investment from Samsung Open Innovation Center and Vodafone Ventures Egypt," *Zawya*, September 9, 2014, www.zawya.com/story/Kngine_Announces_New_Round_of_Investment_from _Samsung_Open_Innovation_Center_And_Vodafone_Ventures_Egypt-ZAWYA2014 0909103000/; Elizabeth MacBride, "Silicon Wadi," *Forbes Middle East*, August 24, 2015, www.forbesmiddleeast.com/en/news/read/2015/silicon-wadi/articleid/9314.

30. Anthony Ha, "Kngine Aims to Build a Natural Language-Driven App that Can Answer Any Question," *TechCrunch*, November 30, 2012, http://techcrunch.com/2012 /11/30/kngine.

31. Hannah Seligson, "Arab Spring, Start-Up Summer? Egypt's Entrepreneurs Look Beyond the Revolution," *New York Times*, July 16, 2011, www.nytimes.com/2011 /07/17/business/global/egypts-entrepreneurs-look-beyond-the-revolution.html.

32. Sawari Ventures, "Press Release: Sawari Ventures Launches Fund, Announces Fund Sponsor Naguib," *PRNewswire*, January 18, 2011, www.prnewswire.com/news -releases/sawari-ventures-launches-fund-announces-fund-sponsor-naguib-sawiris-and -investments-in-feature-phone-platform-company-alzwad-and-top-selling-iphone-app -developer-vimov-114128219.html.

33. American Chamber of Commerce in Egypt, "AmCham Egypt 'GEP Closing Ceremony and Grand Finale Event,'" *American Chamber of Commerce in Egypt*, January 12, 2011, www.amcham.org.eg/events_activities/events/details/default.asp?ID =406&P=1.

34. Flat6Labs, "Flat6Labs," www.flat6labs.com/; Sawari Ventures, "Home | Sawari Ventures," www.sawariventures.com/; Asma Ajroudi, "In Abu Dhabi, a New Start-Up 'Accelerator' Promises More Success Stories," *Al Arabiya News*, November 21, 2014, http://english.alarabiya.net/en/business/2014/11/21/In-Abu-Dhabi-a-new-start-up -accelerator-is-promising-more-success-stories-.html.

35. Christopher M. Schroeder, *Startup Rising: The Entrepreneurial Revolution Remaking the Middle East* (Palgrave Macmillan, 2013).

36. Hernando de Soto, "What the Arab World Really Wants," *The Spectator*, July 13, 2013, www.spectator.co.uk/features/8959621/what-the-arab-world-really -wants.

37. Jeremy M. Sharp, *Egypt: Background and U.S. Relations* (Congressional Research Service, June 27, 2013), www.fas.org/sgp/crs/mideast/RL33003.pdf.

38. Author's calculations. Figures and methodology presented in chapter 5.

39. Pew Research Center Global Attitudes Project, *Global Opinion of Obama Slips, International Policies Faulted: Drone Strikes Widely Opposed* (Pew Research Center, June 13, 2012), www.pewglobal.org/2012/06/13/global-opinion-of-obama-slips -international-policies-faulted.

Chapter Two

Epigraph 1: Hernando de Soto, "What the Arab World Really Wants," *The Spectator*, July 13, 2013, www.spectator.co.uk/features/8959621/what-the-arab-world-really-wants.

Epigraph 2: George C. Marshall, "The 'Marshall Plan' Speech at Harvard University, June 5, 1947," www.oecd.org/general/themarshallplanspeechatharvarduniversity5june1947.htm.

Epigraph 3: Hillary Rodham Clinton, *Hard Choices* (Simon & Schuster, 2014), pp. xii–xiii.

1. The World Bank Group, "Unemployment, Youth Total (% of Total Labor Force Ages 15–24) (modeled ILO Estimate) | Data | Table," http://data.worldbank.org/indicator/SL.UEM.1524.ZS; International Labor Office, *Global Employment Trends for Youth 2013*, May 2013, www.ilo.org/wcmsp5/groups/public/—dgreports/—dcomm/documents/publication/wcms_212423.pdf; World Economic Forum, *Addressing the 100 Million Youth Challenge: Perspectives on Youth Employment in the Arab World in 2012*, 2012, www.weforum.org/reports/addressing-100-million-youth-challenge.

2. Hernando de Soto, "The Capitalist Cure for Terrorism," *Wall Street Journal*, October 10, 2014, http://online.wsj.com/articles/the-capitalist-cure-for-terrorism-1412973796.

3. IRIN, "Analysis: Understanding Nigeria's Boko Haram Radicals," *IRIN*, July 18, 2011, www.irinnews.org/report/93250/analysis-understanding-nigeria-s-boko-haram-radicals.

4. International Labor Office, *Global Employment Trends for Youth 2012* (Geneva: International Labour Organization, May 2012), www.ilo.org/wcmsp5/groups/public/—dgreports/—dcomm/documents/publication/wcms_180976.pdf; Kwabena Gyimah-Brempong and Mwangi S. Kimenyi, *Youth Policy and the Future of African Development*, Africa Growth Initiative, 2013, www.brookings.edu/research/reports/2013/04/15-youth-policy-african-development-kimenyi; African Economic Outlook, "Promoting Youth Employment in Africa," 2013, www.africaneconomicoutlook.org/en/in-depth/youth_employment.

5. Hannah Roberts, "The Unlikely Jihadi: How Party-Loving Paris Bomber Drank and Ran a Club Closed Down for Drugs in the Belgian Hotbed of Terror," *Daily Mail Online*, November 16, 2015, www.dailymail.co.uk/news/article-3319932/Guns-Cod-grievances-Belgiums-Islamist-airbase.html.

6. CSIS Executive Council on Development, *Our Shared Opportunity: A Vision for Global Prosperity*, 2013, http://csis.org/publication/our-shared-opportunity, p. xii.

7. John Thorne, "No Terrorist 'Safe Haven' in North Africa? That's a Tall Order," *Christian Science Monitor*, January 22, 2013, www.csmonitor.com/World/Africa/2013/0122/No-terrorist-safe-haven-in-North-Africa-That-s-a-tall-order.

8. Adeel Malik and Bassem Awadallah, *The Economics of the Arab Spring*, vol. 44, CSAE Working Paper WPS/2011T23, 2011, www.csae.ox.ac.uk/workingpapers/pdfs/csae-wps-2011-23.pdf, p. 2.

9. Hernando de Soto, *The Other Path: The Economic Answer to Terrorism* (Basic Books, 2002); Hernando de Soto, *Mystery of Capital: Why Capitalism Triumphs in the West and Fails Everywhere Else* (Basic Books, 2003).

10. Thomas L. Friedman, "The World According to Maxwell Smart, Part 1," *New York Times*, July 12, 2014, www.nytimes.com/2014/07/13/opinion/sunday/thomas-l-friedman-the-world-according-to-maxwell-smart-part-1.html; Thomas L. Friedman, "Order vs. Disorder, Part 2," *New York Times*, July 15, 2014, www.nytimes.com/2014/07/16/opinion/thomas-friedman-israeli-palestinian-conflict-order-disorder.html.

11. Jim Tankersley, "This Might Be the Most Controversial Theory for What's behind the Rise of ISIS," *Washington Post*, Wonkblog, November 30, 2015, www.washingtonpost.com/news/wonk/wp/2015/11/30/why-inequality-is-to-blame-for-the-rise-of-the-islamic-state; Thomas Piketty, "Le Tout-Sécuritaire Ne Suffira Pas," *Le Monde*, Le Blog de Thomas Piketty, November 24, 2015, http://piketty.blog.lemonde.fr/2015/11/24/le-tout-securitaire-ne-suffira-pas-2.

12. "Unemployment and Informality Beset Latin American Youth," *International Labour Organization*, February 13, 2014, www.ilo.org/global/about-the-ilo/newsroom/news/WCMS_235661/lang—en/index.htm; Ian Gordon, "70,000 Kids Will Show Up Alone at Our Border This Year. What Happens to Them?," *Mother Jones*, 2014, www.motherjones.com/politics/2014/06/child-migrants-surge-unaccompanied-central-america.

13. The World Bank Group, "Unemployment, Youth Total (% of Total Labor Force Ages 15–24) (modeled ILO Estimate) | Data | Table."

14. Gyimah-Brempong and Kimenyi, *Youth Policy and the Future of African Development*; Edward Miguel, Shanker Satyanath, and Ernest Sergenti, "Economic Shocks and Civil Conflict: An Instrumental Variables Approach," *Journal of Political Economy* 112, no. 4 (2004), www.jstor.org/stable/10.1086/421174; African Economic Outlook, "Promoting Youth Employment in Africa."

15. Reuters, "Kenya: Two Charged with Terrorism-Related Offenses," *New York Times*, March 19, 2014, www.nytimes.com/2014/03/20/world/africa/kenya-two-charged-with-terrorism-related-offenses.html.

16. Philipp Sandner, "Kenya: Nation Goes On the Offensive Against Muslims," *Deutsche Welle*, February 5, 2014, http://allafrica.com/stories/201402060159.html?viewall=1.

17. Adam Smith International, "Potential for Pwani: Creating Jobs and Skills on Kenya's Coast | Adam Smith International Partner Zone | Guardian Professional," *The Guardian*, www.theguardian.com/global-development-professionals-network/adam-smith-international-partner-zone/mombasa-economy-youth-employment.

18. Government of India, *Creating a Vibrant Entrepreneurial Ecosystem in India*, 2012, www.planningcommission.nic.in/reports/genrep/rep_eco2708.pdf, p. 3.

19. "Daily Chart: Africa's Impressive Growth," *The Economist*, January 6, 2011, www.economist.com/blogs/dailychart/2011/01/daily_chart; McKinsey Global Institute, *Lions on the Move: The Progress and Potential of African Economies* (McKinsey & Company, June 2010), www.mckinsey.com/insights/africa/lions_on_the_move.

20. Amadou Sy, "Jobless Growth in Sub-Saharan Africa," *Brookings Institution Africa in Focus*, January 30, 2014, www.brookings.edu/blogs/africa-in-focus/posts/2014/01/30-jobless-growth-africa-sy#.UvTffP_f7HE.email.

21. Jan Rieländer and Henri-Bernard Solignac-Lecomte, "Jobs: A Tough Time to Be Young in Africa," *GREAT Insights* 3, no. 2 (2014), http://ecdpm.org/great-insights/fostering-more-and-better-jobs/jobs-tough-time-young-africa.

22. Dan Senor and Saul Singer, *Start-Up Nation: The Story of Israel's Economic Miracle* (Twelve, 2011).

23. Barack Obama, "Remarks by the President on a New Beginning at Cairo University" (2009), www.whitehouse.gov/the_press_office/Remarks-by-the-President-at-Cairo-University-6-04-09.

24. Clinton's QDDR was published in 2010. The State Department, under Secretary John Kerry, finalized a second QDDR in 2015.

25. Department of State and USAID, "Leading Through Civilian Power: The First Quadrennial Diplomacy and Development Review" (QDDR) (Department of State; USAID, 2010), p. 11.

26. Ibid, p. 14.

27. "The Quadrennial Diplomacy and Development Review," U.S. Department of State, www.state.gov/s/dmr/qddr.

28. Clinton, *Hard Choices*.

29. Hillary Clinton, "Council on Foreign Relations Address by Secretary of State Hillary Clinton," July 15, 2009, www.cfr.org/diplomacy-and-statecraft/council-foreign-relations-address-secretary-state-hillary-clinton/p19840.

30. The Business Growth Initiative at USAID wrote a report during my tenure at the State Department that captures many of the central concepts behind GEP's ecosystem approach to entrepreneurship: Business Growth Initiative and USAID, *The Entrepreneurship Toolkit: Successful Approaches to Fostering Entrepreneurship*, September 21, 2011, www.state.gov/documents/organization/175149.pdf.

31. Hillary Clinton, "Closing Remarks at the Presidential Summit on Entrepreneurship" (Washington, D.C., 2010), www.state.gov/secretary/20092013clinton/rm/2010/04/140968.htm.

32. GEP entrepreneurship delegation participants included: Shervin Pishevar, Managing Director of Sherpa Ventures and an early investor in the taxi-hailing app Uber; Loretta McCarthy, now Managing Director of the women-focused angel network Golden Seeds; venture capitalist Faisal Sohail; Mike Cassidy of Google; Seth Goldstein, a well-known Silicon Valley social media entrepreneur; CarMax founder Austin Ligon; and Chris Schroeder, who, as mentioned, went on to write a book about the undiscovered Middle East startup scene.

33. Telephone interview with author, January 12, 2015.

34. Dane Stangler and Robert E. Litan, *Where Will the Jobs Come From?* (Ewing Marion Kauffman Foundation, November 31, 2009), http://papers.ssrn.com/abstract=1580139.

35. Jon Clifton, "More Than 100 Million Worldwide Dream of a Life in the U.S.," *Gallup World*, March 21, 2013, www.gallup.com/poll/161435/100-million-worldwide-dream-life.aspx.

36. Stangler and Litan, *Where Will the Jobs Come From?*, p. 2.

37. See Thomas B. Edsall, "Has American Business Lost Its Mojo?," *New York Times*, April 1, 2015, www.nytimes.com/2015/04/01/opinion/thomas-edsall-has-american -business-lost-its-mojo.html.

38. McKinsey & Company, *The Power of Many: Realizing the Socioeconomic Potential of Entrepreneurs in the 21st Century* (October 2011), www.g20yea.com/en/wp -content/uploads/The_Power_of_Many-_McKinsey_Report.pdf.

39. National Endowment for Science Technology and the Arts, *The Vital 6 Percent: How High-Growth Innovative Businesses Generate Prosperity and Jobs* (October 2009), www.nesta.org.uk/sites/default/files/vital-six-per-cent.pdf.

40. Chiara Criscuolo, Peter N. Gal, and Carlo Menon, "DynEmp: New Evidence on Young Firms' Role in the Economy," *Vox: CEPR's Policy Portal*, May 26, 2014, www .voxeu.org/article/dynemp-new-evidence-young-firms-role-economy.

41. McKinsey & Company, *The Power of Many: Realizing the Socioeconomic Potential of Entrepreneurs in the 21st Century*, p. 16.

42. Angel Gurría, "SMEs and Entrepreneurship: The Way Forward to Job Creation and Growth," *OECD |"Bologna+10" High-Level Meeting |* "SMEs and Entrepreneurship: The Way Forward to Job Creation and Growth" (Paris, 2010), www.oecd.org /economy/smesandentrepreneurshipthewayforwardtojobcreationandgrowth.htm.

43. Government of India, *Creating a Vibrant Entrepreneurial Ecosystem in India*, p. 3.

44. Ngozi Okonjo-Iweala, "How Can We Provide Enough Jobs for Young People in Africa?," *The Guardian:* Poverty Matters Blog, July 8, 2013, www.guardian.co.uk /global-development/poverty-matters/2013/jul/08/jobs-young-people-africa-nigeria.

45. e4e, *Education for Employment: Realizing Arab Youth Potential*, April 2011, www.e4earabyouth.com; OECD and IDRC, *New Entrepreneurs and High Performance Enterprises in the Middle East and North Africa*, Competitiveness and Private Sector Development (OECD Publishing, 2013), www.oecd-ilibrary.org/industry-and -services/new-entrepreneurs-and-high-performance-enterprises-in-the-middle-east -and-north-africa_9789264179196-en.

46. Joseph A. Schumpeter, *Capitalism, Socialism And Democracy (1947)* (Kessinger Publishing, 2010).

47. National Endowment for Science Technology and the Arts, *The Vital 6 Percent: How High-Growth Innovative Businesses Generate Prosperity and Jobs*.

48. McKinsey & Company, *The Power of Many*.

49. Thorsten Beck, Asli Demirguc-Kunt, and Ross Levine, "SMEs, Growth, and Poverty: Cross-Country Evidence," *Journal of Economic Growth* 10, no. 3 (September 2005), pp. 199–229, p. 201.

50. Legatum Institute, "The 2012 Legatum Prosperity Index" (2012), www.prosperity .com.

51. Norbert Berthold and Klaus Gründler, *Entrepreneurship and Economic Growth in a Panel of Countries* (2012), http://econstor.eu/bitstream/10419/67487/1/732095115 .pdf, p. 1, p. 27.

52. M.A. Carree and A.R. Thurik, "The Impact of Entrepreneurship on Economic Growth," *International Handbook of Entrepreneurship Research* (2002), http:// hadjarian.org/esterategic/tarjomeh/2-89-karafariny/1.pdf.

53. Aspen Network of Development Entrepreneurs, *ANDE Impact Report 2012: Engines of Prosperity* (Aspen Network of Development Entrepreneurs, 2013), www .aspeninstitute.org/publications/ande-2012-impact-report.

54. Josh Lerner, *Boulevard of Broken Dreams: Why Public Efforts to Boost Entrepreneurship and Venture Capital Have Failed, and What to Do About It* (Princeton University Press, 2012).

55. The World Bank Group, "Population (Total) | Data | Table," http://data .worldbank.org/indicator/SP.POP.TOTL.

56. Lerner, *Boulevard of Broken Dreams*, p. 18.

57. Senor and Singer, *Start-Up Nation: The Story of Israel's Economic Miracle*; Patricia Crisafulli and Andrea Redmond, *Rwanda, Inc.: How a Devastated Nation Became an Economic Model for the Developing World* (Palgrave Macmillan, 2012).

58. International Labor Office, *Global Employment Trends for Youth 2012*, p. 11.

59. Gyimah-Brempong and Kimenyi, *Youth Policy and the Future of African Development*, p. 8.

60. African Economic Outlook, "Promoting Youth Employment in Africa."

61. Miguel, Satyanath, and Sergenti, "Economic Shocks and Civil Conflict: An Instrumental Variables Approach," p. 727.

62. See, for example, Christopher Blattman and Edward Miguel, "Civil War," *Journal of Economic Literature* 48, no. 1 (March 2010), pp. 3–57; Christopher Blattman, Nathan Fiala, and Sebastian Martinez, *Employment Generation in Rural Africa: Mid-Term Results from an Experimental Evaluation of the Youth Opportunities Program in Northern Uganda* (Innovations for Poverty Action, 2011).

63. Sebastian Tong, "Give Me Liberty and Give Me Cash!," *Reuters*, MacroScope, June 22, 2011, http://blogs.reuters.com/macroscope/2011/06/22/give-me-liberty-and -give-me-cash.

64. Vali Nasr, *Forces of Fortune: The Rise of the New Muslim Middle Class and What It Will Mean for Our World* (Free Press, 2009).

65. McKinsey Global Institute, *Lions on the Move: The Progress and Potential of African Economies*; Nicholas Kulish, "Africans Open Fuller Wallets to the Future," *New York Times*, July 20, 2014, www.nytimes.com/2014/07/21/world/africa/economy -improves-as-middle-class-africans-open-wallets-to-the-future.html.

66. *Constitution of the United States*, 1787, www.archives.gov/exhibits/charters /constitution_transcript.html.

67. U.S. Department of Defense, www.defense.gov/casualty.pdf, n.d., www.defense .gov/casualty.pdf; Brown University Watson Institute for International Studies, "Home | Costs of War," *Costs of War Project*, http://watson.brown.edu/costsofwar/; Linda J. Bilmes, *The Financial Legacy of Iraq and Afghanistan: How Wartime Spending Decisions Will Constrain Future National Security Budgets*, HKS Faculty Research Working

Paper Series, March 26, 2013, https://research.hks.harvard.edu/publications/workingpapers/citation.aspx?PubId=8956&type=WPN.

68. Vali Nasr, *The Dispensable Nation: American Foreign Policy in Retreat* (Doubleday, 2013).

69. Stuart W. Bowen, *Learning from Iraq: A Final Report from the Special Inspector General for Iraq Reconstruction* (Special Inspector General for Iraq Reconstruction, March 2013), p. x.

Chapter Three

1. "EcoPost Limited Kenya," www.ecopost.co.ke; Lovelyn Okafor, "Lorna Rutto—Recycling Trash to Cash," *Konnect Africa*, February 5, 2014, www.konnectafrica.net/lorna-rutto-recycling-trash-to-cash; Chege Muigai, "She Quit a Job at the Bank to Make Millions from Waste," *Business Daily*, October 5, 2011, www.businessdailyafrica.com/She-quit-a-job-at-the-bank-to-make-millions-from-waste-/-/539444/1248630/-/item/0/-/ek57x4z/-/index.html.

2. Rob Crilly, "After Violence, Kenya Tourism Struggles," *Christian Science Monitor*, March 4, 2008, www.csmonitor.com/World/Africa/2008/0304/p07s03-woaf.html; "Kenya Tourism in Middle of 'Perfect Storm' as Visitors Stay Away," *Business Day Live*, March 10, 2014, www.bdlive.co.za/africa/africanbusiness/2014/03/10/kenya-tourism-in-middle-of-perfect-storm-as-visitors-stay-away.

3. Philipp Sandner, "Kenya: Nation Goes On the Offensive against Muslims," *Deutsche Welle*, February 5, 2014, http://allafrica.com/stories/201402060159.html?viewall=1; Mark Lowen, "Kenya al-Shabab Terror Recruits 'in It for the Money,'" *BBC News*, January 29, 2014, www.bbc.co.uk/news/world-africa-25934109; "Kenya Arrests Two after Bombs 'Found in Car,'" *BBC News*, March 18, 2014, www.bbc.com/news/world-africa-26624387; "Al Shabaab Planned to Bomb Mombasa Buildings," *The Star*, March 19, 2014, http://allafrica.com/stories/201403191125.html; Tom Odula and Christopher Torchia, "One Kenyan Gumnan, a 'Brilliant Upcoming Lawyer,' Highlights Challenge of Domestic Threats," *Christian Science Monitor*, April 5, 2015, www.csmonitor.com/World/2015/0405/One-Kenyan-gumnan-a-brilliant-upcoming-lawyer-highlights-challenge-of-domestic-threats.

4. Guled Mohammed, "Kenya: The Cost of Harassing Somalis Over Terror," *The Star*, January 9, 2013, http://allafrica.com/stories/201301100532.html.

5. Nick Glass and Tim Hume, "The 'Hallelujah Moment' behind the Invention of the Post-It Note," *CNN.com*, April 4, 2013, http://edition.cnn.com/2013/04/04/tech/post-it-note-history.

6. Hernando de Soto, *Mystery of Capital: Why Capitalism Triumphs in the West and Fails Everywhere Else* (Basic Books, 2003), p. 6.

7. Ibid.

8. Simon Butt, "Taxing Questions," *Inside Indonesia*, 2011, www.insideindonesia.org/feature-editions/taxing-questions.

9. De Soto, *Mystery of Capital*.

10. "Arab Women Entrepreneurs: Untraditional Choice," *The Economist*, July 13, 2013, www.economist.com/news/business/21581740-middle-east-beats-west-female-tech-founders-untraditional-choice.

11. U.S. Department of Commerce, "Foreign Trade: Trade in Goods with Germany | 2013, www.census.gov/foreign-trade/balance/c4280.html.

12. Raymond Gilpin and Steven R. Koltai, *PeaceBrief 134: Using Entrepreneurship to Promote Stability in Fragile Regions* (United States Institute of Peace, 2012).

13. Patricia Crisafulli and Andrea Redmond, *Rwanda, Inc.: How a Devastated Nation Became an Economic Model for the Developing World* (Palgrave Macmillan, 2012), Kindle Locations 1309–10.

14. Jonathan Ortmans, "Rwanda's Rush to Recovery," *Entrepreneurship.org*, 2013, www.entrepreneurship.org/en/Blogs/Policy-Forum-Blog/2013/April/Rwandas-Rush-to-Recovery.aspx; Jeff Chu, "Rwanda Rising: A New Model of Economic Development," *Fast Company*, April 1, 2009, www.fastcompany.com/1208900/rwanda-rising-new-model-economic-development.

15. "Schumpeter: Mammon's New Monarchs," *The Economist*, January 5, 2013, www.economist.com/news/business/21569016-emerging-world-consumer-king-mammons-new-monarchs; McKinsey & Company, "Capturing the $30 Trillion Emerging Market Opportunity," *McKinsey & Company Consumer & Shopper Insights*, May 2013, www.mckinseyonmarketingandsales.com/capturing-the-30-trillion-emerging-market-opportunity.

16. Ibid.

17. John Greenwood, "Kenya Dominating Global Mobile Payments Industry, Posing Monopolistic Threat: World Bank," *Financial Post*, July 24, 2012, http://business.financialpost.com/2012/07/24/kenya-dominating-global-mobile-payments-industry-posing-monopolistic-threat-world-bank.

18. Ignacio Mas and Dan Radcliffe, "Mobile Payments Go Viral: M-PESA in Kenya," *The Capco Institute Journal of Financial Transformation* 32 (2011), pp. 169–82, p. 169.

19. Vanessa Clark, "The Need for Mobile Money Spawns a Startup Ecosystem Across Africa," *TechCrunch*, November 23, 2012, http://techcrunch.com/2012/11/23/mobile-money-spawns-a-startup-ecosystem-across-africa.

20. "Islam and Science: The Road to Renewal," *The Economist*, January 26, 2013, www.economist.com/news/international/21570677-after-centuries-stagnation-science-making-comeback-islamic-world-road; "Arabs and Jews in High-Tech Israel: Bring Them Together," *The Economist*, May 18, 2013, www.economist.com/news/middle-east-and-africa/21578087-can-israeli-arabs-benefit-countrys-start-up-boom-bring-them-together.

21. Neil Ketchley, "How Social Media Spreads Protest Tactics from Ukraine to Egypt," *Washington Post: The Monkey Cage*, February 14, 2014, www.washingtonpost.com/blogs/monkey-cage/wp/2014/02/14/how-social-media-spreads-protest-tactics-from-ukraine-to-egypt.

Chapter Four

1. Interbrand, *Best Global Brands 2013*, 2013, www.rankingthebrands.com/PDF /Best%20Global%20Brands%202013,%20Interbrand.pdf.

2. "Eepybird Studios | Ads People Want to Watch," http://eepybirdstudios.com.

3. United States Census Bureau, 2007 figures, http://quickfacts.census.gov/qfd/states /12/1236550.html.

4. United States Census Bureau, 2007 figures, http://quickfacts.census.gov/qfd/states /12/1245000.html.

5. United States Census Bureau, 2007 figures, http://quickfacts.census.gov/qfd/states /12/12086.html.

6. See, for example, "News—Research Triangle Region, NC," *Research Triangle Regional Partnership*, 2013, www.researchtriangle.org/news-and-events?cat =Rankings.

7. Dane Stangler and Robert E. Litan, *Where Will the Jobs Come From?* (Ewing Marion Kauffman Foundation, November 31, 2009), http://papers.ssrn.com/abstract =1580139.

8. Jon Clifton, "More Than 100 Million Worldwide Dream of a Life in the U.S.," *Gallup World*, March 21, 2013, www.gallup.com/poll/161435/100-million-worldwide -dream-life.aspx.

9. Dane Stangler and Jason Wiens, *The Economic Case for Welcoming Immigrant Entrepreneurs*, March 27, 2014, www.kauffman.org/what-we-do/resources /entrepreneurship-policy-digest/the-economic-case-for-welcoming-immigrant -entrepreneurs.

10. Barack Obama, "President Obama Campaign Rally Roanoke | Video | C -SPAN.org," 2012, www.c-span.org/video/?307056-2/president-obama-campaign-rally -roanoke.

11. Mary Shirley, "Why Institutions Are Essential to Entrepreneurship," in *Creating the Environment for Entrepreneurial Success* (Center for International Private Enterprise, 2013), pp. 12–14, p. 12.

12. Hernando de Soto, *Mystery of Capital: Why Capitalism Triumphs in the West and Fails Everywhere Else* (Basic Books, 2003).

13. The World Bank Group, "Doing Business: Measuring Business Regulations | World Bank Group," www.doingbusiness.org.

14. Mariana Mazzucato, *The Entrepreneurial State: Debunking Public* vs. *Private Sector Myths* (Anthem Press, 2013), p. 66.

15. Ibid.; Mariana Mazzucato, "Mariana Mazzucato: Government—Investor, Risk-Taker, Innovator | Talk Video | TED.com," *TED.com*, June 2013, www.ted.com /talks/mariana_mazzucato_government_investor_risk_taker_innovator; "Association of American Universities," www.aau.edu/research/smartphone.aspx.

16. David Hart, "On the Origins of Google," *National Science Foundation Discoveries*, August 17, 2004, www.nsf.gov/discoveries/disc_summ.jsp?cntn_id=100660.

17. Scott Pace and others, "The Global Positioning System" (RAND Corporation, 1995), www.rand.org/pubs/monograph_reports/MR614.html.

18. Robert D. Hof, "Lessons from Sematech," *MIT Technology Review*, July 25, 2011, www.technologyreview.com/news/424786/lessons-from-sematech.

19. Small Business Innovation Research, "SBIR.gov," www.sbir.gov; Jeff Madrick, "Innovation: The Government Was Crucial After All by Jeff Madrick," *The New York Review of Books*, April 24, 2014, www.nybooks.com/articles/archives/2014/apr/24/innovation-government-was-crucial-after-all.

20. Mazzucato, *The Entrepreneurial State*.

21. John Maynard Keynes, *The End of Laissez-Faire: The Economic Consequences of the Peace* (Prometheus Books, Great Minds Series, 2004).

22. Mazzucato, *The Entrepreneurial State*, p. 73, p. 83.

Chapter Five

1. Lewis Carroll, *Alice's Adventures in Wonderland & Through the Looking-Glass* (CreateSpace Independent Publishing Platform, 2014).

2. Congressional Budget Office, *The Budget and Economic Outlook: Fiscal Years 2013 to 2023*, February 2013, www.cbo.gov/sites/default/files/cbofiles/attachments/43907-BudgetOutlook.pdf.

3. The Henry J. Kaiser Family Foundation, "2013 Survey of Americans on the U.S. Role in Global Health," November 7, 2013, http://kff.org/global-health-policy/poll-finding/2013-survey-of-americans-on-the-u-s-role-in-global-health; Curt Tarnoff and Marian Leonardo Lawson, *Foreign Aid: An Introduction to U.S. Programs and Policy* (Congressional Research Service, April 20, 2012), http://usoda.eads.usaidallnet.gov/docs/foreign-aid-intro.pdf.

4. Ibid.

5. CSIS Executive Council on Development, *Our Shared Opportunity: A Vision for Global Prosperity*, 2013, http://csis.org/publication/our-shared-opportunity, p. 9.

6. USAID, "Foreign Aid Explorer" https://explorer.usaid.gov.

7. See, for example, Kori N. Schake, *State of Disrepair: Fixing the Culture and Practices of the State Department* (Hoover Institution Press, 2012).

8. OECD, "International Development Statistics (IDS) Online Databases," 2014, www.oecd.org/dac/stats/idsonline.htm. Full methodology is on file with the author.

9. Costs of War, "Pentagon Budget | Costs of War," www.costsofwar.org/article/pentagon-budget.

10. ANDE also relied on OECD's CRS data, and the organization's 2014 Impact Report and informal conversations with ANDE Executive Director Randall Kempner confirm that ANDE and I employed similar methodologies. See Aspen Network of Development Entrepreneurs, "ANDE 2014 Impact Report: State of the SGB Sector," 2015, www.andeglobal.org/blogpost/737893/220813/Impact-Report-State-of-the-Small-and-Growing-Business-Sector.

11. A complete description of the methodology is on file with the author.

12. See The White House: Office of the Press Secretary, "FACT SHEET: U.S. Investment in Entrepreneurship," July 25, 2015, www.whitehouse.gov/the-press-office/2015/07/25/fact-sheet-us-investment-entrepreneurship.

13. Author's notes.

14. The Millennium Challenge Corporation compact with Indonesia was finalized at $600 million, and the country received over $500 billion from USAID between 2010 and 2012. Millennium Challenge Corporation, "Indonesia Compact | Millennium Challenge Corporation," www.mcc.gov/pages/countries/program/indonesia-compact; United States Government, "ForeignAssistance.gov," n.d., www.foreignassistance.gov /web/Default.aspx.

15. Millennium Challenge Corporation, "Indonesia Compact | Millennium Challenge Corporation"; "Millennium Challenge Compact between the United States of America Acting through The Millennium Challenge Corporation and the Republic of Indonesia," 2011, https://assets.mcc.gov/agreements/compact-indonesia .pdf.

16. Chemonics International Inc., *Egypt's Competitiveness Program, Fourteenth Quarterly Report, January 1–March 31, 2014*, May 11, 2014, http://pdf.usaid.gov/pdf_docs /pa00jtr9.pdf.

17. Ernesto Londoño, "U.S. to Partially Resume Military Aid to Egypt," *Washington Post*, April 23, 2014, www.washingtonpost.com/world/national-security/us-to-partially -resume-military-aid-to-egypt/2014/04/22/b25f68c6-ca91-11e3-93eb-6c0037dde2ad _story.html.

18. Congressional Budget Office, *Modernizing the Army's Rotary-Wing Aviation Fleet*, November 2007, www.cbo.gov/sites/default/files/cbofiles/ftpdocs/88xx/doc8865 /11-30-helicopters.pdf.

19. USAID, "Strengthening Entrepreneurship and Enterprise Development (SEED) | Fact Sheet | Egypt," https://www.usaid.gov/egypt/fact-sheets/strengthening -entrepreneurship-and-enterprise-development-seed.

20. "Fact Sheet: A New Beginning—The Presidential Summit on Entrepreneurship," www.whitehouse.gov, 2010, www.whitehouse.gov/sites/default/files/rss_viewer /fact_sheet_entrepreneurship_summit_deliverables.pdf.

21. OPIC, "OPIC Board Approves $455 Million for Five Investment Funds Targeting Middle East & North Africa," June 24, 2010, www.opic.gov/press-releases /2010/opic-board-approves-455-million-five-investment-funds-targeting-middle-east -nort.

22. Vali Nasr, *The Dispensable Nation: American Foreign Policy in Retreat* (Doubleday, 2013), p. 30.

23. David Rohde, *Beyond War: Reimagining American Influence in a New Middle East* (Viking Adult, 2013), Kindle Locations 1561–62.

24. Paul Brinkley, *War Front to Store Front: Americans Rebuilding Trust and Hope in Nations Under Fire* (Turner Publishing Company, 2014).

25. Schake, *State of Disrepair: Fixing the Culture and Practices of the State Department*, Kindle Locations 1883–86.

26. Jose Fernandez, "Remarks at the North Africa Partnership for Economic Opportunity (NAPEO) Conference," in *Second NAPEO U.S.—Maghreb Entrepreneurship Conference* (Marrakesh, Morocco, 2012), www.state.gov/e/eb/rls/rm/2012/181519 .htm; U.S. Department of State, "State Dept. Fact Sheet on U.S.—Maghreb Entrepre-

neurship Conference | IIP Digital," January 16, 2012, http://iipdigital.usembassy.gov/st
/english/texttrans/2012/01/20120116143059su0.3981549.html#axzz31aHIDRTW.

27. U.S. Department of State and the Broadcasting Board of Governors—Office
of the Inspector General—Office of Inspections, *Inspection of the Bureau of Economic and Business Affairs*, February 2014, https://oig.state.gov/system/files/222651
.pdf, p. 1, p. 8.

Chapter Six

1. Thomas L. Friedman, "Start-Up America: Our Best Hope," *New York Times*,
February 15, 2014, www.nytimes.com/2014/02/16/opinion/sunday/friedman-start-up
-america-our-best-hope.html.

2. Partnership for Public Service and Booz Allen Hamilton, *Building the Enterprise:
A New Civil Service Framework*, April 1, 2014, http://ourpublicservice.org/publications
/download.php?id=18.

3. Kori N. Schake, *State of Disrepair: Fixing the Culture and Practices of the State
Department* (Hoover Institution Press, 2012), Kindle Locations 717–21.

4. Susan Dominus, "Megan Smith: 'You Can Affect Billions of People,'" *New York
Times*, October 31, 2014, www.nytimes.com/2014/11/02/magazine/megan-smith-you
-can-affect-billions-of-people.html.

5. Max Stier, "Written Testimony of Max Stier President and CEO Partnership for
Public Service: 'A More Efficient and Effective Government: Cultivating the Federal
Workforce,'" 2014, http://ourpublicservice.org/publications/download.php?id=349.

6. Ibid.

7. Quintan Wiktorowicz, "Challenges for Public Sector Innovation," *Designing for
Government*, January 15, 2014, www.designingforgovernment.com/1/post/2014/01
/challenges-for-public-sector-innovation-by-quintan-wiktorowicz.html.

8. Schake, *State of Disrepair*, Kindle Locations 736–38.

9. Joshua Miller, "'Millennials' Cynical about Politics," *The Boston Globe*, April 29,
2014, www.bostonglobe.com/metro/2014/04/29/millenials-cynical-about-politics-new
-harvard-poll-year-olds-finds/7f6e3tRFBS2GioZvkf71XL/story.html.

10. Steve Coll, "Hard on Obama," *New York Review of Books*, July 11, 2013, www
.nybooks.com/articles/archives/2013/jul/11/vali-nasr-hard-on-obama.

11. Ian Urbina, "The Shopping List as Policy Tool," *New York Times*, January 25,
2014, www.nytimes.com/2014/01/26/sunday-review/the-shopping-list-as-policy-tool
.html; Josh Hicks, "No One Knows the Size of the Government's Contracted Workforce," *Washington Post*, March 12, 2015, www.washingtonpost.com/blogs/federal-eye
/wp/2015/03/12/no-one-knows-the-size-of-the-governments-contracted-workforce;
CSIS Defense-Industrial Initiatives Group, *Defense Contract Trends: U.S. Department
of Defense Contract Spending and the Supporting Industrial Base* (Center for Strategic
and International Studies, May 2011), http://csis.org/files/publication/110506_CSIS
_Defense_Contract_Trends-sm2.pdf.

12. "Global Supplier Diversity Program," AT&T, www.att.com/gen/corporate
-citizenship?pid=17724.

13. Wal-Mart Stores Inc., "U.S. Securities and Exchange Commission Filing: Form 10-K for the Fiscal Year Ended January 31, 2014," March 21, 2014, www.sec.gov /Archives/edgar/data/104169/000010416914000019/wmtform10-kx13114.htm.

14. In the interest of full disclosure, my firm, Koltai & Co. LLC, is a small outfit that pursues work in the entrepreneurship (and economic development) sectors, but has never sought or received a U.S. government contract in this space.

15. Lorenzo Piccio, "Top USAID Contract Awardees: A Primer," Devex, 2013, www.devex.com/news/top-usaid-contract-awardees-a-primer-81198.

16. "U.S. Agency for International Development," www.usaid.gov.

17. "USAID: A History of US Foreign Aid," *Devex*, 2014, https://pages.devex.com /usaid-history.

18. Schake, *State of Disrepair*, Kindle Locations 1549–50.

19. IRD's rise from mom-and-pop humanitarian NGO to "beltway bandit" behemoth has been the subject of investigations by the *Washington Post* and federal auditors. In January 2015 USAID announced it would suspend IRD from work due to "serious misconduct in IRD's performance, management, internal controls, and present responsibility." A U.S. district judge overturned the suspension in August 2015, but, as of November 2015, IRD claims USAID has nonetheless unfairly kept it in "suspension-related purgatory." See Scott Higham, Jessica Schulberg, and Steven Rich, "Big Budgets, Little Oversight in War Zones," *Washington Post*, May 5, 2014, www .washingtonpost.com/investigations/doing-well-by-doing-good-the-high-price-of -working-in-war-zones/2014/05/04/2d5f7ca8-c715-11e3-9f37-7ce307c56815_story.html; Scott Higham and Steven Rich, "Auditors Examining Nonprofit Organization's Confidentiality Agreements, 'Revolving Door,'" *Washington Post*, May 6, 2014, www.washingtonpost.com/investigations/auditors-examining-nonprofits -confidentiality-agreements-and-revolving-door/2014/05/06/92c2723a-d539-11e3-95d3 -3bcd77cd4e11_story.html; Scott Higham and Steven Rich, "USAID Suspends IRD, Its Largest Nonprofit Contractor in Iraq and Afghanistan," *Washington Post*, January 26, 2015, www.washingtonpost.com/investigations/usaid-suspends-ird-its-largest -nonprofit-contractor-in-iraq-and-afghanistan/2015/01/26/0cafe16a-a599-11e4-a2b2 -776095f393b2_story.html; Molly Anders, "USAID Ordered to Undo Illegal IRD Suspension," Devex, August 5, 2015, www.devex.com/news/usaid-ordered-to-undo-illegal -ird-suspension-86665; Bryan Koenig, "Nonprofit Says USAID Shut It Out Despite Lifted Suspension," *Law360*, November 11, 2015, www.law360.com/articles/725302 /nonprofit-says-usaid-shut-it-out-despite-lifted-suspension.

20. Greg Jaffe and Jim Tankersley, "Capital Gains: Spending on Contracts and Lobbying Propels a Wave of New Wealth in D.C.," *Washington Post*, November 18, 2013, www.washingtonpost.com/national/capital-gains-spending-on-contracts-and -lobbying-propels-a-wave-of-new-wealth-in-d-c/2013/11/17/6bd938aa-3c25-11e3-a94f -b58017bfee6c_story.html.

21. Piccio, "Top USAID Contract Awardees: A Primer."

22. Ibid.

23. Higham, Schulberg, and Rich, "Big Budgets, Little Oversight in War Zones."

24. Steven Tomanelli, FAR Workshop, November 4–5, 2014, Sterling, Virginia.

25. Ibid.

26. Interview with Nancy Glaser, June 10, 2014.

27. Ibid.

28. Stuart W. Bowen, *Learning from Iraq: A Final Report from the Special Inspector General for Iraq Reconstruction* (Special Inspector General for Iraq Reconstruction, March 2013), p. x.

29. Farhad Manjoo, "Why Government Tech Is So Poor," *The Wall Street Journal*, October 16, 2013, http://online.wsj.com/news/articles/SB10001424052702304384104579139461596987366.

30. Ibid.

31. Craig Timberg and Lena H. Sun, "Some Say Health-Care Site's Problems Highlight Flawed Federal IT Policies," *Washington Post*, October 9, 2013, www.washingtonpost.com/business/technology/some-say-health-care-sites-problems-highlight-flawed-federal-it-policies/2013/10/09/d558da42-30fe-11e3-8627-c5d7de0a046b_story.html.

32. Jerry Markon and Alice Crites, "Accenture, Hired to Help Fix HealthCare.gov, Has Had a Series of Stumbles," *Washington Post*, February 9, 2014, www.washingtonpost.com/politics/accenture-hired-to-fix-healthcaregov-has-troubled-past/2014/02/09/3d1a2dc4-8934-11e3-833c-33098f9e5267_story.html.

33. Interview with David van Slyke, Syracuse University, January 23, 2014.

34. David Rohde, *Beyond War: Reimagining American Influence in a New Middle East* (Viking Adult, 2013), Kindle Locations 125–26.

Chapter Seven

1. "MEST: School and Incubator for African Startups," http://mestghana.wpengine.com.

2. Kwabena Gyimah-Brempong and Mwangi S. Kimenyi, *Youth Policy and the Future of African Development*, Africa Growth Initiative, 2013, www.brookings.edu/research/reports/2013/04/15-youth-policy-african-development-kimenyi, p. 16; Alicia Robb, "Ghana and the Next Wave of Entrepreneurship in Africa," *Entrepreneurship.org*, 2013, www.entrepreneurship.org/en/Blogs/Policy-Forum-Blog/2013/May/Ghana-and-the-Next-Wave-of-Entrepreneurship-in-Africa.aspx.

3. My firm, Koltai & Co. LLC, performed an analysis of Ghana's entrepreneurship ecosystem for the United Kingdom's Department for International Development. See Steven R. Koltai, Matthew Muspratt, and Victor Mallet, *Final Report: Ghana Entrepreneurship Ecosystem Analysis* (Koltai & Co. LLC, October 25, 2013), http://koltai.co/notebook/ghana-report.

4. See Mary Shirley, "Why Institutions Are Essential to Entrepreneurship," in *Creating the Environment for Entrepreneurial Success* (Center for International Private Enterprise, 2013), pp. 12–14.

5. Reuters, "Israel Tech Firms Raise $930 Mln in Q2 from Venture Capital," *Reuters*, July 15, 2014, http://in.reuters.com/article/2014/07/15/israel-venturecapital-idINL6N0PQ1UV20140715.

6. Fareed Zakaria, "Under Netanyahu, Israel Is Stronger than Ever," *Washington Post*, May 9, 2012, http://articles.washingtonpost.com/2012-05-09/opinions/35455414 _1_meir-dagan-existential-threat-kadima-party.

7. Dan Senor and Saul Singer, *Start-Up Nation: The Story of Israel's Economic Miracle* (Twelve, 2011), p. 11.

8. Ibid.

9. See George Foster and others, *Entrepreneurial Ecosystems Around the Globe and Company Growth Dynamics* (World Economic Forum, September 2013), www3 .weforum.org/docs/WEF_EntrepreneurialEcosystems_Report_2013.pdf; Omidyar Network, *Accelerating Entrepreneurship in Africa: Understanding Africa's Challenges to Creating Opportunity-Driven Entrepreneurship*, 2013, www.omidyar.com/news /omidyar-network-releases-report-challenges-faced-african-entrepreneurs-and -recommendations; "Tech Entrepreneurs in the Middle East: Start-Up Spring," *The Economist*, July 13, 2013, www.economist.com/news/business/21581737-clusters-internet -firms-are-popping-up-all-over-region-start-up-spring; Jonathan Ortmans, "Starting Up Africa," *Entrepreneurship.org*, February 3, 2014, http://entrepreneurship.org/Blogs /Policy-Forum-Blog/2014/February/Starting-Up-Africa.aspx.

10. The World Bank Group, "Ranking of Economies: Doing Business," *Doing Business*, 2015, www.doingbusiness.org/rankings.

11. "GEM Global Entrepreneurship Monitor," www.gemconsortium.org.

12. Global Entrepreneurship and Institute, "GEDI Index," *GEDI Index*, 2013, www .thegedi.org/research/gedi-index.

13. Startup Genome, *Startup Ecosystem Report 2012: Part One*, 2012, doi: 10.4324/9780203165829_PART_ONE.

14. Aspen Network of Development Entrepreneurs, *Entrepreneurial Ecosystem Diagnostic Toolkit*, December 2013, www.aspeninstitute.org/publications/entrepreneurial -ecosystem-diagnostic-toolkit.

15. Ibid.

16. "Start-Up Chile," n.d., www.startupchile.org; "Entrepreneurs in Latin America: The Lure of Chilecon Valley," *The Economist*, October 13, 2012, www.economist.com /node/21564589.

17. Vanessa Van Edwards, "Start-Up Chile: Growing Pains of the Chilecon Valley," *Huffington Post*, May 7, 2013, www.huffingtonpost.com/vanessa-van-edwards /start-up-chile_b_3225480.html; "Entrepreneurs in Latin America: The Lure of Chilecon Valley."

18. "Start-Up Chile: Heading toward Failure or Success?," *Entrepreneurship Ecosystem Insights by Endeavor Insight*, September 9, 2014, www.ecosysteminsights.org /start-up-chile-heading-toward-failure-or-success.

19. Senor and Singer, *Start-Up Nation: The Story of Israel's Economic Miracle*; "BIRD Foundation," www.birdf.com/?CategoryID=317&ArticleID=374.

20. Senor and Singer, *Start-Up Nation*.

21. Brad Feld, *Startup Communities: Building an Entrepreneurial Ecosystem in Your City* (Wiley, 2012); Antonio Regalado, "It's Up to You, Entrepreneurs," *MIT Tech-*

nology Review, July 15, 2013, www.technologyreview.com/news/516521/its-up-to-you
-entrepreneurs.

22. "Entrepreneurs: If in Doubt, Innovate," *The Economist,* February 2, 2013, www
.economist.com/news/special-report/21570834-nordic-region-becoming-hothouse
-entrepreneurship-if-doubt-innovate.

23. Patricia Crisafulli and Andrea Redmond, *Rwanda, Inc.: How a Devastated Nation Became an Economic Model for the Developing World* (Palgrave Macmillan, 2012); Raymond Gilpin and Steven R. Koltai, *PeaceBrief 134: Using Entrepreneurship to Promote Stability in Fragile Regions* (United States Institute of Peace, 2012).

24. Michael Goldberg, "Beyond Silicon Valley: Growing Entrepreneurship in Transitioning Economies," *Coursera,* 2014, www.coursera.org/course/entpecon.

25. Ibid.

26. In the interests of full disclosure, I am a board member of Babson Global.

27. Diane Mulcahy, "Six Myths about Venture Capitalists," *Harvard Business Review,* May 2013, http://hbr.org/2013/05/six-myths-about-venture-capitalists/ar/1.

28. Aspen Network of Development Entrepreneurs, *Entrepreneurial Ecosystem Diagnostic Toolkit.*

29. Business Growth Initiative and USAID, *The Entrepreneurship Toolkit: Successful Approaches to Fostering Entrepreneurship,* September 21, 2011, www.state.gov /documents/organization/175149.pdf.

30. Koltai, Muspratt, and Mallet, *Final Report: Ghana Entrepreneurship Ecosystem Analysis.*

31. Endeavor Global, "Impact Dashboard | Endeavor Global," accessed February 26, 2014, www.endeavor.org/impact/assessment.

Chapter Eight

1. Omidyar Network, *Accelerating Entrepreneurship in Africa: Understanding Africa's Challenges to Creating Opportunity-Driven Entrepreneurship,* 2013, www .omidyar.com/news/omidyar-network-releases-report-challenges-faced-african -entrepreneurs-and-recommendations.

2. Asma Ajroudi, "In Abu Dhabi, a New Start-Up 'Accelerator' Promises More Success Stories," *Al Arabiya News,* November 21, 2014, http://english.alarabiya.net/en /business/2014/11/21/In-Abu-Dhabi-a-new-start-up-accelerator-is-promising-more -success-stories-.html.

3. Monitor Deloitte and Aspen Network of Development Entrepreneurs, *Growth and Opportunity: The Landscape of Organizations That Support Small and Growing Businesses in the Developing World,* September 2013, www.aspeninstitute.org /publications/growth-opportunity-landscape-organizations-support-small-growing -businesses-developing.

4. Endeavor Global, "Impact Dashboard | Endeavor Global," www.endeavor.org /impact/assessment; Endeavor Global, *Endeavor Global: Goals and Impact,* 2012, https:// www.yumpu.com/en/document/view/48034782/endeavors-goals-and-impactpdf.

5. Startup Weekend, "Startup Weekend," http://startupweekend.org; Regina Schrambling, "How Startup Weekend Got Its Start," *Entrepreneur*, February 22, 2011, www.entrepreneur.com/article/218104.

6. Artha Venture Challenge, "Get Funding | Raise Funds | Artha Venture Challenge," www.arthaventurechallenge.com.

7. Rice Alliance for Technology and Entrepreneurship, "Rice Business Plan Competition," http://ricebusinessplancompetition.com/about.html; Tara Henke and others, *Entrepreneurial Impact: The Rice Business Plan Competition, 2001–12*, August 2012, http://alliance.rice.edu/uploadedFiles/RBPC/2012_RBPC_ImpactReport.pdf.

8. Anya Kamenetz, "General Assembly Provides Entrepreneurial Skills to a Chosen Few," *Fast Company*, January 2012, www.fastcompany.com/1793488/general-assembly-provides-entrepreneurial-skills-chosen-few.

9. General Assembly, "Transforming Thinkers into Creators," https://generalassemb.ly.

10. "Startup Institute," www.startupinstitute.com.

11. "Top 25 Colleges for Entrepreneurship for 2015 (Undergrad)," *Entrepreneur*, October 2014, www.entrepreneur.com/slideshow/237330; "Top 25 Colleges for Entrepreneurship for 2015 (Graduate Programs)," *Entrepreneur*, October 2014, www.entrepreneur.com/article/237323.

12. One Hen Inc., "One Hen Inc: Learn, Play, Make a Difference," www.onehen.org.

13. Lemonade Day, "Lemonade Day," http://lemonadeday.org.

14. Babson College, "Babson Global | About Babson | Babson College," www.babson.edu/about-babson/global/babson-global/pages/home.aspx.

15. "GEM Global Entrepreneurship Monitor," www.gemconsortium.org.

16. "VentureWell Lean LaunchPad," http://venturewell.org/lean-launchpad.

17. "PechaKucha 20x20," www.pechakucha.org.

18. Impact Hub, "What Is Impact Hub," www.impacthub.net/what-is-impact-hub/.

19. Entrepreneurs' Organization, "About EO: Entrepreneurs' Organization," www.eonetwork.org/about.

20. The Indus Entrepreneurs, "Entrepreneurship: Largest Entrepreneurs Network Worldwide," http://tie.org.

21. The Organization of Pakistani Entrepreneurs of North America, "About OPEN DC," www.openwashingtondc.org/index.php?option=com_content&task=view&id=111&Itemid=54.

22. "SEED | Stanford Institute for Innovation in Developing Economies," https://seed.stanford.edu.

23. Demeter Network, "DEMETER Entrepreneurs Support Network," www.demeternetwork.com.

24. Kim Lachance Shandrow, "This Firm Offers Startups Mentorship for a Fee, Not an Equity Stake," *Entrepreneur*, March 17, 2014, www.entrepreneur.com/article/232292.

25. Tomio Geron, "Top Startup Incubators and Accelerators: Y Combinator Tops with $7.8 Billion in Value," *Forbes.com*, April 30, 2012, www.forbes.com/sites

/tomiogeron/2012/04/30/top-tech-incubators-as-ranked-by-forbes-y-combinator-tops
-with-7-billion-in-value; Y Combinator, "Y Combinator," www.ycombinator.com.

26. J.J. Colao, "MassChallenge: A Colossal Startup Accelerator That's 100% Free,"
Forbes.com, March 13, 2012, www.forbes.com/sites/jjcolao/2012/03/13/masschallenge
/2; MassChallenge, "MassChallenge," http://masschallenge.org.

27. Nina Lincoff, "Tech Haven Venture Hive Puts Focus on Education," *Miami
Today*, October 1, 2014, www.miamitodaynews.com/2014/10/01/tech-haven-venture
-hive-puts-focus-education; "Venture Hive," *Venture Hive*, www.venturehive.co.

28. Lauren Granger, "From iHub to the BRCK: How Ushahidi Became an African
Success Story," *Ventureburn*, February 26, 2014, http://ventureburn.com/2014/02/from
-ihub-to-the-brck-how-ushahidi-became-an-african-success-story; iHub, "iHub | Tech-
nology, Innovation, Community," www.ihub.co.ke.

29. "Unreasonable East Africa," *Unreasonable East Africa*, http://unreasonable
eastafrica.org.

30. Flat6Labs, "Flat6Labs," www.flat6labs.com; Sawari Ventures, "Home | Sawari
Ventures," www.sawariventures.com; Ajroudi, "In Abu Dhabi, a New Start-Up 'Accelerator' Promises More Success Stories."

31. Ibid.

32. OECD, *Entrepreneurship at a Glance 2014* (OECD Publishing, July 14, 2014),
www.oecd-ilibrary.org/industry-and-services/entrepreneurship-at-a-glance-2014
_entrepreneur_aag-2014-en; Diane Mulcahy, "Six Myths about Venture Capitalists,"
Harvard Business Review, May 2013, http://hbr.org/2013/05/six-myths-about-venture
-capitalists/ar/1.

33. Carol Tice, "Money for Startups: Top 10 Seed Funders of 2013," *Forbes.com*,
January 15, 2014, www.forbes.com/sites/caroltice/2014/01/15/money-for-startups-top
-10-seed-funders-of-2013; "Number of Active Seed Venture Capital Investors in 2013
Matches Record High. Here's Who Did the Most Seed Deals," *CB Insights*, January 3,
2014, www.cbinsights.com/blog/2013-seed-venture-capital-investors.

34. 500 Startups, "We are #500 Strong," http://500.co; SeedInvest, "FAQs," https://
www.seedinvest.com/faqs.

35. Golden Seeds, "Golden Seeds," www.goldenseeds.com.

36. U.S. National Advisory Board on Impact Investing, *Private Capital, Public
Good*, June 2014, www.nabimpactinvesting.org/s/Private_Capital_Public_Good-pamn
.pdf.

37. "Kickstarter," www.kickstarter.com/help/stats.

38. Katherine Noyes, "Why Investors Are Pouring Millions into Crowdfunding,"
Forbes.com, April 17, 2014, http://fortune.com/2014/04/17/why-investors-are-pouring
-millions-into-crowdfunding.

39. Ibid.

40. Small Enterprise Assistance Funds, "SEAF," accessed November 26, 2014,
http://seaf.com.

41. Hernando de Soto, *Mystery of Capital: Why Capitalism Triumphs in the West
and Fails Everywhere Else* (Basic Books, 2003).

42. First Access, "First Access," www.firstaccessmarket.com.

43. Adam Koppeser, "Flat6Labs Demo Day Shines Spotlight on Egyptian Entrepreneurship," *Daily News Egypt*, May 21, 2014, www.dailynewsegypt.com/2014/05/21/flat6labs-demo-day-shines-spotlight-egyptian-entrepreneurship.

44. Najib Razak, "4th Global Entrepreneurship Summit 2013," 2013, https://najibrazak.com/blog/4th-global-entrepreneurship-summit-2013.

45. Jonathan Ortmans, "Malaysia in the Limelight," *Ewing Marion Kauffman Foundation Policy Dialogue on Entrepreneurship*, 2013, www.kauffman.org/blogs/policy-dialogue/2013/july/malaysia-in-the-limelight.

46. Barack Obama, "Remarks by President Obama in Address to the United Nations General Assembly" (The White House, 2014), www.whitehouse.gov/the-press-office/2014/09/24/remarks-president-obama-address-united-nations-general-assembly.

47. SRI International, *Making an Impact: Assessing the Benefits of Ohio's Investment in Technology-Based Economic Development Programs*, September 2009, http://development.ohio.gov/files/otf/Final_OH_Impact_Exec_Sum_SRI.pdf.

48. Ibid, p. 4.

49. "Investment Climate | Embassy of the United States Kigali, Rwanda," http://rwanda.usembassy.gov/investment_climate_.html.

50. AsiaBiz, "Entrepreneur Pass (EntrePass) Scheme," www.asiabiz.sg/how-to/relocate/entrepass-guide.

51. Tobias Buck, "Spain Hopes New Law to Cut Red Tape Will Attract Entrepreneurs," *The Financial Times*, June 2, 2013, www.ft.com/intl/cms/s/0/fe6c8276-ca0b-11e2-8f55-00144feab7de.html?siteedition=intl#axzz3KxrPbN36; Nick Leiber, "At Spain's Door, a Welcome Mat for Entrepreneurs," *New York Times*, November 22, 2014, www.nytimes.com/2014/11/23/business/international/at-spains-door-a-welcome-mat-for-entrepreneurs-.html?_r=0.

52. Patricia Crisafulli and Andrea Redmond, *Rwanda, Inc.: How a Devastated Nation Became an Economic Model for the Developing World* (Palgrave Macmillan, 2012).

53. Türkiye Ekonomi Politikaları Araştırma Vakfı and Global Entrepreneurship Program Turkey, *Global Entrepreneurship Program Turkey Activity Report 2011–2012*, 2012.

54. "US EY Entrepreneur of the Year Program—EY—United States," www.ey.com/US/en/About-us/Entrepreneurship/Entrepreneur-Of-The-Year.

55. "Distinguished Entrepreneurs | Blank Center | Babson College," www.babson.edu/Academics/centers/blank-center/academy-of-distinguished-entrepreneurs/Pages/home.aspx.

56. "Thiel Fellowship," https://web.archive.org/web/20150525111157/http://www.thielfellowship.org/2014/06/peter-thiel-announces-2014-class-of-thiel-fellows/

57. Richard Feloni, "Mark Cuban Explains the Real Reason He Joined the *Shark Tank* Cast," *Business Insider*, December 1, 2014, www.businessinsider.com/mark-cuban-on-shark-tank-2014-12.

58. "Inspiring, Empowering and Connecting Entrepreneurs | Wamda.com," *Wamda*, www.wamda.com.

59. Global Entrepreneurship Week, "About | Global Entrepreneurship Week," *Wamda*, www.gew.co/about. See also, Rebecca Burn-Callander, "Global Entrepre-

neurship Week: What You Need to Know," *The Telegraph*, November 16, 2014, www
.telegraph.co.uk/finance/businessclub/11234163/Global-Entrepreneurship-Week-what
-you-need-to-know.html.

Chapter Nine

1. Tom Burridge, "Funding Jihad: Al-Shabab Cash Lures in Young Kenyans,"
BBC News, December 11, 2014, www.bbc.com/news/world-africa-30419987. See also
Mark Lowen, "Kenya Al-Shabab Terror Recruits 'In It for the Money,'" *BBC News*,
January 29, 2014, www.bbc.co.uk/news/world-africa-25934109.

2. Hernando de Soto, "The Capitalist Cure for Terrorism," *Wall Street Journal*,
October 10, 2014, http://online.wsj.com/articles/the-capitalist-cure-for-terrorism
-1412973796.

3. Dan Senor and Saul Singer, *Start-Up Nation: The Story of Israel's Economic
Miracle* (Twelve, 2011), p. 206.

4. International Labor Office, *Global Employment Trends 2014*, January 21, 2014,
www.ilo.org/global/research/global-reports/global-employment-trends/2014/WCMS
_233953/lang—en/index.htm, p. 62.

5. Stuart W. Bowen, *Learning from Iraq: A Final Report from the Special Inspector
General for Iraq Reconstruction* (Special Inspector General for Iraq Reconstruction,
March 2013); The Editorial Board, "The Afghan Legacy," *New York Times*, July 4,
2013, www.nytimes.com/2013/07/05/opinion/the-afghan-legacy.html?hp&_r=0.

6. Author discussion with Steven Tomanelli at FAR Workshop, November 4–5,
2014, Sterling, Virginia.

7. Bowen, *Learning from Iraq: A Final Report from the Special Inspector General
for Iraq Reconstruction*, p. x.

8. John F. Sopko, *Statement for the Record: Reducing Waste, Improving Efficien-
cies, and Achieving Savings in U.S. Reconstruction of Afghanistan* (Special Inspector
General for Afghanistan Reconstruction, April 18, 2013), www.sigar.mil/pdf/testimony
/2013-04-18 SIGAR Written Testimony_Senate State and Foreign Ops Sub.pdf, p. 1.

9. See, for example, USAID Office of the Inspector General, *Semiannual Report
to the Congress: April 1–September 30, 2012* (USAID, 2012), http://oig.usaid.gov
/node/1439.

10. Scott Higham and Steven Rich, "Whistleblowers Say USAID's IG Removed
Critical Details from Public Reports," *Washington Post*, October 22, 2014, www
.washingtonpost.com/investigations/whistleblowers-say-usaids-ig-removed-critical
-details-from-public-reports/2014/10/22/68fbc1a0-4031-11e4-b03f-de718edeb92f_story
.html.

11. Organization for Economic Cooperation and Development, "Creditor Reporting System," *OECD.StatExtracts*, http://stats.oecd.org/Index.aspx?DataSetCode
=crs1.

12. USAID Office of the Inspector General, *Audit of USAID/Pakistan's Firms Project (Audit Report No. G-391-12-001-P)*, November 3, 2011, https://oig.usaid.gov/sites
/default/files/audit-reports/g-391-12-001-p.pdf, p. 1.

13. USAID Office of the Inspector General, *Audit of USAID/Sri Lanka's Biz Plus Program (Audit Report No. 5-383-14-005-P)*, September 8, 2014, http://oig.usaid.gov /sites/default/files/audit-reports/5-383-14-005-p.pdf, p. 2.

14. USAID Office of the Inspector General, *Audit of USAID/West Africa's Peace through Development II Program (Audit Report No. 7-625-14-001-P)*, March 28, 2014, http://oig.usaid.gov/sites/default/files/audit-reports/7-625-14-001-p.pdf p. 2.

15. Congressional Budget Office, *Modernizing the Army's Rotary-Wing Aviation Fleet*, November 2007, www.cbo.gov/sites/default/files/cbofiles/ftpdocs/88xx/doc8865 /11-30-helicopters.pdf; Department of the Air Force, *United States Air Force FY 2011 Budget Estimates*, February 2010, www.saffm.hq.af.mil/shared/media/document/AFD -100128-072.pdf.

16. The World Bank Group, "United States Overview," 2014, www.worldbank.org /en/country/unitedstates/overview#1; The World Bank Group, "IBRD: Percentage of Total Shares by Country," https://finances.worldbank.org/Shareholder-Equity/IBRD -Percentage-of-Total-Shares-by-Country/rnib-fv94.

17. Rebecca M. Nelson, *Multilateral Development Banks: U.S. Contributions FY2000–FY2013* (Congressional Research Service, 2013), http://fas.org/sgp/crs/misc /RS20792.pdf.

18. The World Bank Group, "United States Overview."

19. The World Bank Group, *Annual Report 2014*, 2014, www.worldbank.org/en /about/annual-report.

20. George Ingram, "Building Aid Transparency: More Data, Better Data," *Brookings Institution UpFront Blog*, June 13, 2014, www.brookings.edu/blogs/up-front/posts /2014/06/13-building-aid-transparency-ingram.

21. Myra Sessions, "Overview of the President's Emergency Plan for AIDS Relief (PEPFAR)," *Center for Global Development*, n.d., www.cgdev.org/page/overview-president ?s-emergency-plan-aids-relief-pepfar; U.S. Department of State, "The United States President's Emergency Plan for AIDS Relief," n.d., www.pepfar.gov.

22. Ibid.

23. See, for example, the *Washington Post* Editorial Board, "How a Bush Administration Initiative to Combat HIV/AIDS Is Saving Lives," *Washington Post*, April 9, 2009, www.washingtonpost.com/wp-dyn/content/article/2009/04/08/AR2009040803706 .html; Nicholas D. Kristof, "The Coffin-Maker Benchmark," *New York Times*, July 7, 2012.

24. U.S. Department of State, "International Programs to Combat Trafficking in Persons," June 20, 2014, www.state.gov/j/tip/rls/fs/2014/227662.htm.

25. International Justice Mission, *Human Trafficking Prioritization Act*, n.d., http:// freedomcommons.ijm.org/sites/all/modules/ijm/custom_pages/resources/1-Step-1 -Voice-FAQ.pdf?v=1.0.

26. "OPIC: Overseas Private Investment Corporation," www.opic.gov.

27. Todd Moss, Benjamin Leo, and Beth Schwanke, *OPIC Unleashed: Strengthening US Tools to Promote Private-Sector Development Overseas*, August 14, 2013, www .cgdev.org/publication/opic-unleashed-strengthening-us-tools-promote-private-sector -development-overseas.

28. U.S. National Advisory Board on Impact Investing, *Private Capital, Public Good*, June 2014, www.nabimpactinvesting.org/s/Private_Capital_Public_Good-pamn.pdf.

29. George Ingram, *Adjusting Assistance to the 21st Century: A Revised Agenda for Foreign Assistance Reform* (The Brookings Institution, July 2014), www.brookings.edu /research/papers/2014/07/22-foreign-assistance-reform-ingram; George Ingram and others, "Strengthening U.S. Government Development Finance Institutions," *Brookings Institution UpFront Blog*, December 16, 2013, www.brookings.edu/blogs/up-front /posts/2013/12/16-strengthening-development-finance-kharas-ingram.

30. Todd Moss and Benjamin Leo, *A Consolidated U.S. Development Bank: Reorganizing Private Sector Policy Tools in Emerging Markets and Fragile States* (Center for Global Development, April 6, 2011), www.cgdev.org/doc/blog/globaldevelopment /USDB White Paper - April 2011.pdf, p. 1.

31. Sarah Jane Staats, "Can You Hear Me Now? Obama's Global Development Council Listening, Not Yet Talking," *Center for Global Development*, July 1, 2013, http://international.cgdev.org/blog/can-you-hear-me-now-obama?s-global -development-council-listening-not-yet-talking.

32. President's Global Development Council, *Beyond Business as Usual*, April 14, 2014, www.whitehouse.gov/sites/default/files/docs/gdc_memo_for_the_president_final .pdf.

33. Curt Tarnoff, *Millennium Challenge Corporation* (Congressional Research Service, July 1, 2014), http://fas.org/sgp/crs/row/RL32427.pdf; "Millennium Challenge Corporation," www.mcc.gov.

34. Lorenzo Piccio, "Top USAID Contract Awardees: A Primer," *Devex*, 2013, https://www.devex.com/news/top-usaid-contract-awardees-a-primer-81198.

35. Farhad Manjoo, "Why Government Tech Is So Poor," *Wall Street Journal*, October 16, 2013, http://online.wsj.com/news/articles/SB1000142405270230438410457 9139461596987366; Craig Timberg and Lena H. Sun, "Some Say Health-Care Site's Problems Highlight Flawed Federal IT Policies," *Washington Post*, October 9, 2013, www.washingtonpost.com/business/technology/some-say-health-care-sites-problems -highlight-flawed-federal-it-policies/2013/10/09/d558da42-30fe-11e3-8627 -c5d7de0a046b_story.html.

36. Josh Hicks, "Watchdog's View: An Interview with the Department of Energy Inspector General," *Washington Post*, October 20, 2014, www.washingtonpost.com /blogs/federal-eye/wp/2014/10/20/watchdogs-view-an-interview with-the-department -of-energy-inspector-general.

37. Author discussion with Steven Tomanelli at FAR workshop, November 4–5, 2014, Sterling, Virginia.

38. See U.K. Parliament Public Accounts Committee, *Forty-Seventh Report: Contracting Out Public Services to the Private Sector*, February 26, 2014, www.publications .parliament.uk/pa/cm201314/cmselect/cmpubacc/777/77702.htm. The U.K. government encounters problems similar to the United States vis-à-vis contracting.

39. "VEGA: Volunteers for Economic Growth Alliance," http://vegaalliance.org.

40. U.K. Department for International Development, *DFID Smart Rules: Better Programme Delivery*, July 17, 2014, www.gov.uk/government/publications/dfid-smart

-rules-better-programme-delivery; Tom Wingfield and Pete Vowles, "DFID Is Changing Its Approach to Better Address the Underlying Causes of Poverty and Conflict: Can It Work?," *World Bank People, Spaces, Deliberation Blog*, October 21, 2014, http://blogs .worldbank.org/publicsphere/dfid-changing-its-approach-better-address-underlying -causes-poverty-and-conflict-can-it-work-guest.

41. Interview with Steven Schooner, George Washington University, October 2, 2014.

42. Interview with David van Slyke, Syracuse University, January 23, 2014.

43. Interview with Steven Schooner, George Washington University, October 2, 2014.

44. Josh Hicks, "No One Knows the Size of the Government's Contracted Workforce," *Washington Post*, March 12, 2015, www.washingtonpost.com/blogs/federal-eye /wp/2015/03/12/no-one-knows-the-size-of-the-governments-contracted-workforce.

45. Nancy Birdsall and William D. Savedoff of the Center for Global Development are strong advocates for "cash on delivery" arrangements in aid. See Nancy Birdsall and William D. Savedoff, *Cash on Delivery: A New Approach to Foreign Aid*, 2011, www .cgdev.org/publication/9781933286600-cash-delivery-new-approach-foreign-aid.

46. "Federal Employment | Peace Corps," *Peace Corps*, www.peacecorps.gov/about /jobs/workingpc/fedemp.

47. Tom Fox, "Critiques of the Presidential Management Fellows Program," *Washington Post*, November 17, 2014, www.washingtonpost.com/blogs/on-leadership /wp/2014/11/17/critiques-of-the-presidential-management-fellows-program.

48. Juliet Eilperin and Nancy Scola, "White House Launches Digital Team for Online Upgrades," *Washington Post*, August 11, 2014, www.washingtonpost.com /business/economy/white-house-launches-digital-team-for-online-upgrades/2014/08 /11/ee7f3830-217c-11e4-8593-da634b334390_story.html.

49. Susan Dominus, "Megan Smith: 'You Can Affect Billions of People,'" *New York Times*, October 31, 2014, www.nytimes.com/2014/11/02/magazine/megan-smith -you-can-affect-billions-of-people.html.

50. Mohana Ravindranath, "HHS Adds New Class of 'Entrepreneurs-in-Residence,'" *Washington Post*, December 7, 2014, www.washingtonpost.com/business/on-it/hhs -adds-new-class-of-entrepreneurs-in-residence/2014/12/05/92a4cfd6-7a71-11e4-9a27 -6fdbc612bff8_story.html.

51. "Partnership for Public Service: Good Government Starts with Good People," *Partnership for Public Service*, http://ourpublicservice.org.

52. Partnership for Public Service and IDEO, *Innovation in Government*, February 3, 2011, http://ourpublicservice.org/OPS/publications/viewcontentdetails.php?id=155.

53. Quintan Wiktorowicz, "Challenges for Public Sector Innovation," *Designing for Government*, January 15, 2014, www.designingforgovernment.com/1/post/2014/01 /challenges-for-public-sector-innovation-by-quintan-wiktorowicz.html.

54. Scott Higham, Jessica Schulberg, and Steven Rich, "Big Budgets, Little Oversight in War Zones," *Washington Post*, May 5, 2014, www.washingtonpost.com /investigations/doing-well-by-doing-good-the-high-price-of-working-in-war-zones/2014 /05/04/2d5f7ca8-c715-11e3-9f37-7ce307c56815_story.html.

55. USAID, *USAID Forward Progress Report 2013*, 2013, www.usaid.gov /usaidforward.

56. USAID, U.S. Global Development Lab: The Catalog (version 1.5), 2014, www.usaid.gov/sites/default/files/documents/15396/USAID_Lab_The_Catalog_V1 _5.pdf.

57. As noted in chapter 5, the White House issued a press release in 2015 during the Global Entrepreneurship Summit in Kenya that outlines United States' entrepreneurship efforts. See the White House: Office of the Press Secretary, "FACT SHEET: U.S. Investment in Entrepreneurship," July 25, 2015, www.whitehouse.gov /the-press-office/2015/07/25/fact-sheet-us-investment-entrepreneurship.

58. USAID, "Grand Challenges for Development," www.usaid.gov/grandchallenges.

59. Telephone interview with author, January 12, 2015.

60. Ibid.

Index

Surnames starting with "al" and "el" are alphabetized by the following portion of name.

AAAS Science & Technology Policy Fellowships, 167
Abraham, Magid, xx
Abu Dhabi, 11, 130–31
Accelerating Entrepreneurship in Africa (Monitor Group), 101
Accelerators: connecting and sustaining entrepreneurs via, 127, 142; and entrepreneurship ecosystems, 108; and GEP, 117; government role in, 171; as key to startups, 102–03; role of, 131–35. *See also specific incubators and accelerators*
Accenture, 95
Adobe, 124
Advertising Age, 51
Afghanistan: economic development efforts in, 149, 152; foreign aid to, 91–94, 152; U.S. invasion and occupation of, 35, 71, 154
Africa: barriers to entrepreneurism in, 119; economic development in, 20–21, 23; entrepreneurial ecosystem in, 101–02, 109; foreign investment

regulations in, 137; incubators and accelerators in, 130; innovation in, 7; microfinance in, 158; nongovernmental organizations in, 89; poverty in, 23. *See also* East Africa; Middle East and North Africa (MENA); West Africa; *specific countries*
African Development Bank, 70, 154
African Development Foundation, 70
Agriculture, 8, 70, 73, 91, 123, 132, 155
Agriculture Department (U.S.), 70
Agriculture Education Health Entrepreneurship, 73
AH-64 Apache helicopter, 78, 144, 154
AIDS. *See* HIV/AIDS programs
Airbnb, 129
Alan, Jonathan, xix
El Alfi, Ahmed, xx, 10, 11, 28, 171
Algeria, 1, 27
al-Qaeda, 2–3, 20, 35
al-Qaeda in the Maghreb (AQIM), 35

al-Shabaab, 35, 38, 147
Altop, Didem, xx
Amazon, 101
American University in Cairo, 10–11
ANDE. *See* Aspen Network for Development Entrepreneurs
Android, 10
Angel investors, 10, 43, 61, 74, 102, 113, 132, 150, 170
Ansari, Shahid, xx
Apache helicopters, 78, 144, 154
Apple, 7, 53, 59, 89, 95, 102–03
AQIM (al-Qaeda in the Maghreb), 35
Arab Spring, 9, 12, 19–20, 22, 33, 77, 81, 89, 147
Arellano, Hilda "Bambi," xx, 77–78
Arista Networks, 140
Armenia, 4, 158
ARPANET, 63
Artha Networks Inc., 121
Artha Venture Challenge (AVC), 123
Ashley, Bennett, xxi
Asian Development Bank, 70, 154
Aspen Institute, 81
Aspen Network for Development Entrepreneurs (ANDE), 71, 106, 115, 133
AT&T, 90
Auditude, 124
AVC (Artha Venture Challenge), 123
Awadallah, Bassem, 21

Babson College, 106, 113, 121, 126, 138, 140
Babson Global, 113, 121, 126, 143
Ballinger, Peter, xx
Banks, funding from, 43, 58, 102, 113–14, 154
Bayh-Dole Act of 1980, 58
Bayrasli, Elmira, xx
Bean, Leon Leonwood, 53
Beatty, Pete, xxi
Bechtolsheim, Andreas, 140
Behrman, Greg, xix, 116
Belgium, 20
Bell, Alexander Graham, 55
Berliner, Jim, xxi
Bernstein, Carl, 146

Berthold, Norbert, 31
BIRD Foundation, 105, 107, 108, 135
Biz plus program, 153
Blank, Steve, 127
BNSF Railway, 46
Boeing, 54, 62
Boko Haram, 20, 35
Bolivia, 8
Boly, Richard, xx
Bondy, Buffy, xxi
Boorstin, Louis, xxi
Borofsky, Yael, 63
Bouazizi, Mohamed, 20, 33, 147
Boulevard of Broken Dreams (Lerner), 32
Bowen, Stuart, 94, 152
Branson, Richard, 6–7
Breakthrough Institute, 63
Brightsen, Laura, xx
Brin, Sergey, 59
Brinkley, Paul, 80
Britain. *See* United Kingdom
Brookings Institution, 158
Bujorean, Ovi, xx
Bureaucracy, 13–14, 80, 87–88, 146, 168
Bureau of Economic, Energy, and Business Affairs (EEB), 66–67, 75
Bureau of Economic and Business Affairs (EBA), 66
Burgess, Anthony, 146
Bush, George W., 36, 60, 80, 157, 160
Business climate, 107, 111, 135, 138. *See also* Entrepreneurship ecosystems
Business plan competitions: and entrepreneurship ecosystems, 27, 111–17, 122–24, 140, 142, 171; GEP sponsorship of, 10, 75; identification of entrepreneurs via, 150

Caglar, Esen, xx
Cairo Initiative, 24, 27, 36, 74–75, 79–80, 82, 116, 170
Cakmakci, Canan, xx
Cakmakci, Mete, xx
Callear, Mildred, xxi
Camp, Garrett, 7
Campbell Soup Company, 53
Canada, 52, 72

Capital in the Twenty-First Century (Piketty), 22
CarMax, 10
Case Western Reserve University, 108
Cassidy, Mike, xx, 10, 11
CBA (Office of Commercial and Business Affairs), 65–66
Census Bureau, 62
Center for Entrepreneurship and Executive Development (CEED), 134
Center for Global Development, 159
Center for Strategic and International Studies (CSIS), 20, 70
Central African Republic, 119
Chang, Ha-Joon, 7
Charles, Cleveland, xx
Chemonics, 78, 91–92, 153
Chile, 107–08, 136
China: economic growth in, 47; entrepreneurial ecosystem in, 105; foreign assistance to, 91; labor pool in, 22
Christian Science Monitor on economic development in Africa, 21
Cisco, 11, 53
Civil society, 2–3, 13, 19, 29, 33–34, 49, 170
ClaimSync, 101
Clinton, Hillary: on foreign policy tools, 19, 36; on GEP, xx, 27, 66, 75–77, 149; and QDDR, 24–25; and women's empowerment, 45
Coca-Cola, 26, 51, 114
Cold War, 75, 134
Coll, Steve, 89
Commerce Department (U.S.), 70
Commercialization, 5, 39–40, 60–61
Commission on Wartime Contracting in Iraq and Afghanistan (U.S.), 93
Congressional Research Service, 69
Consumers, 32, 34, 42, 82
Contracting. *See* Government contracting and procurement
Cornell University, 106
Corruption, 21, 42, 94, 110, 114, 138
Costco, 46
Cotton, Anthony, xx
Coworking spaces, 127

Creativity, 146. *See also* Innovation
Creditor Reporting System (CRS), 70–71, 73–74
Crowdfunding, 133
Crowley, Michael, xxi
CSIS (Center for Strategic and International Studies), 20, 70
Cuban, Mark, 141
Curley, Nina, 131

DARPA. *See* Defense Advanced Research Projects Agency
Dasewicz, Agnes, xxi
Dead capital, 134
Defense Advanced Research Projects Agency (DARPA), 58, 60, 63, 135
Defense Department (U.S.), 60–61, 70, 90, 152, 154–55
Dehgan, Alex, xx
Demeter Network, 128, 142
DEMO Africa, 101
Democracy: as American value, 53, 61, 170; and Arab Spring protests, 12, 19; economic growth linked to, 33; as foreign policy tool, 24
Department for International Development (DFID, UK), 41, 117
de Soto, Hernando, 2, 12, 19, 21, 43, 134, 147
Development banks, 155, 159–60. *See also specific development banks*
Development Innovation Ventures, 169
DFID (Department for International Development, UK), 41, 117
Disney, Walt, 3
Disrupt Battlefield (*TechCrunch*), 101
Dropbox, 129
Drucker, Peter, 5
Ducker, Mike, xx

E-Agency proposal, 150–51, 159
Ease of doing business, 135, 138
East Africa, 4, 23, 38, 46–47, 57. *See also specific countries*
EBA (Bureau of Economic and Business Affairs), 66
Economic development, 15, 25, 35, 45, 68, 110, 149, 153, 155, 162, 169

The Economist on small technology
  firms in Middle East, 7
EcoPost, 38–39
ECP (Egypt Competitiveness Project),
  77–78, 153
Edison, Thomas, 3
Education, 41–42, 44, 69, 73, 91, 140,
  148, 160
EEB (Bureau of Economic, Energy, and
  Business Affairs), 66–67, 75
EepyBird Studios, 51–52, 55
Egypt: Arab Spring protests in, 19–20,
  33; entrepreneurship ecosystem in,
  110, 117, 122, 131, 136, 142, 144, 171;
  GEP in, 9–13, 27–28, 48–49, 77–79,
  96, 154, 170; and NAPEO, 82; public
  opinion of U.S. in, 55–56;
  unemployment in, 1
Egypt Competitiveness Project (ECP),
  78, 153
Einstein, Albert, 148
Elete Salon & Spa, 53
Embassies, 76–77, 82
Emerging economies, 30, 40, 46, 120,
  130, 151
Endeavor, xx, 41, 118, 120
Energy Department (U.S.), 60, 70
EntrePass (Singapore), 137–38
Entrepreneurship: benefits of, 37–49;
  defined, 3–8, 29, 71–72; as effective
  foreign assistance, 42–45, 65–83; as
  equalizing force, 48–49; as investment
  opportunity, 45–48; job creation via,
  19–36, 170–72; peace through,
  170–72; pedagogy, 112, 125–26;
  policy support for, 12–15, 61–64;
  programming, 13–14, 26, 35, 66,
  68, 80, 120, 150, 156, 162, 172; as
  U.S. value, 51–64. *See also*
  Entrepreneurship ecosystems;
  specific programs
Entrepreneurship ecosystems, 9–12,
  101–44; celebrating entrepreneurs,
  139–44; connecting and sustaining
  entrepreneurs, 127–31;
  Entrepreneurship Ecosystem Model,
  12, 27, 104, 111–12; foreign aid
  investment in, 42, 155; funding

startups, 131–35; and GEP, 26, 30;
  identification of entrepreneurs,
  122–24; and public policy, 135–38;
  training for entrepreneurs, 124–27;
  in U.S., 56–58
Entrepreneurs' Organization (EO), 128
Environmental Protection Agency,
  69–70
Equity, 44, 46, 97, 107, 123, 129–31, 158
Eritrea, 58, 106
Ernst & Young, 123, 140
Ethiopia, 126
Europe and European Union, 2, 46, 55,
  85, 125, 151. *See also specific countries*
Export-Import Bank, 70
Exports, 8, 44, 46, 54
Extremism, 2, 33, 144, 147

F-14 aircraft, 64
F-35 aircraft, 92
Facebook, 6–7, 9, 89, 102–03
ElFadeel, Ashraf & Haytham, xx,
  9–10, 11
Fakharany, Wael, xx
Fast Company: on entrepreneurship,
  139; on General Assembly, 125
FDI. *See* Foreign direct investment
Federal Trade Commission (FTC), 70
FedEx, 6
Feld, Brad, 108, 113
Fenn, Donna, 140
Ferguson, Dave, xxi
First Access, 134–35
FitzGerald, Des, xxi
500 Startups, 101, 132
Flat6Labs, 11, 130–32, 136, 170–71
FMO (development bank), 41
Forbes: on entrepreneurship, 139; on
  incubators, 132; on MEST, 101; on
  Y Combinator, 129
Forces of Fortune (Nasr), 34
Ford, Henry, 55
Foreign assistance: for entrepreneurship
  programs, 44, 65–83, 104; on
  entrepreneurship programs, 13; as
  foreign policy tool, 25; procurement
  system for, 161. *See also specific aid
  agencies*

Foreign direct investment (FDI), 45, 108, 112, 114, 137, 143, 159
Foreign policy: and entrepreneurship ecosystems, 104, 144; entrepreneurship promotion as, 14–15, 41, 43, 49, 54, 56, 75, 77, 172; and foreign direct investment, 89; QDDR on, 24–25
Foreign Service Institute, 66
Fortune on entrepreneurship, 139
Fragile states, 20, 33, 35, 40, 171
France, 29, 61
Franklin Fellowship Program, 24, 87, 167
Freedom Support Act of 1992 (FSA), 134
Friedman, Thomas, 21, 85
Fry, Art, 39
FTC (Federal Trade Commission), 70
Funding: from banks, 43, 58, 102, 113–14, 154; crowdfunding, 133; for GEP, 75–79, 115–17, 156; for startups, 43–44, 131–35, 170; for World Bank, 70. *See also* Grants; Seed funds; *specific funding sources*

Garissa University College, 38
Garrett, Anthony, xxi
Gates, Bill, 6, 55, 119
Gates Foundation, 89
Gedalin, Martin, xx
GEDI (Global Entrepreneurship and Development Institute), 106, 138
GEM. *See* Global Entrepreneurship Monitor
General Assembly (entrepreneurship program), 125, 129
GEP. *See* Global Entrepreneurship Program
Germany, 45–46, 61, 72, 151, 158
Gerson Lehrman Group (GLG), 128
Ghana: economic development in, 23; entrepreneurship ecosystem in, 101–02, 104, 114, 117; entrepreneurship in, 8, 139; labor market in, 102; startups in, 102, 125, 128. *See also* Meltwater Entrepreneurial School of Technology (MEST)
Ghandour, Fadi, 148
Ghonim, Wael, 48–49

Gillon, Peter, xxi
Ginting, Eka, xx
Gittleman, Sol, xxi
Glaser, Nancy, 93, 94
Glass, Randy, xxi
GLG (Gerson Lehrman Group), 128
GLG Share, 128–29
Global Attitudes Project (Pew Research Center), 56
Global Consortium of Entrepreneurship Education, 126
Global Development Council, 160, 170
Global Entrepreneurship and Development Institute (GEDI), 106, 138
Global Entrepreneurship Monitor (GEM), 5, 106, 126, 138
Global Entrepreneurship Program (GEP): author's experience running, 34, 65–66; and business plan competitions, 124; creation of, 9, 25; in Egypt, 9–13, 96, 122, 136, 153–54, 170; funding constraints for, 75–79, 115–17, 156; in Indonesia, 110; and job creation, 26–28; and State Department bureaucracy, 67; in Turkey, 122, 136, 140, 170; and USAID, 87, 153–54
Global Entrepreneurship Summit, 72, 136
Global Impact Investing Network, 133
Global Innovation Index, 106
Global Social Benefit Institute, 126
Globe & Mail on EepyBird, 52
Goldberg, Michael, 108–09
Golden Seeds, 133
Goldman Sachs, 114
Google: in Egypt, 11, 49; and entrepreneurship ecosystems, 101, 103; executives entering government service, 168; foreign policy influence of, 89; and GEP, 28; innovation by, 53; job creation by, 6–7; in Rwanda, 46
Government contracting and procurement: entrepreneurism lacking in, 14, 68; flaws in, 68, 86, 149, 161; and foreign aid, 71; grants

Government contracting and
procurement (cont.)
vs., 165; modernization of, 77;
recommendations for, 162–63, 164;
and small businesses, 91–93, 151, 161.
See also specific departments
Grand Challenges for Development
initiative, 169
Grants: for accelerators and seed
funding, 130–31, 137; for Afghanistan
reconstruction, 93; contracting and
procurement vs., 165; and NAPEO,
82; for research and innovation,
59–60, 135; for startups, 122–23.
See also specific organizations
Green, Janice, xxi
Griffin, Sean, xxi
Grobe, Fritz, 51–52
Gross, Leo, xxi
Gründler, Klaus, 31
Guantanamo Bay detainees, 2, 35
The Guardian on MEST, 101
Guatemala, 63
Guinea, 103
Gupta, Kapil, xx

H-1B visas, 55
Haiti, 105, 121, 130
Hamas, 35
Hariton, Lorraine, 45
Hartono, Martin, xx
Harvard University Innovation Lab,
126
Health and Human Services
Department (U.S.), 70
Healthcare.gov, 36, 90, 95, 96, 149
Helms, Jesse, 42
Helmy, Atef, 136
Heritage Foundation, 106
Hersman, Erik, 7
Hessan, Diane, xxi, 125
Hewlett, William, 105, 111
Hezbollah, 35
Higgins, Jackie Strasser, xx
High-growth businesses, 5, 31
HIV/AIDS programs, 156–57, 160
Hollerith, Herman, 62
Holthouse, Michael, 126

Homeland Security Department
(U.S.), 70
Hook, Lisa, xxi
Hormats, Bob, xx, 159
Human trafficking, 157
Hume, Cameron, xix, 76–77
Humphreys, Mark, xxi
Hungary, 134
Hunnicutt, Travis, xx
Hynes, Ken, xxi

ICC (International Criminal Court), 38
IDEO (design consultancy), 169
Idowu, Daniel, xxi
IEEE Global History Network, 63
iHub, 130
Incubators: connecting and sustaining
entrepreneurs via, 127, 142; and
entrepreneurship ecosystems, 108; and
GEP, 117; government role in, 171; as
key to startups, 102–03; role of,
131–35. *See also specific incubators
and accelerators*
India: economic growth in, 47;
foreign assistance to, 91; job
creation in, 23, 30
Indiegogo, 133
Indonesia: and Cairo Initiative, 27–28;
entrepreneurship ecosystems in,
110–11, 139; entrepreneurship in, 4;
GEP in, 27–28, 76, 79; tax revenues
in, 44
infoDev, 41
Infrastructure, 44, 88, 105, 160
Ingram, George, 158
Innovation: bureaucracy vs., 88, 97; and
commercialization, 39; as core of
entrepreneurship, 4–7, 146; and
education, 41, 148–49; and
entrepreneurship ecosystems, 43, 106,
107, 135; government contracting and
procurement lacking, 14, 67–69, 166,
169–70; in U.S. entrepreneurship,
52–54, 56, 58–61, 63
Instagram, 7, 46, 103, 150
Intel, 60, 63
Intellectual property (IP), 6, 40, 42–43,
48, 57, 112, 135

Inter-American Development Bank, 70, 154

Inter-American Foundation, 70

International Criminal Court (ICC), 38

International Justice Mission, 157

International Labor Organization, 148

International Relief and Development (IRD), 92

International trade, 8, 44, 46, 54

Internet, 8, 57, 59–60, 63

IP. *See* Intellectual property

iPhone, 59, 95

Iraq: counterinsurgency in, 3; reconstruction and economic development efforts, 90, 92–94, 149, 152, 155; unemployment in, 1, 20, 22; U.S. invasion and occupation of, 35, 71

IRD (International Relief and Development), 92

Islamic State, 2–3, 20, 22, 147

Israel: entrepreneurship ecosystem in, 103, 105, 107–08, 135–36; entrepreneurship in, 32; unemployment in, 2; venture capital in, 131

Jamaica, 32

Japan, 47, 60–61

Jenkins, Jesse, 63

Jimmy Buffett's Margaritaville Café, 52

Job creation, 19–36; economic growth linked to, 28–34, 153–55; and entrepreneurship ecosystem, 109, 118; funding for programs, 77–78; and GEP, 24–28; government's role in, 34–36, 153–55; peace linked to, 28–34; in U.S., 54; via entrepreneurship, 3, 5

Jobs, Steve, 6, 52, 55, 59, 102, 105, 139

JOBS Act of 2013, 110, 133

John Snow Inc., 91

Jordan, 1–2, 6, 27–28, 48, 55–56, 79, 97

JPMorgan Chase, 46

J/TIP (Office to Monitor and Combat Trafficking in Persons), 157

Jump, Leslie, xx, 10

Justice Department (U.S.), 70

Kabak, Wayne, xxi

Kagame, Paul, 46

Kalanick, Travis, 7

Kalil, Tom, 169

Kamdani, Shinta, xx

Kamel, Sherif, xx

Kamel, Tarek, xx

Karabey, Ali, xx

Kauffman Foundation, 29, 106

Kelley, Donna, xxi

Kempner, Randall, xx

Kenya: EcoPost in, 38–39; entrepreneurship ecosystem in, 57; Global Entrepreneurship Summit in, 72; incubators and accelerators in, 130–31; innovation in, 7, 46–47; microfinance in, 158; unemployment in, 22

Keshishian, Peggy, xx

Keynes, John Maynard, 61

Kickstarter, 133

Kimathi, Al-Amin, 23

Kimmel, Wayne, 133

Kiper, Selcuk, xx

Kirsner, Scott, 140

Kirusa, 101

Kiser, Cheryl, xxi

Kngine, 10–11

Kodak, 7

Kofi Annan Centre, 117

Koh, Cindy, xx

Koko King, 8

Koltai & Co., 117

Koltai, Benjamin, xxi

Koltai, Katherine, xxi

Koltai, Nicholas, xxi

Koltai-Levine, Marian, xxi

Kranenburg, Rik, xxi

Kubrick, Stanley, 146

Kullman, Rebecca, xxi

Kuwait, 1

Labor Department (U.S.), 70

Landais, Alix, xxi

Lanier, Jaron, 7

Latin America, 107, 118, 135, 158. *See also specific countries*

Laurent, Pierre, xxi

Lean LaunchPad Educator Seminars, 127
Lebanon, 27–28, 55–56, 79
Legatum Institute, 31, 106
Legatum Prosperity Index, 138
Legvold, Robert, xxi
Lemonade Day, 126
Leo, Benjamin, 158, 159–60
Lerner, Josh, 32
Letterman, David, 51
Ley de Emprendedores
    (Entrepreneurship Law, Spain), 138
Libya, 82
Ligon, Austin, 10–11
Lincoln, Abraham, 82
Litan, Bob, 5
Lockheed Martin, 96
Lucas, Paul, xxi
Lyseggen, Jorn, 102

Malaysia, 136
Mali, 21
Malik, Adeel, 21
Manjoo, Farhad, 94
Mann, Vanessa Holcomb, xx
Marciel, Scot, xix, 76
Marcopoulos, George, xxi
Margolis, Jeff, xx
Marshall, George C., 19
Marshall Plan approach, 19, 24, 46, 96,
    151–52, 154
Massachusetts Institute of Technology
    (MIT), 128
MassChallenge, 129, 132
Mauritania, 81
Maxmin, Jim, xxi
Mayer, Jane, xxi
Mazzucato, Mariana, 59, 61
MCC. *See* Millennium Challenge
    Corporation
McCarthy, Loretta, xx
McClure, Dave, 101, 132
McKinsey & Company, 29–30, 47
Medicaid & Medicare, 69
Meltwater Entrepreneurial School of
    Technology (MEST), 101–04, 111–18,
    125, 130, 132, 139
MENA. *See* Middle East and
    North Africa

Mentorship programs, 150
Microfinance programs, 124, 157–58
Microsoft, 129
Middle class, 33–34, 47
Middle East and North Africa (MENA):
    demographics in, 1; entrepreneurship
    ecosystems in, 108, 118, 119, 120, 130,
    139, 141; entrepreneurship promotion
    in, 12, 24, 28–30, 54, 75, 154, 170–71;
    and GEP, 25; social unrest in, 3,
    21–23, 147–48; unemployment in, 1;
    and USAID, 92; women entrepreneurs
    in, 7, 45. *See also specific countries*
Millennium Challenge Corporation
    (MCC), 70, 76–77, 115, 155, 158,
    160, 165
Millennium Development
    Corporation, 155
Miller, Mark, xxi
Mills, Cheryl, xx
MIT (Massachusetts Institute of
    Technology), 128
MIT Technology Review, 60
Mohammad, Ramez, 119
Mo Ibrahim Foundation, 106
Monitor Group, 101
Moore's Law, 21
Morocco, 6, 27, 81
Morrill Land-Grant Act of 1862, 59
Mortgages, 43–44, 76, 113, 134
Moss, Todd, 158, 160
M-PESA, 47
MQ-1 Predator drones, 147, 154
Mubarak, Hosni, 48
Mulholland, Daniel, xxi
Muslim Brotherhood, 33
Muslim Human Rights Forum, 23
Muspratt, Matthew, xxi

NAPEO. *See* North African Partnership
    for Economic Opportunity
Nasr, Vali, 1, 34, 80, 89
National Business Incubator
    Association, 129
National Nanotechnology Initiative, 63
National Science Foundation, 59,
    63, 70
National Security Council, 80

Naval Appropriations Act of 1915, 62
Netherlands, 72, 75, 158
New York Times: on entrepreneurship,
139; on entrepreneurship in refugee
camps, 6; on Middle East conflicts,
21; on Silicon Valley vs.
Washington, D.C., 85
Nicaragua, 113
Nicolosi, Giuseppe, xxi
Nides, Tom, xx, 159
Niger, 21, 113
Nigeria, 30, 147
Noah, Jason, xxi
Nokia, 108
Nongovernmental organizations
(NGOs), 41, 89, 104, 111, 115–20, 139,
143, 169. *See also specific
organizations*
Nonprofits, 92, 120, 129, 133, 157–58,
169–70
North Africa. *See* Middle East and
North Africa (MENA)
North African Partnership for Economic
Opportunity (NAPEO), 81–82, 96
Noyce, Robert, 60

Obama, Barack: Cairo Initiative, 24–25,
27, 36, 75, 79–80, 82, 116, 149, 170;
and entrepreneurship promotion,
57–58, 66, 77; Global Entrepreneurship
Summit (2015), 72; on Malaysia's
entrepreneurship, 136; Summit on
Entrepreneurship (2010), 13
OECD countries: economic growth in,
46; job creation in, 30
OECD Creditor Reporting System
(CRS), 70–71, 73–74
Office of Commercial and Business
Affairs (CBA), 65–66
Office of Global AIDS Coordinator
(OGAC), 157
Office of Multilateral Trade Affairs, 81
Office of Technology and Policy, 169
Office to Monitor and Combat
Trafficking in Persons (J/TIP), 157
OGAC (Office of Global AIDS
Coordinator), 157
Ohio Third Frontier programs, 137, 142

Omidyar Network, 5, 41, 101, 106, 119
One Hen, 126
O'Neill, Maura, xx
Open Society Foundations, 89
Open World Leadership Center, 70
OPIC. *See* Overseas Private Investment
Corporation
Organization for Economic Cooperation
Development (OECD), 70–71, 73–74.
See also OECD countries
Organization of Pakistani Entrepreneurs
of North America, 128
Ortmans, Jonathan, xx
Osei, Albert, 8
Other Transaction Authorities
(OTAs), 165
Overseas Private Investment
Corporation (OPIC), 70, 79, 155–60
Ozen, Emir, xx

PACE (Partnering to Accelerate
Entrepreneurship), 73, 169
Pacific Railway Act of 1862, 62
Pacific Telegraph Act of 1860, 62
Packard, David, 105
Page, Larry, 59
Pakistan, 35, 91, 153, 158
Palaniswamy, Vimala, xxi
PandoDaily on entrepreneurship, 139
Park, Anne, xx
Partnering to Accelerate
Entrepreneurship (PACE), 73, 169
Partnership for Economic
Opportunity, 82
Partnership for Public Service, 88,
169–70
Partnership for Supply Chain
Management, 91
Patterson, Anne, xix
Peace Corps, 70, 155, 157, 167
Penfold, Nigel, xxi
PEPFAR (President's Emergency Plan
for AIDS Relief), 156–57, 160
Peru, 43–44, 147
Pew Research Center, 56
Piercy, Jan, xx
Piketty, Thomas, 22
Pinelli, Maria, xxi, 140

Pipia, Natalia, xx
Pishevar, Shervin, xx
PMFs (Presidential Management
  Fellows), 75, 167
Poland, 134
Pope, Bill, 87
Postel, Eric, xx
Poverty, 21, 23, 70, 77, 130, 136
Predator drones, 147, 154
Presidential Global Entrepreneurship
  Summit, 80
Presidential Management Fellows
  (PMFs), 75, 167
Presidential Summit on
  Entrepreneurship, 25, 27, 75, 116,
  149
President's Emergency Plan for AIDS
  Relief (PEPFAR), 156–57, 160
Princeton Review on Babson College
  entrepreneurship program, 125
Pritzker, Penny, 102
Procurement. *See* Government
  contracting and procurement
Prosperity Index, 31
Public–private partnerships, 53, 60,
  115–16

Qatar, 63
Quadrennial Diplomacy and
  Development Review (QDDR), 24–25
Qualcomm, 61

Radelet, Steve, xx
RAND Corporation, 60
Rasuanto, Sati, xx
Razak, Najib, 136
RBPC (Rice Business Plan
  Competition), 123–24
Reagan, Ronald, 60, 154
reddit, 129
Reeves, James, xxi
Rensselaer Polytechnic Institute, 126
Research Triangle Park, 53
RetailTower, 101
Rice Business Plan Competition
  (RBPC), 123–24
Rieländer, Jan, 23
Rifkind, Noam, xxi

Righi, Peter, xxi
Rios, Brenda, xx
Rockefeller, Liv, xxi
Rohde, David, xxi, 80, 95
Ronald Coase Institute, 57
Rosen, Harold, xxi
Ross, Gail, xxi
Rottenberg, Linda, xx
Russia, 4, 47–48. *See also* Soviet Union
Rutto, Lorna, 37–39
Rwanda, 32, 46, 103, 137, 138
Ryder, Jim, 52
Ryder System, Inc., 52–53

Saarnio, Sue, xx, 116
Sabanci, Ali, xx
el-Sadany, Tarek, xx
Safaricom, 47
Sahbaz, Ussal, xx, 170
Sak, Guven, xx
Salamon, Julie, xxi
Samsung, 10
Santa Clara University Global Social
  Benefit Institute, 126
Saudi Arabia, 1, 11, 122, 130
Saving Lives at Birth program, 169
Sawari Ventures, 10–11, 28, 49
SBA. *See* Small Business Administration
SBIR (Small Business Innovation
  Research), 60, 61–62
Schadlow, Nadia, xxi
Schake, Kori, 80, 81, 87, 88, 92
Schmidt, Eric, 104
Schooner, Steve, 163, 164
Schramm, Carl, 5
Schroeder, Chris, xx, 11
Schumpeter, Joseph, 5, 31, 57
Schwanke, Beth, 158
Scobey, Margaret, xix
SEAF (Small Enterprise Assistance
  Funds), 134
SEED (Support for East European
  Democracy Act of 1989), 134
Seed funds: connecting and sustaining
  entrepreneurs via, 127, 142; and
  entrepreneurship ecosystems, 108; and
  GEP, 117; government role in, 171; as
  key to startups, 102–03; role of,

131–35. *See also specific incubators and accelerators*
Selian, Audrey, xxi
SEMATECH, 60
Senor, Dan, 105
SeventySix Capital, 133
SGBs (small and growing businesses), 133
Shaffer, Lynda, xxi
Shah, Rajiv, 92, 169
Shark Tank (television program), 14, 140–41
Shirley, Mary, 57–58
Shure, Ken, xxi
Siemietkowski-Needham, Marianne, xx
Silicon Valley, 26, 85, 101–09, 114, 129–30
Silver, Spencer, 39
Simon, Bill, xxi
Singapore, 32, 58, 106, 137
Singer, Saul, 105
Singh, Tom, 123
Siri voice recognition, 10, 59
Siriklioglu, Nihan, xx
Six+Six Entrepreneurship Ecosystem Model, 111–18
Skype, 88
Slaughter, Anne-Marie, xix, 24, 45
Slavery, 157
Small and growing businesses (SGBs), 133
Small and medium-sized enterprises (SMEs), 30, 160
Small Business Administration (SBA), 60, 69, 130, 135
Small Business Innovation Research (SBIR), 60, 61–62
Small Enterprise Assistance Funds (SEAF), 134
SMEs (small and medium-sized enterprises), 30, 160
Smith, Jonathan, xx
Smith, Megan, 168
Smith, Tony, xxi
Social media, 49. *See also specific platforms*
Sohail, Faysal, xx
Solignac-Lecomte, Henri-Bernard, 23
Al Sonbaty, Hany, xx, 10–11
Sonenshine, Tara, xx, 159
Sosnicky, Jim, xxi

South Africa, 23
Soviet Union, 20, 86. *See also* Russia
SRI International, 137
Sri Lanka, 22, 153
Stanford University, 102, 105, 117, 128, 137, 139
Starbucks, 7, 46, 52, 150
Start-Up Chile program, 135
Startup Communities (Feld), 113
StartUp Cup, 117
Startup Institute, 121, 125
Start-Up Nation (Senor & Singer), 105
Startup Rising (Schroeder), 11–12
Startups: corruption's impact on, 43; in Egypt, 11, 78; and entrepreneurship ecosystems, 6–7, 14, 57, 102–07, 109, 113–14, 119–25, 129–33, 137–43; funding for, 43–44, 131–35, 170; and GEP, 26–32; high-growth, 76, 118; in Israel, 48; job creation by, 49; in United States, 53–54
Startup Weekend, 122
State Department (U.S.): bureaucracy in, 14, 85–90; foreign assistance for entrepreneurship programs, 69–70, 75–76, 80; and Iraq reconstruction efforts, 152; Office of Inspections, 82; and public–private partnerships, 115–16; and QDDR, 24–25. *See also* Global Entrepreneurship Program (GEP)
Stern, Alissa, xxi
Stewart, Rory, 3
Stier, Max, 88
Strengthening Entrepreneurship and Enterprise Development, 79
Stringer, Bob, xx
Sudirman, Jalan, 4
Support for East European Democracy Act of 1989 (SEED), 134
Sweden, 72, 75
Swezey, Devon, 63
Switzerland, 133
Syria, 1, 3, 20–22

Tahrir Square, Egypt, 9, 12, 22, 48, 77–78
Takkenberg, Wouter, xxi
Tamil Tigers, 22

Tankersley, Jim, 22
TechCrunch: Disrupt Battlefield, 101; on entrepreneurship, 139; on Kngine, 10
Technical assistance, 134, 158–59
TechStars startup accelerator, 53
Terrorism, 2, 20, 22, 35–36, 90, 130, 154
Texas Instruments, 60
Thiel, Peter, 139–40
Thiel Fellowship, 139–40
Tomanelli, Steven, 93, 152, 162
Tourism, 38
Trade, international, 8, 44, 46, 54
Trader Joe, 8
Training programs, 71–72, 102, 115, 125
Transparency International, 106, 138
Transportation Department (U.S.), 70
Trueman, Brett, xxi
Tunisia, 1, 27, 33, 55–56, 79, 81
Turkey: angel investors in, 79, 117, 124; GEP initiatives in, 27–28, 79, 117, 122, 136, 140, 170; media in, 140; startups in, 170; unemployment in, 1–2, 33
Twain, Mark, 140

Uber, 7
Uganda, 130
Ukraine, 48–49
Ullal, Jayshree, 140
Unemployment: entrepreneurship as solution for, 13, 30; in MENA, 1, 153; social unrest resulting from, 20–23, 33; in Spain, 138; women, 1; youth, 8–9, 26, 30, 35, 75, 110, 142
Union Pacific, 62
United Kingdom: development finance in, 158; DFID, 48, 67, 163; economic growth in, 47; entrepreneurship in, 31, 56; foreign assistance for entrepreneurship promotion by, 72, 158; job creation in, 31
United Nations, 31, 136
Universities, 26, 53, 104–05, 108, 115, 125–26, 169. *See also specific institutions*
Unreasonable Institute, 113
US Agency for International Development (USAID): and CEED, 134; contracting and procurement for,

78, 90–94, 152–58, 163–64, 165–66; and entrepreneurship ecosystem, 116; entrepreneurship promotion by, 26, 41, 168–70; and entrepreneurship training, 124; funding of entrepreneurship programs by, 69–70; and GEP, 75–77, 110; impact of, 13; inter-agency coordination by, 70, 160; and SEAF, 134; SEED project, 79; and VEGA, 163
Ushahidi (Kenyan tech startup), 7, 130

Vanuatu, 160
VEGA (Volunteers for Economic Growth Alliance), 163
Venture capital, 10, 52, 59, 93, 102, 113, 127, 131, 134
Venture Hive, 129–30
Verveer, Melanne, xix, 45
The Viral Video Manifesto (Grobe & Voltz), 52
Visa, 46
Vocational training, 71–72. *See also* Training programs
Vodaphone, 10
Volker, Karen, xx
Voltz, Stephen, 51–52
Volunteers for Economic Growth Alliance (VEGA), 163

Walgreens, 52
Wall Street Journal: on Afghanistan and Iraq reconstruction contracts, 94–95; on entrepreneurship, 139
Walt Disney Company, 89
Walton, Sam, 3
Wamda Capital Fund, 141
Washington Post: on economics in Middle East, 22; on Presidential Management Fellows, 167
Wasielewski, John, xx
West Africa, 101, 117, 128, 161. *See also specific countries*
Western Union, 47
Whitney, Eli, 62
Who Owns the Future? (Lanier), 7
Wiktorowicz, Quintan, xx, 169
Winchester, Simon, 63

Winfrey, Oprah, 6–7
Wired on entrepreneurship, 139
Wolfram Alpha, 10
Women: business plan competitions for, 122; empowerment of, 40, 45; as entrepreneurs, 4–7, 28, 39–40, 133
Woodward, Bob, 146
Workarounds, 65–67
World Bank: contracting and procurement for, 92; *Doing Business Project*, 46, 58, 106, 108, 138; on economic growth, 31; and entrepreneurship programs, 154; and infoDev, 41; U.S. funding for, 70
World Economic Forum, 106
World War II, 45, 151

Y Combinator, 7, 129, 132, 135
Yemen, 1
Young Presidents' Organization (YPO), 128
Youth unemployment, 8–9, 26, 30, 35, 75, 110, 142
YouTube, 51
Yozma program, 105, 108, 135
Yu, Wenchi, xix

Zambia, 23
Zentall, Kate, xxi
Ziesing, Lucinda, xxi
Zuboff, Shoshana, xxi
Zuckerberg, Mark, 6–7, 52, 102, 119, 139